The Politics of Market Discipline in Latin America

The Politics of Market Discipline in Latin America uses a multimethod approach to challenge the conventional wisdom that financial markets impose broad and severe constraints over leftist economic policies in emerging market countries. It shows, rather, that in Latin America this influence varies markedly among countries and over time, depending on cycles of currency booms and crises exogenous to policy making. Market discipline is strongest during periods of dollar scarcity that, in the low-savings, commodity-exporting countries of the region, happen when commodity prices are high and international interest rates are low. In periods of dollar abundance, when the opposite occurs, markets' capacity to constrain leftist governments becomes very limited. Ultimately, Daniela Campello argues that financial integration should force a long-term moderation of the Left in economies less subject to these cycles, but not in those most vulnerable to them.

Daniela Campello is an assistant professor of politics and international affairs at the Getúlio Vargas Foundation (FGV), Brazil. Before joining the FGV in July 2013, Campello was an assistant professor in the department of politics and at the Woodrow Wilson School of Public and International Affairs at Princeton University. Her work has been published in *Comparative Political Studies*, *Review of International Political Economy*, and *The Oxford Handbook of Latin American Political Economy*, and in edited volumes published in the United States, Spain, Uruguay, and Brazil.

The Politics of Market Discipline in Latin America

Globalization and Democracy

DANIELA CAMPELLO
Getúlio Vargas Foundation (FGV), Brazil

CAMBRIDGE
UNIVERSITY PRESS

32 Avenue of the Americas, New York, NY 10013-2473, USA

Cambridge University Press is part of the University of Cambridge.

It furthers the University's mission by disseminating knowledge in the pursuit of education, learning, and research at the highest international levels of excellence.

www.cambridge.org
Information on this title: www.cambridge.org/9781107039254

© Daniela Campello 2015

This publication is in copyright. Subject to statutory exception
and to the provisions of relevant collective licensing agreements,
no reproduction of any part may take place without the written
permission of Cambridge University Press.

First published 2015

A catalog record for this publication is available from the British Library.

Library of Congress Cataloging in Publication data
Campello, Daniela, 1970–
The politics of market discipline in Latin America : globalization and
democracy / Daniela Campello.
  pages   cm
Includes bibliographical references and index.
ISBN 978-1-107-03925-4 (hardback)
1. Capital market–Political aspects–Latin America.   2. Finance–Political aspects–Latin
America.   3. Right and left (Political science)–Economic aspects–Latin America.
4. Elections–Economic aspects–Latin America.   5. Latin America–Politics and
government.   6. Latin America–Economic policy.   I. Title.
HG5160.5.A3C35   2014
332′.0415098–dc23   2014032392

ISBN 978-1-107-03925-4 Hardback

Cambridge University Press has no responsibility for the persistence or accuracy of
URLs for external or third-party Internet Web sites referred to in this publication
and does not guarantee that any content on such Web sites is, or will remain,
accurate or appropriate.

To Georgette and Manoel

Contents

List of Illustrations	*page*	viii
List of Tables		x
Acknowledgments		xi
1 Globalization, Democracy, and Market Discipline		1
2 Between Votes and Capital: Redistribution and Uncertainty in Unequal Democracies		26
3 Investors' "Vote" in Presidential Elections		45
4 The Politics of Currency Booms and Crises: Explaining the Influence of Investors' "Vote"		64
5 Currency Crisis, Policy Switch, and Ideological Convergence in Brazil		87
6 Exogenous Shocks and Investors' Political Clout in Ecuador		118
7 One President, Different Scenarios: Crisis, Boom, and Market Discipline in Venezuela		136
8 "Vivir con Lo Nuestro": Default and Market Discipline in Argentina		159
9 Who Governs? Market Discipline in the Developed World		188
10 Conclusion: Markets' Vote and Democratic Politics		214
References		221
Index		233

Illustrations

1.1	Capital Account Liberalization in Latin America	*page* 7
1.2	The Evolution of Financial Markets	8
1.3	Commodity Exports	14
1.4	Commodity, Interest Rates, and GDP in Latin America	15
1.5	Government Revenues between Good and Bad Times	17
1.6	Commodity Prices and Interest Rates	18
1.7	Vulnerability, International Scenario, and Market Discipline	21
1.8	Vulnerability, International Scenario, and Economic Policy Making	22
2.1	Capital Flight and Income of the Poor as Function of Taxation	32
2.2	Financial Globalization and Optimal Taxation	33
2.3	Left–Right Policy Distance as a Function of Income Inequality	34
2.4	State of the Economy and Optimal Taxation	38
2.5	Exogenous Shocks and Policy Switches	41
3.1	Causal Model	53
3.2	International Scenario: The "Good Economic Times" Index and Its Components	56
4.1	Policy Switches and Currency Crises in Latin America	66
4.2	Impact of Crises and Booms on Policy Switches	77
4.3	Impact of Political Factors on Policy Switches	78
4.4	Robustness Check – Case-wise Deletion	79
5.1	Stock Market Behavior: 1994 and 2002 Presidential Elections	96
5.2	Currency Pressures in the Brazilian 2002 Election	101

Illustrations ix

5.3	Brazilian Sovereign Spread: 2002 and 2006 Presidential Elections	109
5.4	Currency Pressures in the Brazilian 2006 Election	110
5.5	Evolution of Real Minimum Wage	111
5.6	Evolution of Bolsa Família Program	112
5.7	Brazilian Sovereign Spread: 2010 Presidential Election	115
6.1	Currency Pressures in Ecuadorian Elections: 2002 and 2006	121
6.2	Ecuadorean Sovereign Spread: 2002 Presidential Election	126
6.3	Ecuadorean Sovereign Spread: 2006 Presidential Election	131
6.4	Ecuador – Central Government Budget (% GDP)	133
7.1	Venezuelan Sovereign Spread: 1998 Election	144
7.2	Oil Reference Price (WTI, U.S.$ per barrel) – Pre-Chávez	145
7.3	Oil Reference Price (WTI, U.S.$ per barrel) – Chávez Presidency	147
7.4	Foreign Direct Investment, Oil Prices, and Economic Growth	152
7.5	Chávez's Popularity	153
7.6	Venezuelan Sovereign Risk, Compared to Latin America	154
7.7	Venezuelan Debt Composition	155
7.8	Venezuelan Sovereign Spread: 2006 Election	155
7.9	Currency Pressures in Venezuelan Elections: 1998 and 2006	156
8.1	Trade Balance (% GDP)	163
8.2	Balance of Payments (U.S.$ billion)	165
8.3	Argentine Sovereign Spread: 2003 Presidential Election	174
8.4	Currency Pressures in the Argentine 2003 Election	174
8.5	Balance of Payments in the Kirchner Years	179
9.1	The Eurozone Boom	192

Tables

3.1	Ideology and Economic Policy Making (2007–2011)	*page* 49
3.2	Country Risk Ratings in Latin America	52
3.3	Sovereign Bond Spreads: Summary Data	55
3.4	Impact of Ideology on Sovereign Risk (dependent variable: spread of the JP Morgan EMBIg)	57
3.5	Impact of Ideology on Sovereign Risk (3-point scale, dependent variable: spread of the JP Morgan EMBIg)	58
3.6	Impact of Elections on Sovereign Risk (dependent variable: spreads of JP Morgan EMBIg)	60
3.7	Countries' Fixed-Effects and Sovereign Risk	61
3.8	Coding of Campaigns and Economic Programs	62
3.9	Two Lefts in Latin America	63
4.1	Summary Statistics of Explanatory Variables: All Campaigns	75
4.2	Summary Statistics: Market-Oriented Campaigns	75
4.3	Impact of Explanatory Variables on the Probability of a Policy Switch (dependent variable: switch)	76
4.4	Impact of Explanatory Variables on Left to Right Policy Switches (dependent variable: switch)	82
4.5	Coding of Campaigns and Economic Programs	83
5.1	Brazil Reform Scorecard – Merrill Lynch	102
6.1	Economic Indicators: 2002 and 2006 Presidential Elections	120
8.1	Fiscal Results under Convertibility (% GDP)	164
8.2	Macroeconomic Indicators (% GDP) – Kirchner Years	179
9.1	Fiscal Results (% GDP)	193
9.2	Current Account (% GDP)	194
9.3	Government Debt (% GDP)	195

Acknowledgments

For most of my life I have been interested in the means through which economic power translates into political power.

Born and raised in Brazil, a country where inequality is huge and highly visible in daily life, one does not need to be a scholar to realize that, even though democracy presupposes one person one vote, some votes matter far more than others. How they mattered and how to make sure they did [not] were concerns I had since very early on, and that may explain why, after graduating and working as an industrial engineer, I ended up pursuing an academic career in political science.

It was only during my Ph.D. studies, however, when I was first exposed to the concept of a structural power of business, that I managed to transpose these personal concerns into a research agenda. Since then, my efforts have been devoted to understanding the relative power of creditors vis-à-vis voters to influence governments' choices in Latin America.

When I first formulated this problem, in the early 2000s, creditors' influence seemed determinant, almost inescapable, in a region in which governments from right to left had advanced some measure of a neoliberal program under the pressure of capital flight and IMF conditionality. In that period, these cases seemed to somehow replicate relations I observed in the last job I held in Brazil before moving to the United States, in the planning secretariat of the Rio de Janeiro state government. There, having the opportunity to watch the dynamics of multilateral conditionality very closely, I gathered that, regardless of ideology, when money is badly needed creditors rule.

Interestingly, as I explored theses questions during my Ph.D. studies at UCLA the scenario changed quite dramatically. Governments on the left were elected in a number of Latin American countries and, differently from what happened in previous decades, they actually pursued the redistributive and interventionist policies promised during campaigns. Interviews with fund managers and government officials in countries like Argentina, Ecuador, and Venezuela would later reveal, somewhat to my surprise, that markets' agenda had become close to irrelevant in these countries.

If there is one advantage to embarking on such a long-term project as a book, it is that reality changes over time in ways that are very informative; as this book is concluded, building and maintaining markets' confidence has become, once again, a top concern among Latin American governments. Observing these cycles allowed me not only to develop my theory but also to test it as the wind turned once again.

Another advantage of long-term projects is that they afford the opportunity to incorporate criticisms and suggestions along the way. Even though any mistakes made here are mine, this book could not possibly be the same without the help of my advisors, colleagues, interviewees, and friends.

From my early times in a master's program in IUPERJ, I thank Maria Regina Soares, my advisor and mentor from day one. Many thanks also to Renato Lessa, Cesar Guimarães, and José Eisenberg, for political theory classes that still frame the way I see the political world, and to Renato Boschi and Eli Diniz for great feedback and support. I am also in debt to Wanderley Guilherme dos Santos; working as his research assistant was the equivalent of taking a second master's. Wanderley also taught me a lesson on the importance of honesty and integrity (or the consequences of the lack thereof) in academic and professional life. I owe much to Octavio Amorim Neto, advisor, role model, and later a friend, without whom I would certainly not have come this far.

Immense gratitude goes to my advisors at UCLA who, in very different ways, helped me to frame my interests and inspired me to pursue questions I had been asking myself for a long time. It was a privilege to work with Barbara Geddes. Barbara went way beyond what one would expect from an advisor, providing me with personal guidance and offering extensive feedback on every piece of material. Most importantly, she challenged me to balance passion and rigor during all these years. There are not enough thanks to give her.

Ron Rogowski was also a great interlocutor, who understood my research sometimes better than I did and provided me with insights that for a long time managed to put me back on track whenever I risked deviating from my core interests. Robert Brenner was also a never-ending

Acknowledgments

xiii

source of inspiration and intelligent critique; I cannot overestimate his influence on my work.

I also owe a great deal to Geoff Garrett, for his permanent support even after leaving UCLA. Most of all I thank Geoff for his always challenging critique, which pushed me to move forward. Miriam Golden, Kathy Bawn, and James DeNardo were also very influential and of great help during the development of this research.

I was lucky enough to have a unique group of cohorts at UCLA who discussed and read parts of this work – Zachariah Mampilly, Joe Wright, Dan Young, Julia Gray, Tyson Roberts, David Dayan-Rosenman, among many others. To my friend Marcela Meirelles I owe many hours of discussion, but I will never forget the ones spent before her working hours revising my job talk word by word, nor the great insights she provided on the framing of my research from an economist's point of view. Special thanks to Paulo Melo-Filho, without whom the second chapter of this book would not have been possible as it is.

Many other people – at UCLA and elsewhere – commented on previous versions of the manuscript and on related work. Among others, thanks to Dan Posner, Dan Treisman, Mike Thies, Javier Santiso, Aaron Tornell, James Galbraith, David Leblang, Gustavo Flores-Macías, Ben Ross Schneider, Stephen Kaplan, Maria Victoria Murillo, Robert Kaufman, Scott Desposato, and participants of seminars at UCLA, UCSD, Cornell, the LBJ School of Public Affairs at University of Texas–Austin, Princeton, and Tulane.

At Princeton, I could not have asked for more generous colleagues than Carles Boix, Deborah Yashar, Amaney Jamal, Larry Bartels, Chris Achen, Christina Davis, Miguel-Angel Centeno, Grigore Pop-Eleches, Joanne Gowa, Rafaela Dancygier, Kosuke Imai, Robert Keohane, Nolan McCarthy, and Brandice Canes-Wrone. Thanks also to participants in my book conference: Jeffry Frieden, Layna Mosley, Alberto Diaz Cayeros, Ken Roberts, and Erik Wibbels, as well as to Michele Epstein, without whose efficiency and intelligence the conference would not have happened.

I also want to acknowledge help and support received during fieldwork. In Ecuador, Pablo Andrade from the Universidad Andina Simón Bolívar and Simón Pachano from FLACSO introduced me to local colleagues and facilitated my research tremendously. I was lucky to have fantastic research assistants, without whom the last chapters of this book would not have been possible. Many thanks to Salvador Mendez in Venezuela; Maria Laura Callegari, Guadalupe Tuñón, and Julieta Lenarduzzi in Argentina; and Clayton Mendonça and Cintia de Souza in Brazil.

xiv *Acknowledgments*

The following institutions provided generous financial support for this project: at UCLA, the International Center, Latin American Center, and the Graduate Division; the University of California Institute for Global Cooperation and Conflict; and at Princeton, the Office of the Dean of Faculty, the Program in Latin American Studies, and the Bobst Center. The Ministry of Education of Brazil partly funded my Ph.D. studies in the United States.

I am grateful to my family for the high expectations that always inspired me to be truthful to my capabilities and weaknesses. I am especially thankful to Caio, my oldest son, who shares with me the deepest belief that, without joy, not even the greatest task is worth pursuing. Thanks also for the time he spent playing alone while I worked, and for understanding nights, weekends, and even months of research abroad when I was not physically there for him. Enzo came much later in the process, but his calm and effortless happiness helped to make the conclusion of this project more bearable.

Finally, I cannot express how much I owe to my husband, Cesar Zucco Jr., my love who also happens to be my colleague and co-author. Many thanks for his help, patience, criticism, and encouragement, and also for setting the bar high, as the great researcher he is. Above all, I thank Cesar for providing my life with joy and peace, without which the conclusion of this book would not have been possible.

1

Globalization, Democracy, and Market Discipline

Early in 2002, Brazil was considered an example of a successful emerging economy, praised in international financial markets for its sound economic conditions. Despite concerns over the country's public debt, long-term prospects seemed promising. Optimism was such that the president of the Brazilian central bank was elected "Man of the Year" by *Latin Finance* magazine after his successful managing of the country's 1998 financial crisis.

In the course of the year, however, the country risk doubled, stock prices fell 50 percent, and the currency plummeted – a remarkable change in market sentiment, driven by investors' anticipation that the leftist Workers' Party (PT) would win the October presidential election. Lula da Silva, PT candidate and formerly a prominent labor leader, had been a vocal opponent of the neoliberal agenda advanced by the incumbent administration, and was expected to reverse it if elected.

The consequences of this so-called confidence crisis were not circumscribed to financial markets; public accounts deteriorated and important sectors of the economy that held a high share of dollar-denominated debt were left in dire straits. Accelerating inflation further raised fears that the country's economic stabilization was in jeopardy.

Even though opponents capitalized on market fears, the crisis did not prevent voters from electing Lula by a landslide. What it did, however, was to change the balance of power within the party leadership in favor of its most conservative members, with important effects on the way the Workers' Party would govern Brazil.

PT's interlocutors with financial markets, who worked to restore investors' confidence by credibly signaling their commitment to economic orthodoxy during the campaign, would later assume key positions in

1

2 *The Politics of Market Discipline in Latin America*

the administration. A former CEO of BankBoston, and member of the opposition, was appointed head of the Brazilian Central Bank, after PT historical economists were set aside for being considered "too partisan" in financial market reports.

The government ended up adopting an investor-oriented agenda, which frustrated traditional allies and provoked the exodus of party members but sparked euphoria among market players and creditor governments. In the words of Myles Frechette, former U.S. consul general in São Paulo and then president of the Council of the Americas in New York, "There is an enormous sense of relief that Lula, despite the rhetoric of his party, has people who understand how the global economy works, and want to be players."[1]

Financial investors' capacity to influence policymaking – or to discipline governments – by "voting with the feet" is by no means limited to Brazil. In other Latin American countries such as Venezuela, Argentina, and Ecuador, speculative attacks triggered by fears of a left-wing victory in presidential elections severely constrained governments' economic programs. Beyond the region, India and South Korea, as well as Australia, New Zealand, and France, went through comparable processes.

Yet important as it seems, the experience of Latin American countries reveals that this mechanism is not always effective. First, investors sometimes do not react to prospects of a left turn in government; this is what happened, for example, in the 2005 presidential election of Tabaré Vázquez, a left-wing outsider in Uruguay's century-long two-party system. In other occasions, markets react but presidents seem to ignore it completely. Rafael Correa, after his victory in the Ecuadorean 2006 election, responded to a sharp rise in the country risk by advising nervous investors to "take a Valium."[2]

It is also perplexing to note that market discipline during elections has enduring effects in some political systems in the region but not in others. After his move to the right in 2002, Lula was reelected in 2006 promising economic policies that bore little distinction from those of his conservative opponent, and markets reacted with indifference. The same happened in the presidential race of 2010, when PT candidate Dilma Rousseff was unequivocal in her commitment with maintaining investors' confidence during the campaign.

---

[1] Alan Clendenning, "Investors' worst fears put to rest: So much for predictions that Brazil's first elected leftist president would lead the country into a financial meltdown," *Ottawa Citizen*, April 18, 2003.

[2] Monthe Hayes, "Ecuadorean Leader Eyes Wealth Distribution," The Associated Press, December 2, 2006.

Globalization, Democracy, and Market Discipline

In Venezuela, conversely, markets' behavior constrained the first years of Hugo Chávez's presidency but did not preclude a later reversal to his original left-wing agenda, nor its radicalization after the 2006 reelection.

The puzzles just stated suggest that, although the claim that the internationalization of financial markets increases investors' influence on policymaking is quite established among students of international political economy, the understanding of the *causal links* between investors' capacity to move capital across borders and governments' economic policymaking, as well as of the factors that mediate these relations are still tentative, particularly in the emerging world.

This book employs a combination of formal and empirical analyses, as well as extensive case studies in Brazil, Ecuador, Venezuela, and Argentina, to unveil these links. I focus on the interaction between bondholders and politicians during presidential elections held in Latin America, and examine the following questions: How do investors react to the election of the Left? When and how do markets' reactions effectively curb governments' leftist agenda? Why does market discipline have enduring effects in some political systems, while in others leftist incumbents later revert to their original program?

I show that creditors react negatively whenever they anticipate a leftist victory in presidential elections, and punish a leftist government by charging higher interest rates to fund public debt. Yet these responses are not always consequential.

Rather, bondholders' leverage to discipline leftist governments in Latin America varies substantially depending on cycles of abundance and scarcity of foreign currency that are very common in the region and are *exogenous* to policymaking. These cycles are particularly pronounced owing to the region's dependence on commodity exports and low domestic savings. In countries that display these characteristics, economic performance turns out to be very influenced by fluctuations in commodity prices and international interest rates.

When commodity prices are high, strong export revenues reduce governments' demand for foreign currency to tap external financial obligations, at the same time that the acceleration of economic growth improves risk/return ratios, making economies more attractive to foreign finance. Low international interest rates further increase this attractiveness by making creditors more risk-prone and willing to divert capital from developed markets into the emerging world. High supply and low demand for foreign funds release governments from the urgency to attract additional finance. As a result, those on the Left elected during currency booms are in better conditions to deviate from markets' preferences and to pursue their preferred agenda.

When the opposite occurs, however, low export revenues reduce the supply of foreign currency, at the same time that slower economic growth makes countries less attractive to investors. High interest rates increase risk aversion, further depressing capital inflows. It is during these "bad times" that bondholders' negative reactions to the election of the Left are most consequential. The necessity of attracting capital in a scenario of low supply and high demand for hard currency prompts leftist presidents to abandon their original agenda in favor of policies expected to win the confidence of the international financial community.

In the long run, market discipline should have different consequences for leftist parties depending on countries' exposure to cycles of currency booms and crises. In economies that are relatively stable and less subject to these cycles, as financial integration advances the urge to build market confidence should become more constraining to leftist governments, and likely to prompt their convergence toward neoliberal policies.

More vulnerable economies, however, in which bondholders' leverage to influence policymaking varies substantially over time, should not experience the same convergence. Instead, leftist governments in these countries should display diverging patterns, embracing conservative economic policies in bad times and promoting radical redistribution in good times.

After placing the internationalization of finance in Latin America in historical perspective, the remainder of this introductory chapter examines the state of the current theoretical and empirical debates on the political implications of financial globalization, identifying contributions and discussing the main problems scholars face when attempting to explain the impact of increased capital mobility on the functioning of Latin American democracies. Next, I propose a framework to analyze the interactions between governments and markets in which income inequality, capital mobility, and economic uncertainty are key explanatory factors, and present the research project. The final section details how the book is organized.

The Globalization of Finance in Emerging Economies

Latin America, like other less developed regions, was shut out from international financial markets after the wave of defaults that followed the Great Depression (Drake 1989; Edwards 1998). After the first oil price shock in 1973, however, banks' efforts to recycle petrodollars coupled with the necessity of oil-importing countries to fund their

Globalization, Democracy, and Market Discipline 5

current account paved the return of private lending to non-OECD[3] economies. Differently from the financial boom of the 1920s, when banks served as intermediaries between governments and investors, in the 1970s they became the direct financiers of governments' debt (Dornbusch 1989; Drake 1989; Sachs 1989).

The magnitude of investment flows to Latin America in this period is striking; net loans amounted to U.S.\$61.3 billion between 1971 and 1980, compared to U.S.\$7.3 billion between 1961 and 1970 (Thorp 1998).[4] The oversupply of international credit forced interest rates down, sometimes reaching negative real levels. Fierce competition among creditors discouraged oversight, and loans were offered with no strings attached. Most of the capital was channeled to the public sector and provided governments with plenty of room to use it at their own discretion (Stallings 1987).

The boom came to a halt in the early 1980s. The escalation of inflation in the United States prompted a sudden hike in American interest rates, dramatically raising the costs of capital between 1979 and 1982. In addition, the widespread panic caused by the Mexican default in 1982 impelled investors to reassess their exposure to risk in other less developed economies, triggering a sudden reversal of capital flows.

As a result, average real interest rates went from negative 6 percent in 1981 to 14.6 percent in 1982, and net transfers of resources across borders dropped from about 25 percent in 1978 to negative 40 percent of the region's exports in 1987 (Thorp 1998).

Despite the severe costs of adjustment imposed by the debt service, creditors' successful use of "carrots and sticks" prevented debtor countries from renegotiating their obligations collectively. The power asymmetry established between uncoordinated debtors and a cartel of creditors that included a few large banks, with the support of their home governments and the International Monetary Fund (IMF), guaranteed debt repayment and prevented a collapse of the international financial system, as happened in the 1930s.

Yet this was done at the expense of debtor countries' policymaking autonomy (Drake 1989; O'Donnell 1985). The necessity of rolling debt and raising new capital subjected these governments to stringent conditions; restricted to macroeconomic adjustment in the early 1980s,

---

[3] Organisation for Economic Co-operation and Development, used in reference to developed economies.
[4] Values in 1980 U.S. dollars.

6   The Politics of Market Discipline in Latin America

these evolved to include massive structural reforms from 1985 onward (Stallings 1992).[5]

The pervasive implementation of painful reforms and the limited number of sovereign defaults provide compelling evidence of creditors' strong influence over policymaking in debtor nations (Drake 1989; Lindert and Morton 1989). Occasional efforts to promote compensatory policies, as attempted by Alan García in Peru and Raúl Alfonsín in Argentina, resulted in complete failure; exclusion from the international financial community accelerated hyperinflation and further worsened the conditions of the poorest segments of the population.

A decade passed before Latin American governments finally regained access to international financial markets. This process ensued with the securitization of bank loans into sovereign bonds promoted by the Brady Plan, which allowed private banks to sell distressed debt off their balance sheets and debtor countries to issue new sovereign bonds.

The securitization of debt under the Brady Plan started in 1989; as of July 1999, twenty governments from various regions of the world had issued Brady bonds, among them Argentina, Brazil, Costa Rica, Dominican Republic, Ecuador, Panama, Peru, Uruguay, and Venezuela.[6] The impact of the plan was dramatic; in 1997, U.S.$305 billion of loans and U.S.$2,403 billion of Brady bonds were traded, compared with the U.S.$70 billion face value of loans traded in secondary markets in 1989 (Buckley 2008, p. 53).

In this same period, countries began deregulating their capital accounts (Figure 1.1), which facilitated the entry of broader classes of investors, and encouraged the expansion and internationalization of Latin American financial markets (Figure 1.2a and 1.2b).[7] This trend is evidenced not only by the greater presence of international financial intermediaries, but also by the fact that issuance and trading of local securities continued to migrate to international markets (Agnoli and Vilán 2007).

Financial globalization, which occurred as countries liberalized their capital accounts, (re)integrated into international financial markets, and

---

[5] See Lora, Panizza, and Quispe-Agnoli (2004) for an encompassing analysis of structural reforms advanced in Latin American countries.

[6] As reported by the Emerging Markets Trading Association, other countries were Albania, Bulgaria, Croatia, Ivory Coast, Jordan, Nigeria, Philippines, Poland, Russia, Slovenia, and Vietnam.

[7] Although the definition of an emerging market has been the subject of increasing debate, a common characteristic of these countries is that financial investment is subject not only to economic, but also to relevant political and regulatory risks. These risks are pervasive to financial markets and direct investment, and they put politics at the center of investment decisions in these countries. See the Emerging Market Trading Association website for a more encompassing definition of emerging markets.

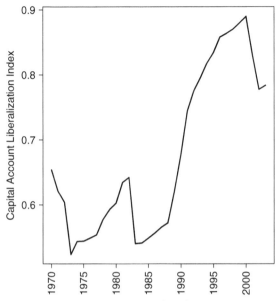

FIGURE 1.1. Capital Account Liberalization in Latin America.
Note: The index is an unweighted average of capital account liberalization in Latin American emerging economies.
Source: Biglaiser and DeRouen Jr. (2007).

accessed an increasingly broad and diversified investor base, initiated a new phase in the relations between now democratic governments and creditors, which is different in many ways from the 1920s to 1930s or 1970s to 1980s. It did not take long for scholars to start investigating these developments.

The Politics of Financial Globalization

The structure of creditor markets that prevailed after the 1970s empowered private banks and creditor governments to use direct leverage to shape the economic policy agenda of less developed countries in the aftermath of the debt crisis (Stallings 1992; Thorp 1987).

In a world of globalized finance, however, in which the creditor base is composed of a large number of investment funds and individual savers, this strategy is no longer an option. Extreme circumstances, like the Argentine default of 2001, reveal the difficulties involved in overcoming creditors' collective action problems to force repayment.

In this new scenario, investors' influence is exerted through a more elusive mechanism, which takes place in the context of what has been referred to as a "confidence game" (Bresser-Pereira 2001; Santiso 2003).

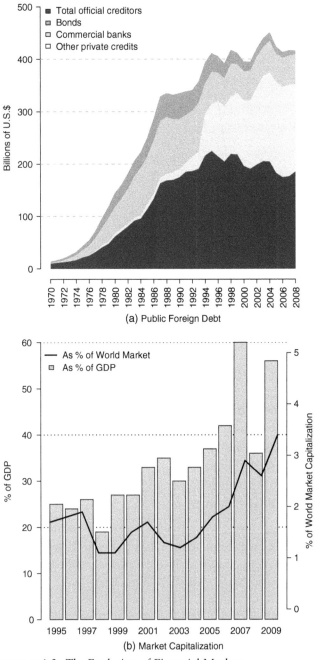

FIGURE 1.2. The Evolution of Financial Markets.
Note: Total public foreign debt outstanding and stock market capitalization of Latin American emerging economies (latter excluding Uruguay and Venezuela).
Source: World Data Bank.

Globalization, Democracy, and Market Discipline 9

In this game, exit is the most likely response of uncoordinated sovereign bondholders to prospects of unfavorable government policies,[8] and signals that either affect or reveal market sentiment become of increasing concern to investors and governments alike.

The first generation of studies on the political implications of financial globalization in Latin America attempted to reproduce research originally focused on OECD countries, and revolved around the debate between what became known as *efficiency* and *compensation* theories.

Efficiency theories[9] posit that the easier it is for asset holders to move capital across borders, the stronger become the incentives for governments to implement policies that increase domestic rates of return on investment (Cerny 1995; Drezner 2001; Dryzek 1996; Kurzer 1993; Strange 1986). Policies deemed unfavorable to financial investment should be subject to the disciplining effects of capital markets; other conditions fixed, investors should exit economies in which they anticipate their adoption. Depending on the magnitude of this exit, countries may experience anything from rises in the cost of capital to speculative attacks, with deleterious economic and political consequences.

As financial integration advances, thus, compensation theorists predicted that market discipline would force governments of different ideological leanings to converge around the neoliberal model of minimal state and deregulation preferred by international financial players. Governments' competition for cross-border capital should promote this convergence not only within, but also between countries.

The response came from theorists who acknowledged the pressures imposed by increased economic integration, yet contended that citizens' demands for compensation and protection could counterbalance – and potentially offset – investors' enhanced leverage to influence policymaking (Boix 2000; Garrett 1998; Rodrik 1998).

Compensation theories argue that parties on the Left, which typically retain stronger support from poorer citizens and labor unions and are ideologically committed to income redistribution, should respond to globalization by furthering welfare policies aimed to maintain social and political stability. Partisan distinctions are therefore predicted to persist,

---

[8] See Hirschman (1977) for a discussion of exit, voice as means of expressing policy preferences, and Santiso (2003) for a comprehensive analysis of how these concepts apply to the operation of integrated financial markets.

[9] See Cohen (1996) and Mosley (2003) for an extensive review of the literature dedicated to OECD countries. Examples of recent work that builds on this framework include Dreher, Sturm, and Ursprung (2008), Hellwig, Ringsmuth, and Freeman (2008), Nooruddin and Simmons (2009), Potrafke (2009), and Yi (2011).

as long as electoral benefits exceed the economic costs leftist governments incur when responding to their core constituencies.

Significant policy distinctions should also remain among countries' political systems, since governments' capacity to pursue a successful leftist agenda depends on domestic social and economic structures and institutions. Garrett (1998), for example, contends this can occur only in countries where encompassing labor unions are able to restrain wage growth and inflationary pressures when the economy is close to full employment.

Empirical work on the political consequences of globalization in the developed world has found considerable support for the compensation hypothesis; more integrated economies have been shown to have larger public sectors (Quinn 1997; Rodrik 1998), and divergence in welfare regimes remains significant in the OECD (Kitschelt, Lange, Marks, and Stephens 1999). Although some authors observe macroeconomic convergence coexisting with distinct partisan strategies in supply-side policies (Garrett 1998), others contend that not even macroeconomic policies converge when properly controlled for exchange rate regimes (Oatley 1999). Nevertheless, studies found that ideological distinctions between Left and Right both within and between countries have decreased in the 1990s (Boix 2000; Garrett 1998), suggesting that it might be early to completely dismiss efficiency claims.

As the prevalence of efficiency or compensation strategies in democratic systems is considered to depend on the balance between citizens' capacity to mobilize around economic interests and investors' ability to impose market discipline, the skepticism with respect to governments' likelihood to adopt compensatory policies in Latin America should be of no surprise.

Citizens' political clout is arguably modest in countries where levels of societal mobilization are low, democratization is still recent, and clientelism is widespread.[10] The absence of strong and encompassing labor unions, labor market informality, and a tradition of corporatism further compromise labor's capacity to shape the political agenda (Kurtz 2004; Song and Hong 2005; Weyland 2004).

Likewise, the dependence on foreign sources of finance due to low levels of domestic savings potentializes the impacts of market sentiment on the economy, and therefore financiers' leverage to influence policymaking.

---

[10] *Clientelism* is defined as transactions between politicians and citizens whereby material favors are offered in return for political support at the polls (Wantchekon 2003).

Globalization, Democracy, and Market Discipline   11

At last, economists have shown that capital flows tend to be pro-cyclical in emerging economies (Reinhart and Rogoff 2009), which further restricts governments' ability to provide compensation and stimulate the economy in response to increasingly frequent financial crises (Griffith-Jones 2000; Wibbels 2006).

In this context, rising insecurity and increasing dislocation resulting from economic openness should curb citizens' capacity to demand, let alone obtain, compensation in Latin America (Kurtz and Brooks 2008).

Notwithstanding all these factors, it is important to note that democratic elections should create strong incentives for governments to promote compensatory policies in very unequal economies (Boix 2003; Meltzer and Richard 1981) such as those in Latin America. In addition, low economic institutionalization and the concentration of power in the hands of presidents convey that, once governments choose a compensatory path, they should find few institutional impediments to pursue it. The prospects for the prevalence of compensation or efficiency policies in the region remain, thus, a matter to be settled empirically.[11]

Yet whereas the empirical literature reached reasonable consensus on the somewhat limited impact of market discipline in the OECD, the same did not happen in cross-national work on Latin America.

On one side, scholars have increasingly acknowledged market pressures (Baiocchi and Checa 2008; Hunter 2011; Murillo, Oliveros, and Vaishnav 2011; Palermo 2005; Samuels 2008; Weyland 2009), pointing to the "continuing influence of macroeconomic constraints" (Hunter 2011, p. 307), the need to maintain market credibility (Samuels 2008), and the "constant threat of capital flight or a fall in investors' confidence"(Baiocchi and Checa 2008, p. 117) as barriers that prevent governments from adopting a leftist agenda in the region. Palermo (2005, p. 5), for example, attributes the rightward move of the Workers' Party in Brazil to the "complications inherent to a government transition led by a party that scares the financial markets."

Notwithstanding, when it comes to comparative studies, results remain remarkably inconclusive; although some authors find negative associations between globalization and measures of the size of the State that are independent of the partisanship in office (Kaufman and Segura-Ubiergo 2001; Orestein and Haas 2005; Rudra 2002), consistent with convergence claims, others contend that political leaders in the region still retain a significant degree of autonomy to respond to

---

[11] The recent diffusion of cash transfer programs offers an example of the type of compensation that might be possible in the context of unequal but demobilized societies.

12 *The Politics of Market Discipline in Latin America*

international market forces (Avelino, Brown, and Hunter 2005; Wibbels and Arce 2003).

In sum, the scholarship dealing with the political impacts of financial integration has not yet grappled comprehensively with the mechanisms through which increasingly mobile financial investors influence governments' choices in Latin American emerging economies.

Empirically, the difficulties involved in quantifying financial integration and the paucity of reliable data exhausted the explanatory power of highly aggregated studies focused on broad associations between indicators of globalization and partisan policymaking.

A temporal coincidence further challenges the suitability of aggregate analyses to studying the political consequences of financial liberalization in Latin America. Different from the developed world, where trade was liberalized decades before finance, most countries in the region have experienced these processes simultaneously. In addition, democratization was also concomitant with economic liberalization in the majority of cases. Considering that trade, financial liberalization, and democratization are all expected to have major impacts on governments' partisan agendas and policy choices, disentangling these simultaneous effects is no simple task.

Unsatisfactory measures of capital mobility; underspecification of causal mechanisms; and the difficulties involved in disentangling the simultaneous effects of trade, financial openness, and democratization vindicate the importance of moving away from macroempirical analyses and instead focus on the microfoundations of creditors' political clout in a world of increasingly mobile capital (Mosley 2003).

This is the strategy I adopt in this book, and that allows me to establish how international creditors respond to partisanship in Latin America, how and when these responses influence the agenda of the Left in the region, and the conditions under which market discipline should lead to economic policy convergence in the long run.

Research Project: The Politics of Market Discipline in Latin America

This book examines how the confidence game is played by international creditors and politicians during presidential elections, unfolding an important mechanism through which market discipline works in Latin American emerging economies.

Elections are particularly important junctures for financial investors because of their potential to bring about major policy changes (Whitehead 2006). This is even more true in Latin America, where

Globalization, Democracy, and Market Discipline

democratization is still recent, and low levels of political institutionalization and concentration of power in the hands of the executive create substantial policy volatility.

Santiso and Frot (2010) note that over the past decades nearly all major financial crises in emerging economies have occurred in synchronization with electoral cycles. As market players perceive parties to have distinct priorities and to seek different economic outcomes, their behavior during elections is driven by expectations about how partisan changes in office will affect these outcomes and, ultimately, investment returns.

In the particular case of sovereign-debt markets, Mosley (2003) argues that investors in emerging economies not only follow governments' macro- and microeconomic agenda to form their expectations about inflation and currency risks, but also pay close attention to supply-side policies and political ideology to estimate governments' willingness and capacity to pay debt. As a result, the prospects of a left-wing agenda that prioritizes employment over inflation and social justice over growth, or that is believed to increase the chances of a default, lowers market sentiment, depresses asset prices, and ultimately triggers capital flight and speculative attacks.

It should be of no surprise, thus, that in a scenario of increasing capital mobility the anticipation of these responses pushes leftist governments toward an agenda closer to investors' preferences. Most importantly, market influence materialized during elections carries long-term implications, for the sets of choices available to governments are often limited by decisions made soon after inauguration.

Both the qualitative and the quantitative evidence presented in this book confirm that sovereign bondholders do care about governments' ideological stance in Latin America, and react negatively to the election of leftist presidents. These reactions are sometimes mitigated by leftist candidates' willingness to signal their intentions to moderate their program if elected, but the credibility of such signals is limited by institutional factors.

Interestingly, investors' reactions fade when the newly elected government moderates its agenda, but otherwise higher bond spreads persist throughout left-wing administrations, indicating another way through which investors' behavior affects the economic success of a leftist government beyond the short term.

Notwithstanding their potentially negative consequences, though, creditors' behavior is not always capable of curbing governments' leftist agenda in Latin America. On the contrary, the main contribution of this

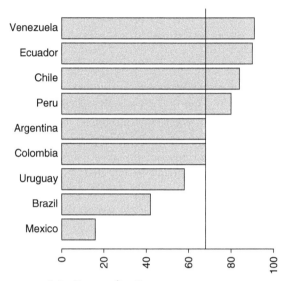

FIGURE 1.3. Commodity Exports.
Note: Commodity as a share of total merchandise exports, year = 2000. The vertical line denotes median share of commodities in the sample.
Source: World Data Bank.

book is to show that the effectiveness of market discipline varies tremendously, not only across countries but also over time, and to explain this variation.

Comparing the economic programs leftist parties announce during electoral campaigns and the policies they enact in office, I show that investors' capacity to constrain the Left in Latin America varies with cycles of currency booms and crises that are exogenous to policymaking.

With the exception of Mexico, and to a lower extent Brazil, most Latin American emerging economies are essentially commodity exporters (Figure 1.3), and therefore highly vulnerable to fluctuations in international commodity prices. Moreover, low levels of domestic savings make economies in the region particularly dependent on international capital, which is itself driven by changes in international interest rates.

As a result, economists have demonstrated that a large share of capital inflows, as well as of Latin America's rates of economic growth, are fundamentally determined by changes in the international interest rates and in commodity prices (Calvo, Leiderman, and Reinhart 1996; Gavin, Hausmann, and Leiderman 1995; Izquierdo, Romero, and Talvo 2008; Maxfield 1998). Figures 1.4a and 1.4b illustrate these relationships.

Globalization, Democracy, and Market Discipline 15

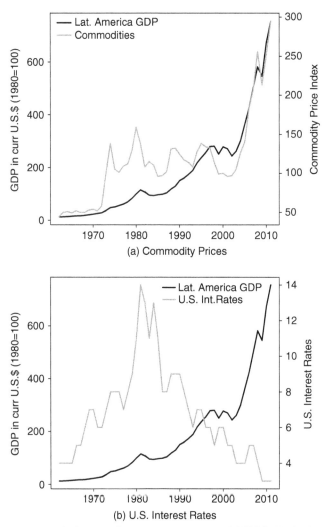

FIGURE 1.4. Commodity, Interest Rates, and GDP in Latin America.
Note: Free Market Commodity Price Index from UNCTAD and U.S. 10-Year Treasury Constant Maturity Rate from the Federal Research Bank of Saint Louis (FRED).

Why does that dependence affect creditors' capacity to influence policymaking? This happens because fluctuations in international interest rates and commodity prices alter the balance between governments' demand for foreign finance and its supply.

In periods when commodity prices are depressed, low export revenues reduce the supply of hard currency in the domestic economy and curtail governments' budgets, either directly, when state companies control commodity exports, or through tax revenue, when the commodity sector is in private hands. Under these circumstances, governments face an increased necessity of raising foreign funds to meet international financial obligations, in a scenario in which poor economic and fiscal prospects make sovereign bonds less appealing to international creditors.

The worst case scenario from the perspective of governments occurs when low commodity prices coincide with high international interest rates, which intensify investors' risk aversion and tendency to flee emerging economies (Reinhart 2005). In these occasions, governments' demand for foreign finance is the highest, while the supply is the lowest.

Moreover, in these "bad times" poor fiscal prospects make default risk non-negligible. Under these conditions, as Mosley (2003) contends, bondholders' range of policy concerns extend beyond macroeconomic indicators, to encompass a wide range of microeconomic policies that have an impact on governments' capacity to repay debt.

Consequently, in these periods market constraints become not only strong but also broad, and newly elected leftist presidents are faced with powerful incentives to adopt conservative economic policies expected to revert market sentiment and attract foreign finance.

Exceptionally high commodity prices have the opposite effect; abundant export revenues boost economic growth, dollar inflows, and public revenue, releasing governments' demand for foreign funds at the same time that favorable fiscal prospects make sovereign bonds more attractive to creditors. Leftist governments' greatest autonomy from market discipline occurs when high commodity prices coincide with low interest rates, which reduce investors' risk aversion and increase their propensity to divert capital to emerging economies. In these periods, governments' demand for foreign finance is at its lowest while supply is at its highest.

Likewise, negligible default risks during booms reduce investors' concerns with governments' microeconomic agenda, provided that macroeconomic indicators remain within an acceptable range – a behavior similar to what has been claimed to be the "norm" in the OECD (Mosley 2003). Presidents ruling in "good times" are thus subject to relatively narrow market constraints, and have a wider room to advance a leftist agenda.

Figure 1.5 illustrates the different conditions Latin American governments are subject to between "good" and "bad" times. By showing the difference of central government revenue as a percentage of GDP in worst

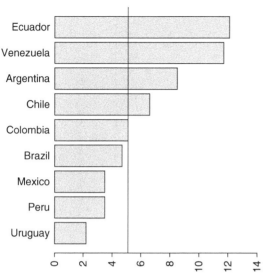

FIGURE 1.5. Government Revenues between Good and Bad Times.
Note: Difference of central government revenues as a percentage of GDP in worst and best years between 1999 and 2010. In most cases the worst year was 1999; exceptions are Chile (2008), Peru (2002), and Uruguay (2000).
Source: Cepalstat.

and best years between 1999 and 2010, it offers an intuition of how governments fiscal position varies between booms and crises.[12]

The figure also indicates how this variation depends on countries' exposure to currency boom and bust cycles. Even though differences are large in most countries in the region, they are dramatic in those highly dependent on commodity exports, such as Ecuador, Venezuela, Chile, and Peru.

Finally, it is worth noting that Ecuador and Venezuela, the extreme cases, are the two countries in which not only is the economy heavily dependent on commodity exports, but also this commodity is oil. Authors have shown that, different from agricultural products, non-renewable commodities are more subject to rent, which accrues to government revenues when prices are rising (Ananchotikul and Eichengreen 2007; Avendaño, Reisen, and Santiso 2008; Collier 2007).

---

[12] The year 1999 was very unfavorable owing to the effects of the Asian and Russian crises, whereas a boom started in most of the region after commodity prices began to rise in 2004.

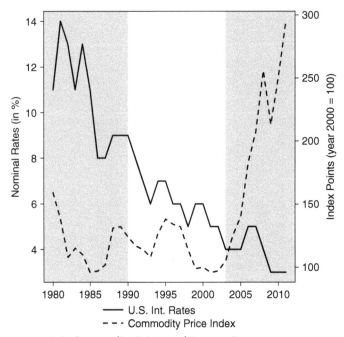

FIGURE 1.6. Commodity Prices and Interest Rates.
Source: Commodity price index and interest rates (American bonds). Data from UNCTAD and International Financial Statistics (IMF).

By examining variations in the effectiveness of market discipline amid "good" and "bad" times, the theory presented here integrates, in a single framework, two phenomena that captured a great deal of attention among students of Latin American political economy: policy switches in the 1990s (Campello 2014; Drake 1991; Roberts 1996; Stokes 2001); and the resurgence of the Left in the 2000s (Castañeda 2006; 2008; Edwards 2010; Roberts and Levitsky 2011; Weyland, Madrid, and Hunter 2010).

As Figure 1.6 illustrates, in the first decade after the securitization of Latin American foreign debt, when financial globalization was consolidating in the region's largest economies, interest rates were still high compared to historical levels,[13] while commodity prices were stagnant for most of the period and in sharp decline after 1995.

During these relatively bad times, most governments still carried a heavy load of debt as a result of the 1980s crises, and were in desperate need of inflows of international capital. Yet, different from the previous decade, these new funds were to be supplied by a large number of

---

[13] Even though they had dropped significantly from the peak reached in 1982.

Globalization, Democracy, and Market Discipline 19

mutual funds and investors, rather than private banks (as in the 1970s), or multilateral agencies (as in smaller and closer economies of the region). To attract this capital, governments could not send officials to personally meet with creditors, or with an IMF designated team, but needed to signal to bond markets with favorable policies.

In their need to attract foreign finance in times of scarcity, leftist presidents inaugurated between the late 1980s and early 2000s thus could hardly afford to risk enacting redistributive or interventionist policies likely to scare investors. Instead, many of them campaigned on a neoliberal agenda, and those who did not frequently abandoned their electoral promises in favor of neoliberal policies immediately after inauguration. As Santiso (2003, p. 27) observes, "Latin America's reform fever of 1990s must be seen in the context of the urgent need for new capital inflows."

Starting in 2003–2004, however, a sharp rise in commodity prices, concurrent with declining interest rates (Figure 1.6), turned the currency scarcity of the previous decade into unprecedented abundance. The boom widened governments' fiscal space to various extents across the region, reducing the necessity of leftist presidents elected in the period to adopt policies aimed at attracting financial capital. It also allowed those that had previously switched to neoliberal programs to boost social expenditures without necessarily confronting market orthodoxy. As a result, after two decades marked by severe constraints, the Latin American Left was more capable of pursuing its own agenda in office.

It follows that, in the long run, market discipline should have different consequences for leftist parties depending on a country's levels of financial integration and exposure of cycles of currency booms and crises.

Other conditions fixed, increased financial integration should moderate the agenda of leftist parties in the long run. This moderation occurs as presidents learn the costs imposed by massive capital flight, and these costs do not vary substantially over time.

This is what happened in Brazil, Latin America's largest financial market and an economy comparatively less dependent on commodity exports where, as a result, the fiscal effect of the boom was less marked and the consequences of a reversal of market sentiment would be more consequential.

After Lula adopted an orthodox economic agenda in response to the confidence crisis of 2002, no other viable leftist candidate ever campaigned on the policies the Workers' Party had defended until the previous year, consolidating a convergence toward a conservative economic agenda in consonance with predictions of efficiency theories of globalization. As the Lula administration gained some wider room to

20 *The Politics of Market Discipline in Latin America*

maneuver after the boom, it managed to expand social policies and the role of the state in the economy, but only within the limits established by macroeconomic orthodoxy.

In economies more vulnerable to currency fluctuations, however, market constraints, and therefore presidents' room to advance a leftist agenda, vary substantially amid "good" and "bad" times. In these countries leftist governments can go from severely constrained to highly autonomous markets, depending on the international economic scenario. As an illustration, during Chávez's first presidency public revenue increased from 18 to 29.7 percent of gross domestic product (GDP) in Venezuela. In Ecuador, it increased from 16.6 percent in 2007 to 25.8 in 2010 under Rafael Correa. In Lula's first year as the president of Brazil, as a comparison, public revenue was 21 percent of the GDP, having reached its maximum in 2010 of 24.3 percent.

It follows that in highly vulnerable countries the promise of leftist policies remains credible to investors and voters, and presidential candidates identified with the Left have an incentive to announce a leftist program whenever they believe this will boost their electoral prospects, even if they are not sure of their capacity to promote these policies in office.

Thus, volatile economies should *not* experience a moderation of the Left in the long run, as observed in more complex and diversified countries. Instead, leftist governments in these countries should pursue radical redistribution when good times create room for that, and switch to a conservative economic program in bad times when market constraints become too strong.

Once again Ecuador illustrates the point; both Lucio Gutiérrez and Rafael Correa ran as left-wing outsiders, with comparable political constituencies. Gutiérrez, elected in bad times, embraced a neoliberal agenda in an attempt to regain the access to international finance that Ecuador had lost after the 1999 crisis. Correa, conversely, was released by the commodity boom from the need to attract foreign funds, and was faithful to the agenda that got him elected.

The remarkable differences between Hugo Chávez's policies in his first years in office, and later when oil prices hiked (Corrales and Penfold 2011; Kaufman 2011; Murillo, Oliveros, and Vaishnav 2011), are further evidence of how sharp differences in market constraints during good and bad times prevent ideological convergence in volatile economies.[14] Policies that limited capital mobility, which could be

---

[14] As widely noted in the scholarly literature, it is no coincidence that both Chávez and Correa found it necessary to concentrate power in the hands of the presidency to advance their preferred agenda. The same happened during the 1990s when, as shown

Globalization, Democracy, and Market Discipline

Scenario

		Bad Times	Good Times
Vulnerability	High	Strong and broad	Weak
	Low	Fairly strong and broad	Fairly strong but narrow

FIGURE 1.7. Vulnerability, International Scenario, and Market Discipline.

adopted only in a country where almost the totality of the inflows of foreign currency are under the government's control, further increased Chávez's room to maneuver.

Argentina also experienced a sharp decrease in market constraints between the governments of Carlos Menem and Fernando De La Rúa, and those of Néstor Kirchner and Cristina Fernández. In this case, though, the change was not primarily caused by exogenous factors like in Ecuador or Venezuela, but by a prior government decision to default on the country's public (and mostly foreign-denominated) debt, which substantially reduced its external financing needs.

The room to maneuver provided by the default, which was later widened by the commodity price boom, explains Kirchner and Fernández's lack of interest in reintegrating the Argentine economy into international financial markets, as well as their capacity to deviate quite radically from investors' macro- and microeconomic preferences, after a decade of investor-oriented policymaking under Menem and De La Rúa.

Figures 1.7 and 1.8 summarize the rationale just stated; the first indicates the nature of market discipline under different scenarios, for vulnerable and nonvulnerable economies, whereas the second displays the predicted outcome in terms of economic policymaking, in the case of left-leaning governments.

Finally, it is important to note that governments' room for radical redistribution in good times, even in countries more subject to variations in commodity prices, is reduced as financial integration increases. Ollanta Humala, in the financially integrated and commodity-dependent Peru,

in Chapter 4, more powerful leftist presidents were the ones most likely to switch to neoliberalism.

	Scenario		
	Bad Times	**Good Times**	*In the Long Run*
High Vulnerability	Extreme macro- and microeconomic orthodoxy	Neither macro-nor microeconomic orthodoxy	*Divergence*
Low Vulnerability	Macro- and microeconomic orthodoxy	Macroeconomic orthodoxy, leftist micro	*Convergence*

FIGURE 1.8. Vulnerability, International Scenario, and Economic Policy Making.

moderated his agenda in response to a preelectoral confidence crisis, even having been inaugurated in the midst of a consolidated commodity price boom.

Yet the opposite is not necessarily true; constraints imposed in bad times do not require that economies are financially integrated. When alternative sources of foreign currency are scarce, governments in more closed economies have an incentive to try to enter – or return to – international financial markets, as did Gutiérrez in Ecuador.

This rationale contributes to explain why a "radical" Left might persist in some Latin American countries but not others, in line with Weyland's (2009) distinction between complex economies and rentier states. Nonetheless, different from Weyland, my theory predicts that this radical Left will coexist with policy switchers *in a same political system*, depending on the strength of market discipline at a given point in time. In that sense, the analysis presented here challenges expectations that the emergence of a moderate Left is country specific.[15]

---

[15] Flores-Macías (2012), for example, argues that the institutionalization of political systems is key to understanding different types of leftist governments in the region. Yet Ecuador's political system had been extremely fragmented and volatile for decades, but this did not prevent Gutiérrez from adopting a conservative economic agenda, whereas Correa governed from the Left. In Venezuela, the collapse of the party system happened before Chávez's election, but as a president he advanced remarkably different policies under different scenarios. The levels of institutionalization of the Argentine party system did not vary markedly in the last decades, but whereas Menem and De La Rúa followed an orthodox path, Kirchner deviated from investors' preferred agenda both at the macro- and at the microeconomic level. All these examples reinforce the claim that the context in which governments are inaugurated is key to understanding the strength of market discipline, which itself determines the room the Left has to advance its own agenda.

Globalization, Democracy, and Market Discipline 23

Plan of the Book

This book adopts a multimethod approach to examine the politics of market discipline in Latin American emerging economies, and is organized as follows. Chapter 2 introduces a model of optimal taxation that depicts how left-wing incumbents' decision concerning levels of income redistribution is affected by increases in capital mobility associated with financial integration. Taxation here is used as a proxy for ideological position – whereas the Left taxes and redistributes to maximize the income of the poor, the Right is assumed to tax as to maximize total investment in the economy.

The model demonstrates why capital should flee economies in which elections are expected to bring about a left turn in government. This effect should be stronger in unequal democracies like those in Latin America, in which the electoral payoff of redistribution is higher and Left and Right should be more polarized.

The model also demonstrates how income inequality and investors' allocative decisions determine the Left's optimal level of taxation, above which the stock of capital that flees the domestic economy outweighs the government's redistributive efforts. It indicates that, under complete information, increased capital mobility should lower this optimal level, forcing the Left to converge to right-wing levels of redistribution.

Next, I examine the conditions under which this convergence does not happen – when investors' exit threat does not moderate leftist redistributive agendas. This outcome is more likely in highly unequal countries in which investors and incumbents are uncertain about each other's behavior. I contend that this uncertainty can be either contingent or structural – contingency being associated with recent financial integration and government's little experience in dealing with mobile capital, and structural uncertainty resulting from economies' exposure to exogenous shocks – and hypothesize that countries highly vulnerable to the structural uncertainties are the ones in which ideological convergence of the Left toward the Right should not occur. The hypotheses raised in Chapter 2 are examined in the remaining chapters of the book, using large-N statistical analyses and case studies.

Chapters 3 and 4 test the basic propositions of the model. Chapter 3 examines bondholders' reactions to government ideology, and how it varies between "good" and "bad" times in Latin American emerging economies. Results show that bond spreads increase as investors anticipate elections to bring about a left turn in office, and decrease when the opposite occurs, consistent with previous scholarly work on the topic

(Block, Vaaler, and Schrage 2005; Renno and Spanakos 2009; Santiso and Martínez 2003).

Also interestingly, higher spreads persist under left-wing administrations, but fade in case a left-wing candidate switches to an investor-friendly agenda after inauguration. Yet investors' perceptions of sovereign risk also depend on international economic factors and, other conditions fixed, worsen in bad times. In good times, not only are spreads lower irrespective of government ideology, but they also reveal no distinction between the risks imposed by conservative governments and those of the "moderate" left – which advance leftist policies within the constraints imposed by macroeconomic orthodoxy.

In Chapter 4, I examine how markets' capacity to discipline governments varies in Latin America. I look at all the presidential elections held since re-democratization, and show that left-leaning presidents inaugurated in the midst of severe currency crises are the ones most likely to embrace a neoliberal agenda. This was true when a restricted number of private banks and multilateral institutions resorted to direct leverage to influence policymaking through loans, and remained so even after the dispersion of the creditor base occurred in the 1990s.

Chapters 5 to 8 present case studies that delve into the mechanisms through which market discipline works. Chapter 5 analyzes presidential elections held in Brazil, with two major purposes. The first is to illustrate the confidence game established between candidates and investors starting in the early campaign through the first year of the newly elected government. The other is to explore how ideological convergence occurs as candidates/presidents and investors repeatedly interact, and uncertainties about each other's behavior disappear.

After depicting the mechanisms that link investors' behavior and ideological convergence in Chapter 5, Chapters 6 and 7 explore cases in which convergence does not occur. They focus on countries that are highly vulnerable to exogenous shocks and where markets' capacity to influence policymaking is subject to significant variation. I demonstrate how these shocks, and the uncertainties they produce, prevent ideological convergence from occurring.

Chapter 6 is devoted to Ecuador, where the elections of two presidents who campaigned on an analogous left-wing discourse and with the support od similar political constituencies help identify how exogenous shocks affect investors' political clout. Whereas Lucio Gutiérrez was elected under a currency crisis, Rafael Correa won during a boom sparked by an unprecedented rise in export prices. These different scenarios contribute to explaining the diverging ways by which each president dealt with investors' reactions during elections and in office.

Globalization, Democracy, and Market Discipline 25

Chapter 7 presents a study of Venezuela, where Chávez's decade-long presidency further evidences the impact of exogenous shocks on bondholders' political influence. In this case, the effects of incumbency are held fixed, whereas exogenous conditions largely vary. This variation explains Chávez's renewed capacity to deviate from investors' preferences and advance his nationalistic and redistributive agenda in Venezuela.

Chapter 8 examines the case of Argentina, where the government's room to maneuver derived not from an exogenous shock but from a prior political decision to default on the country's foreign debt. This chapter explores how the default of December 2001 increased the room to maneuver of the Kirchner administration after a decade in which market confidence remained at the center of the Argentine political stage, and how Fernández used the commodity price boom to further this process.

Chapter 9 builds on the analyses presented in Latin American case studies and that evidences the little effectiveness of market discipline in emerging economies during currency booms, by looking at the opposite case – how sovereign bondholders influence policymaking in developed economies during currency crises. I depict the experience of the eurozone's periphery – Greece, Portugal, and Spain – and show that under extreme currency pressures not only bondholders behaved very similarly to the way they do when investing in emerging economies, but also that in these circumstances leftist governments embraced to orthodoxy and converged toward an investor-oriented economic agenda as it had been shown to happen in Latin America.

The last chapter summarizes the findings presented in the book and analyzes their potential implications for policymaking and for the prospects of democratic accountability in Latin America, in a scenario of increasing financial integration.

2

Between Votes and Capital: Redistribution and Uncertainty in Unequal Democracies

If we lived in a world of complete information, the Brazilian Workers' Party (Partido dos Trabalhadores [PT]) would have anticipated financial market panic during the 2002 presidential election. Knowing the severe consequences it entailed, the then candidate Lula da Silva would probably have moderated his agenda already at the outset of his presidential campaign.

It is also plausible to imagine that Lula's team was aware of the constraints imposed on PT's leftist policies but, assuming that voters were not, deliberately chose to move rightward only after inauguration, not to risk losing the election.

Most probably, however, the PT leadership simply failed to anticipate investors' panic in 2002. It might have overlooked the fact that the Asian and Russian crises of the late 1990s, as well as the Argentine default in 2001 had biased international financial markets against emerging economies, increasing investors' sensitivity to the unfavorable policies associated with Lula's victory. In a more positive scenario, markets' reactions might not have been as severe.

Whatever the real story is, it would be reasonable to expect that after the shift rightward in 2002 Lula would have difficulties reinstating PT's historical agenda when running for reelection in 2006. After all, voters and markets had four years to update their beliefs about the policies likely to be enacted in his second term.

This is, actually, what happened; Lula's presidential program in 2006 by no means resembled the ones announced in the 1989, 1994, or 1998 elections. Rather, it consolidated the move rightward that transpired in 2002, in a trend that persisted with his successor Dilma Roussef in 2010. The Brazilian experience is thus coherent with claims that the threat of capital flight pushes the Left into adopting neoliberal, investor-friendly policies.

Yet, as highlighted in the previous chapter, not all Latin American countries experienced the same policy convergence. In Ecuador, Rafael Correa advanced the left-wing program announced during the 2006 presidential campaign, even though the former leftist president Lucio Gutiérrez had embraced a neoliberal agenda. In Venezuela, Chávez pursued orthodox economic policies during the first years in office, but reverted to his original program afterwards. What explains these different patterns?

This chapter uses formal analysis to examine this question. I start with a model that captures the interaction between leftist presidential candidates and investors during elections in a scenario of complete information. The model determines how mobile capital holders should react when they entertain the election of a leftist president, and how the anticipation of this reaction should influence the president's agenda.

Ultimately, the model evidences why increased capital mobility associated with financial globalization should foster ideological convergence by pushing the Left rightward, toward investors' preferred economic policies.

The following section modifies the model to account for uncertainties in the relations between governments and investors. It shows how miscalculations of each part can provoke currency crises and policy switches that should not occur under complete information.

I finish by discussing how these uncertainties are likely to affect long-run prospects of ideological convergence in the particular case of Latin America.

FINANCIAL GLOBALIZATION AND PROSPECTS FOR THE LEFT

It has long been widely believed that markets' *automatic* resistance to unfavorable policies puts investors in a privileged position to influence political decisions vis-à-vis other groups in society (Lindblom 1977; Mitchell 1997; Przeworski and Wallerstein 1982; Swank 1992).

Governments' attempts to adopt policies perceived to reduce profitability frequently provoke investment strikes that preclude collusion, depending solely on individual appreciations of costs and benefits. The consequences of these strikes can be severe, and their anticipation forces governments of all ideological leanings to consider carefully the effects their policies will have on investor sentiment.

In the past decades, the increased ease with which capital flows can move cross-border has been claimed to further strengthen investors' capacity to influence policymaking (Garrett 1998; Keohane and Milner 1996; Rodrik 2000). The easier it is for asset holders to move capital internationally, the stronger become the incentives for governments to adopt policies that boost investment returns,[1] ultimately limiting the pursuit of an agenda that conflicts with markets' priorities.

The model introduced next relies on partisan theories to examine how market discipline – understood as investors' capacity to push governments toward adopting their preferred policies – works in a scenario of financial globalization.

In a simplification, it assumes that parties on the Left distinguish themselves from those on the Right for the priority they assign to social fairness over economic efficiency, and therefore always prefer to tax and redistribute more than their right-wing counterparts. It follows that investors looking to maximize their profits should favor a right-wing over a leftist agenda.[2]

The model follows Boix (2003) but, instead of assuming countries' capital specificity as a given, it explores the effects of *decreasing capital specificity* – a proxy for increased capital mobility associated with financial globalization – within one country.

Before moving to the next section, there are some aspects of the stylized picture represented in the model that should be clarified. First, it is important to emphasize that the framework proposed in this chapter does not differentiate domestic from foreign investors. Whenever it refers to investors, it alludes to those whose capital is allocated in a given economy at the moment when the game is played, and who can move it with more or less ease depending on levels of capital mobility.

Also, there is in principle no reason why the model could not reflect the behavior of foreign or domestic *direct* investors, who become more mobile as financial globalization advances. Actually, the experience of the countries depicted in the last chapters evidences that business responds, in a longer time horizon, to governments' partisanship.

Yet because this book is particularly concerned with the interactions between governments and investors precisely during elections, the implications of the analysis are discussed with reference to the behavior of *financial investors*. These are the capital holders that react almost immediately to prospects of policy change, and whose behavior can force leftist governments to reconsider their agenda shortly after inauguration.

Finally, following standard practice, redistribution is described in terms of tax and transfers. Notwithstanding, as Przeworski (2007) proposes, taxes and transfers should be read here as representing a broad range of policies that have a redistributive impact.

---

[1] See Cohen (1996) for a review of these arguments.

[2] The next chapter will explore in detail why this assumption holds in the context of sovereign bond markets.

Capital Mobility and the Politics of Redistribution

To examine the conditions that affect a leftist incumbent's decision of how much income to redistribute in an open democracy, consider an economy with two types of individuals, the poor – wage earners – and the wealthy – investors whose capital is allocated in the domestic economy in the moment when the game is played.

Wage earners constitute the majority, represented by a share of $\alpha >$ 1/2 of the population, and own a capital stock of K_p. The income of investors ($1 - \alpha$ of the population) when the game starts is K_w. The total capital in the economy is equal to $K = K_p + K_w$. The aggregate share of capital of each group is, respectively, $k_p = K_p/K$ and $k_w = K_w/K$; therefore $k_p + k_w = 1$.

As a result, the capital held by each wage earner is given by $k_{p_i} = \frac{k_p}{\alpha}$, the same applying to the capital held by an investor, equal to $k_{w_i} = \frac{k_w}{1-\alpha}$, and it necessarily follows that $k_{w_i} > k_{p_i}$.

Finally, the average per capita income in the country is given by:

$$k_a = \alpha k_{p_i} + (1 - \alpha)k_{w_i}$$
$$= \frac{\alpha k_p}{\alpha} + \frac{(1 - \alpha)(1 - k_p)}{(1 - \alpha)}$$
$$= 1$$

The relative productivity of capital at home (σ) is a function of the mobility of capital, as it encompasses the costs investors pay to move capital abroad.[3] Other conditions fixed, and assuming there is some cost associated to sending capital abroad ($\sigma \neq 0$), whenever capital flees the economy, it loses a share of its value. The total cost of this transaction is proportional to σ and represented by a quadratic function of the amount of capital invested abroad. This quadratic relationship implies that the more capital flees the economy, the more costly it gets for investors to send an additional unit of it, and that cost is expressed in Eq. (2.1)[4]:

$$\frac{\sigma(k_{w_{iOUT}})^2}{2} = \frac{\sigma \delta^2 k_{w_i}^2}{2} \tag{2.1}$$

where δ represents the share of investors income that leaves the economy.

Following the standard practice in the political economy literature (Boix 2003; Meltzer and Richard 1981; Persson and Tabellini 2002), the

---

[3] I do not make any assumptions about the costs of moving capital into the economy.
[4] Suppose a capital k, which at home produces $y = k$. If sent abroad, this same capital would produce $y^a = \left(1 - \frac{\sigma \delta^2 k}{2}\right)k$.

state taxes citizens with a linear tax τ on their income k and then redistributes the resulting revenue equally among all individuals. It follows that each individual pays τk_j and receives τk_a. The tax system generates welfare losses represented by the quadratic function $\frac{\tau^2}{2} k_a$. The post-tax income of the poor, then, is given by:

$$\kappa_{p_i} = (1 - \tau)k_{p_i} + \left(\tau - \frac{\tau^2}{2}\right) k_a \tag{2.2}$$

The players in this game are a leftist incumbent P and the wealthy investor I. P establishes a tax rate to maximize the income of the poor median voter, taking into consideration I's capacity to send capital abroad. I decides the share of his capital that should be invested in the domestic economy to maximize his own income, which depends on the relative productivity of capital σ and on the tax level τ.

In this model, the median voter is not aware of the constraints imposed by capital mobility, and votes retrospectively for the incumbent if his income increases during the tenure of one government.[5]

In a game where both I and P have complete information, the total income of an investor is:

$$\kappa_{w_i} = (1 - \tau)k_{w_{i_{IN}}} + \left(1 - \frac{\sigma k_{w_{i_{OUT}}}}{2}\right) k_{w_{i_{OUT}}}$$

$$= (1 - \tau)(1 - \delta)k_{w_i} + \left(1 - \frac{\sigma \delta k_{w_i}}{2}\right) \delta k_{w_i}$$

$$= (1 - \tau)(1 - \delta)k_{w_i} + \delta k_{w_i} - \frac{\sigma \delta^2 k_{w_i}^2}{2}$$

It follows that the share of I's income (δ^*) that is sent abroad to maximize his total income is determined by:

$$\max_\delta[\kappa_{w_i}] = \max_\delta \left[(1 - \tau)(1 - \delta)k_{w_i} + \delta k_{w_i} - \frac{\sigma \delta^2 k_{w_i}^2}{2}\right] \tag{2.3}$$

---

[5] Note that if she pursued complete information, the median voter would always elect the leftist incumbent, to maximize her own income.

Between Votes and Capital

Proposition 1: Solving Eq. (2.3) in δ, we find there is an optimal share of I's capital that, sent abroad, maximizes his total income, and this share is given by $\delta^* = \frac{\tau}{\sigma k_{w_i}}$, $\max[\tau] = \min[1, \sigma k_{w_i}]$.

Proof: See Appendix: Maximization of Investors' Income.

It is worth noting that taxation is applied solely on the share of the income of an investor that remains in the country $(1-\delta)$. For that reason, k_a, which was equal to 1 in Eq. (2.2), is now equal to $k_p + (1-\delta)k_w$, and the income of the poor is given by:

$$\kappa_{p_i} = (1-\tau)k_{p_i} + \left(\tau - \frac{\tau^2}{2}\right)(k_a)$$

$$= (1-\tau)k_{p_i} + \left(\tau - \frac{\tau^2}{2}\right)(\alpha k_{p_i} + (1-\alpha)(1-\delta)k_{w_i}) \qquad (2.4)$$

The level of taxation that maximizes the income of the poor, subject to prospects of capital flight, then, is obtained from:

$$\max_{\tau}[\kappa_{p_i}] = \max_{\tau}[(1-\tau)k_{p_i} + \left(\tau - \frac{\tau^2}{2}\right)(\alpha k_{p_i} + (1-\alpha)(1-\delta)k_{w_i})$$

$$(2.5)$$

Proposition 2: Solving Eq. (2.5) in τ, we find that there is one $0 < \tau^* < \sigma k_{w_i}$ ($\sigma k_{w_i} < 1$), which maximizes the income of the poor (κ_{p_i}) subject to the constraints imposed by capital mobility. This is the level of taxation established by the left-wing incumbent.

Proof: See Appendix: Maximization of the Income of the Poor.

Implications of the Model

CAPITAL MOBILITY AND THE INCOME OF THE POOR Other conditions fixed, the optimal share of investor I's capital that is sent abroad is a positive linear function of the tax τ.

Figure 2.1a illustrates this relationship and shows that, because the level of taxation established by a left-wing government is, by assumption, always higher than the taxation imposed by a right-wing government (in the simulation $\tau_L = 0.45 > \tau_R = 0.20$),[6] the share of I's income

---

[6] This model does not explore the behavior of right-wing incumbents, but it assumes that they maximize the share of capital invested in the country $1 - \delta$ subject to electoral constraints. Because voters chose retrospectively and based on the performance of the economy before and after the current government, this constraint is a corner solution, with $\kappa_{p_i} post > \kappa_{p_i} pre$. It is easy to show that, according to this rationale, $\tau_L > \tau_R$.

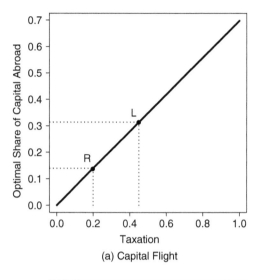

(a) Capital Flight

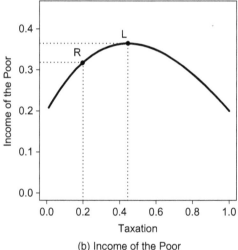

(b) Income of the Poor

FIGURE 2.1. Capital Flight and Income of the Poor as Function of Taxation.
Notes: Simulation of (a) the optimal share of the income of the wealthy sent abroad δ^* and (b) the income of the poor k_{p_i}, as functions of taxation. Parameters of the simulation: share of the poor in the population ($\alpha = 0.70$), relative return to capital ($\sigma = 0.60$), income of one poor ($k_{p_i} = 0.20$), $\tau_{\text{Left}} = 0.45$, $\tau_{\text{Right}} = 0.20$.

that remains in the economy is higher under a conservative government ($\delta_L \cong 0.69 < \delta_R \cong 0.88$). This formulation also implies that, whenever the Left replaces the Right in office, this should trigger some level of capital flight, whereas capital should flow into the economy when the opposite occurs.

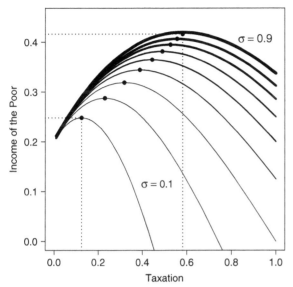

FIGURE 2.2. Financial Globalization and Optimal Taxation.
Notes: Simulation of the optimal level of taxation (τ^*) as a function of the barrier imposed on capital outflows, and reflected on σ. Parameters of the simulation: share of the poor in the population ($\alpha = 0.70$), relative return to capital ($\sigma \epsilon [0.1, 1]$), income of one poor ($k_{p_i} = 0.20$).

From the preceding assumptions it follows that the income of a wage earner (k_{p_i}) is represented by a quadratic function of the level of taxation (τ). This means that redistribution raises this income up to a level where an additional unit of capital transferred to the poor does not compensate for the additional share of I's investment that leaves the economy in consequence of that (Figure 2.1b), and that the income of the poor will be higher under a left-wing government.

FINANCIAL GLOBALIZATION, OPTIMAL TAXATION, AND THE INCOME OF THE POOR Figure 2.2 simulates how financial globalization, by increasing international capital mobility, should affect leftist governments' capacity to tax investors. It shows that the lower are the costs of moving capital abroad (lower σ), the lower is the tax that maximizes the income of the poor.

Other conditions fixed, as barriers to capital decrease, the capacity a leftist incumbent has to tax investors and redistribute income also decreases, in line with "race to the bottom" arguments.[7] Put simply, the

---

[7] See Kaufman and Segura-Ubiergo (2001); Rudra (2002); Rudra (2008); and Abbas, Klemm, Bedi, and Park (2012) for examples of studies of "race to the bottom" dynamics focused on emerging economies.

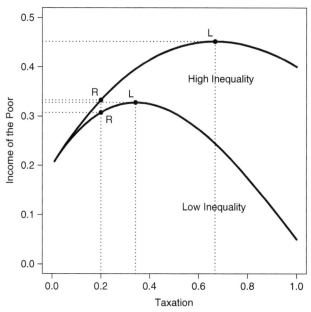

FIGURE 2.3. Left–Right Policy Distance as a Function of Income Inequality.
Notes: Simulation of the policy distance (range of possible levels of τ) as function of levels of income inequality. Parameters of the simulation: share of the poor in the population ($a_{HI} = 0.9$, $a_{LI} = 0.55$), costs of sending capital abroad ($\sigma = 0.50$), income of one poor ($k_{p_i} = 0.20$).

simulation suggests that the utility function of wage earners is reduced with capital mobility, and that even a government that is a perfect agent of a poor median voter will progressively moderate redistributive attempts as mobility advances.

POLICY DISTANCE AS A FUNCTION OF INCOME INEQUALITY The model implies that inequality widens the potential policy distance between the Left and Right (here, depicted as $\tau_L - \tau_R$) in a given polity. Figure 2.3 shows that, for fixed levels of capital mobility and income of the poor, the potential distance between left- and right-wing policies is larger in unequal societies. This is consistent with investors' perception, reported in Mosley (2003, p. 129), that "in emerging market economies, market participants view the range of possible policy outcomes as relatively wide: some governments pursue capital-friendly policies, but others may advocate policies hostile to international investors."

The figure further evidences that income redistribution has greater potential to increase the income of the poor in unequal societies than

Between Votes and Capital 35

in equal ones, and suggests why the electoral payoff of redistributive policies should be higher the more unequal a country is.

SUMMARY The model just presented demonstrates that, even in a scenario of high income inequality, provided that investors and governments have complete information financial integration will moderate the leftist incumbent's attempts to redistribute income to the poor.

If partisan theories are correct, and the Left differentiates itself from the Right in the economic realm by its priority to social fairness and willingness to curb investment returns in favor of income redistribution, capital holders should reduce their exposure to countries where elections are expected to bring about a "move to the Left" in office. Leftist incumbents know that, and accept some capital flight in response to taxation until the level that maximizes the income of the poor.

As capital becomes increasingly mobile, however, this optimal level of taxation decreases. This implies that, under complete information, increased financial integration should reduce governments' room to tax and force a convergence of the Left toward the lower levels of redistribution promoted by the Right.

Yet there are few reasons to expect that, in Latin American emerging economies, the interactions between incumbents and financial investors – the main interest of this analysis – occur in a scenario of complete information. The next section relaxes this assumption, and examines how uncertainty alters the outcomes of the game.

FINANCIAL INTEGRATION, EXOGENOUS SHOCKS, AND UNCERTAINTY

Many factors suggest that financial investors and politicians do not interact in conditions of complete information in Latin American emerging economies. Financial globalization is still quite recent in the region, and most financial markets are illiquid, asymmetric, and volatile, making it hard for politicians to correctly anticipate investors' behavior.

On the political realm, democratization is also a recent process. Moreover, high income inequality, low levels of party and party system institutionalization, and a concentration of power in hands of the executive contribute to high policy volatility, reducing the predictability of policymaking.

In such a scenario, it is not unlikely that investors sometimes overreact to prospects of a left turn in office, causing abnormal[8] capital flight

---

[8] Abnormal here should be understood as capital flight beyond levels anticipated by the incumbent I, given the parameters of the game.

during elections. It is also conceivable that leftist incumbents miscalculate investors' behavior during elections, as well as their consequences. In the model, this would lead candidates to announce policies more "to the Left" than they will be capable of delivering in office considering the existing constraints.

Yet even though these miscalculations should be common in young, recently integrated democracies, they should become less frequent as democratic systems and financial integration consolidate.

A more structural source of uncertainty in the relations between investors and governments in Latin American emerging markets, however, is related to investors' and politicians' knowledge about the true state of the economy. As pointed out in the previous chapter, the performance of Latin American emerging economies depends substantially on circumstances that are beyond governments' control and hard to predict.

A strong dependence on commodity exports and low levels of domestic savings make these economies highly vulnerable to fluctuations in commodity prices and international interest rates. As a result, the relative importance of exogenous ("push") versus domestic ("pull") factors in determining the attractiveness of Latin American emerging markets to foreign capital – and in particular *financial* capital – is significantly higher than in the OECD.

This attractiveness is the highest – and room for redistribution the widest – when commodity prices are high and international interest rates are low. In these periods, economic growth accelerates, increasing the productivity of capital.

This happens through multiple channels. First, faster economic growth promotes gains of scale, allowing for a noninflationary increase in profits and salaries per unit produced. It also boosts jobs and increases average productivity in the economy by removing workers from less to more productive activities. Moreover, faster economic growth creates incentives for companies to increase investment, promoting the expansion and modernization of productive capacity, and allows for the development of new markets, which opens the frontiers to the expansion of the economy. At last, faster economic growth leads to an upward revision of expectations about the economy, and a spread of confidence among private players (Barbosa and Pereira de Souza 2010, p. 11).

In the model, this is captured by an increase in σ which, other conditions fixed, leads to a decrease in the optimal share of investors' capital allocated abroad (δ^*) for a given level of taxation τ. Ultimately, this implies that the optimal share of redistribution promoted by the Left

Between Votes and Capital 37

occurs at a higher level (τ^* increases), increasing the maximum income of the poor compared to "normal times."

When commodity prices drop, conversely, the relative productivity of capital decreases, investors' sensitivity to a leftist agenda increases and, other conditions fixed, the optimum level of taxation shifts downward.

As a result, in countries highly exposed to exogenous shocks, in which the attractiveness to investment varies substantially, candidates and investors have a hard time anticipating the state of the economy in which a new government will operate. This "structural uncertainty," in addition to the contingent uncertainty associated with recent financial liberalization and democratization, modifies the previous assumption of complete information, and allows for miscalculations on the part of each player.

Uncertainties are captured in the model by the inclusion of a draw of nature, which occurs between election and inauguration and can either change or not the conditions incumbents confront when elected. Whenever conditions change, players adjust to the new scenario. As countries' relative productivity varies, investors become more or less reactive to policy choices – in this case, captured by levels of taxation – widening and narrowing leftist governments' room to redistribute income accordingly.

Nature's play: Exogenous Shocks, Currency Crises, and Policy Switches

This game starts with the election of P, a left-wing incumbent who promised to tax $\tau*$, expected to maximize the income of the poor given his beliefs about investors' willingness to send capital abroad.

Next, a draw of Nature establishes the "true state of the economy" (real relative productivity of capital σ_R), which can be "normal" ($\sigma_R = \sigma$, same as assumed by investors and candidates during campaign), "good" ($\sigma_R = \sigma_G > \sigma$) or "bad" ($\sigma_R = \sigma_B < \sigma$). After Nature determines the "true state of the economy," investors and incumbents make their decisions about how much capital to send abroad and how much to tax, respectively.

This Nature's draw aims to capture the effect of exogenous shocks – unexpected fluctuations in international costs of capital or commodity prices – in the relative productivity of capital (σ) in an emerging economy.[9] By changing σ, these shocks also modify investors' propensity to react to taxation, and ultimately leftist governments' room to tax.

---

[9] In the shorter term, it could also reflect uncertainties associated with recent financial globalization.

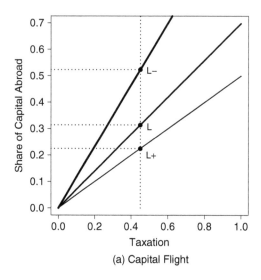

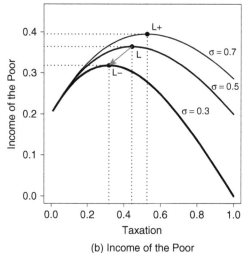

FIGURE 2.4. State of the Economy and Optimal Taxation.
Notes: Simulation of the share of the income of the wealthy sent abroad δ^*, as well as the income of the poor k_{p_i}, as functions of taxation ($\tau_L = 0.45$, $\tau_R = 0.20$), for different scenarios (exogenous shocks): "normal" (L), negative (L−), and positive (L+). Parameters of the simulation: share of the poor in the population ($\alpha = 0.70$), cost of sending capital abroad ($\sigma \in 0.30, 0.50, 0.70$), income of one poor ($k_{p_i} = 0.20$). Policy switches are indicated by the arrow, in graph 2.4b.

As the relative productivity of capital increases with a positive exogenous shock, investor's response to taxation (denoted by the difference in the slopes of lines L and $L+$ in Figure 2.4a) diminishes and they allocate more capital in the economy for a same level of τ. This means that, during booms, investors will send a smaller share of capital abroad than the incumbent initially expected for a tax level of $\tau = \tau*$, creating more room for income redistribution (as shown in curve $L+$ in Figure 2.4b). It is no coincidence that the Latin American "move to the Left" happened in the midst of a boom in commodity prices and in capital inflows started in 2004 (Campello 2014; Kaufman 2011; Murillo, Oliveros, and Vaishnav 2011).

The opposite occurs in "bad times," when the relative productivity of capital decreases, and the elasticity of investment to taxation increases. In this case, capital flight is more severe than the incumbent expected for $\tau = \tau^*$, and the room to redistribute income to wage earners is narrowed down.

In this scenario, leftist incumbents will be forced to "switch to the Right" (tax and transfer less than promised during campaign, evidenced by the arrow from L to $L-$ in Figure 2.4b) to maximize the income of the poor. In case they decided to keep their campaign promise to tax $\tau = \tau^*$, this should prompt a currency crisis – understood here as "abnormal" capital flight – and the income of the poor would be less than optimal. Leftist switches to orthodoxy in periods of currency scarcity, such as those occurred in Latin America in the late 1980s and 1990s and are studied in Chapter 4, are examples of this process.

LONG-TERM IMPLICATIONS FOR IDEOLOGICAL CONVERGENCE

The models introduced in this chapter depicted the interaction between candidates/presidents and investors around elections. They determined how investors should respond to the prospects of a left turn in office, and how the anticipation of these reactions should constrain leftist governments' decision about how much income to redistribute.

I started by examining this interaction in a scenario of complete information, in which incumbents and investors know each others' behavior and the true state of the economy. In such scenario, as financial integration advances investors' increased capacity to move capital cross-borders reduces leftist governments' room to redistribute income. Ultimately, the model points to a convergence of the left toward right-wing levels of redistribution.

The following section relaxed the assumption of complete information, to verify how uncertainties can influence the interaction between investors and leftist incumbents. I argued that these uncertainties could be of two sorts: (1) those contingent on recent financial integration and democratization, which should disappear as investors and governments

40   *The Politics of Market Discipline in Latin America*

repeatedly interact and both processes consolidate and (2) structural uncertainties, which are caused by the vulnerability of Latin American emerging economies to exogenous factors such as fluctuations in international interest rates and commodity prices.

In this second version of the model, countries' relative productivity of capital varies with exogenous factors, and players learn its true value only after inauguration. Whenever this value changes compared to prior expectations, both investors and incumbents respond accordingly. If the true relative productivity is higher than previously expected, investors become more complacent with respect to taxation, and leftist governments are provided with a wider room to redistribute income.

If the true value is lower, investors become more reactive to redistribution, which narrows leftist governments' room to maneuver. In this case, the only way for the Left to maximize the income of the poor is to "shift to the Right," taxing and redistributing less than promised during the campaign. Somewhat paradoxically, if leftist presidents maintain their campaign promises under these circumstances they risk triggering currency crises – excessive capital flight – and delivering less than optimal income to the poor.

As investors and incumbents repeatedly interact in a scenario of increased capital mobility and democratic consolidation, contingent uncertainties diminish as players' behaviors become more predictable. In this scenario, market discipline works as leftist governments learn the limits of how much income they can redistribute (a proxy for their *leftism*) given market constraints, and these constraints do not vary markedly.

Yet there are no reasons, in principle, to expect that structural uncertainties caused by exogenous shocks decrease over time, at least while Latin American economies remain dependent on foreign savings and reliant on commodity exports as they have been historically.

Individual economies' exposure to exogenous shocks varies, though, which means that in the long run uncertainties in the relations between investors and governments should remain in some countries but not others. It follows that the political implications of financial integration should also differ between the two groups.

In countries less exposed to exogenous shocks, and where uncertainties in governments' and markets' relations are mostly contingent, ideological convergence should occur as incumbents learn the constraints imposed by capital mobility, and these constraints do not change substantially between good and bad times (Figure 2.5a).

In the Brazilian case explored in Chapter 5, these uncertainties clearly diminished in the two elections following Lula's victory in 2002. Not

Between Votes and Capital

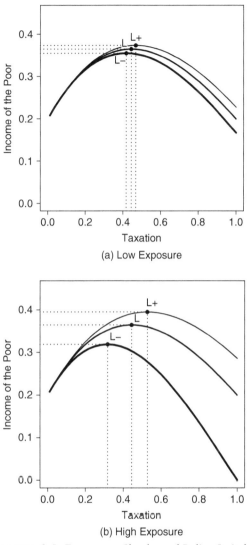

FIGURE 2.5. Exogenous Shocks and Policy Switches.
Notes: Simulation of the income of the poor k_{p_i} as a function of taxation, in "good" and "bad" times. Parameters of the simulation: share of the poor in the population ($\alpha = 0.7$), relative productivity of capital ($\sigma = 0.2$).

only did the president learn investors' sensitivity to his prior agenda and how far he could go without challenging the limits of markets' confidence, but investors also learned Lula's (weak) resolve to confront capital to advance PT's traditional agenda.

In countries in which the exposure to these shocks is high, however, the constraints imposed by capital mobility – and therefore leftist governments' capacity to redistribute income from investors to wage earners – should vary markedly over time (Figure 2.5b). For this reason, incumbents will sometimes be capable of advancing aggressive redistribution, even though in other times they will not.

This uncertainty guarantees that the promise of leftist policies remains credible to investors, and explains the efforts of risk agencies and analysts to scrutinize candidates' background and beliefs. It also explains why, in economies more exposed to exogenous shocks, even after financial integration voters will remain perceiving programmatic divergence between the Left and Right. This perception creates incentives for candidates to keep promising leftist policies whenever they believe this will boost their electoral prospects, even when they are not sure of their capacity to promote these policies in office.

Ultimately, the more volatile economies are, that is, the more dependent on commodity exports and foreign savings, the less likely it is that globalization brings about a long-term moderation of the Left. Instead, leftist governments should alternate aggressive redistribution when good times create room for that, and switches to a neoliberal, investor-driven program in bad times, when market constraints are too strong to bear. Chapters 6 and 7 examine the experiences of Ecuador and Venezuela, respectively, to illustrate these claims.

APPENDIX

Maximization of Investors' Income

$$\max_{\delta} [\kappa_{w_i}] = \max_{\delta} \left[(1 - \delta)(1 - \tau)k_{w_i} + \delta k_{w_i} - \frac{\sigma \delta^2 k_{w_i}^2}{2} \right] \qquad (2.6)$$

Solving that maximization, we have:

$$-(1 - \tau)k_{w_i} + k_{w_i} - \delta(k_{w_i})^2 \sigma = 0$$
$$k_{w_i}(\tau - \delta k_{w_i} \sigma) = 0$$
$$\tau - \delta k_{w_i} \sigma = 0$$
$$\delta^* = \frac{\tau}{\sigma k_{w_i}} \qquad (2.7)$$

Between Votes and Capital

The fact that $0 \leq \delta^* \leq 1$ implies that[10]:

$$\frac{\tau}{\sigma k_{w_i}} \leq 1 \rightarrow \tau \leq \sigma k_{w_i}$$

Hence,

$$\max[\tau] = \min[1, \sigma k_{w_i}] \qquad (2.8)$$

Maximization of the Income of the Poor

From Eq. (2.5) we have that:

$$\max_{\tau}[\kappa_{p_i}] = \max_{\tau}\left[(1-\tau)k_{p_i} + \left(\tau - \frac{\tau^2}{2}\right)(\alpha k_{p_i} + (1-\alpha)(1-\delta)k_{w_i})\right]$$

Rearranging the terms, we have:

$$\max_{\tau}\left[(1-\tau)k_{p_i} + \left(\tau - \frac{\tau^2}{2}\right)(\alpha k_{p_i} + (1-\alpha)(1-\delta)k_{w_i}) = 0\right.$$

$$\max_{\tau}\left[(1-\tau)k_{p_i} + \left(\tau - \frac{\tau^2}{2}\right)\left(\alpha k_{p_i} + (1-\alpha)\left(1 - \frac{\tau}{\sigma k_{w_i}}\right)k_{w_i}\right)\right] = 0$$

Solving it in τ we obtain:

$$-k_{p_i} + (1-\tau)\left[\alpha k_{p_i} + (1-\alpha)k_{w_i} - \frac{(1-\alpha)}{\sigma}\tau\right] - \left(\tau - \frac{\tau^2}{2}\right)\left(\frac{1-\alpha}{\sigma}\right) = 0$$

$$\frac{3(1-\alpha)\tau^2}{2\sigma} - \left(\alpha k_{p_i} + (1-\alpha)k_{w_i} + \frac{2(1-\alpha)}{\sigma}\right)\tau + (1-\alpha)(k_{w_i} - k_{p_i}) = 0$$

$$(2.9)$$

When $\tau = 0$, *LHS* > 0:

$$(1-\alpha)((k_{w_i} - k_{p_i}) > 0$$

When $\tau = 1$, *LHS* < 0:

$$-\frac{(1-\alpha)}{2\sigma} - k_{p_i} < 0$$

---

[10] That condition is binding only when $\sigma k_{w_i} \leq 1$, since $0 \leq \tau \leq 1$.

When $\tau = \sigma k_{w_i}$, $LHS < 0$: To verify the signal of this Eq. (2.9) when $\tau = \sigma k_{w_i}$, one can divide it into three terms:

$$-k_{p_i} + (1 - \tau)(\alpha k_{p_i}) \tag{2.10}$$

$$(1 - \alpha)k_{w_i} - \frac{(1 - \alpha)}{\sigma}\tau \tag{2.11}$$

$$-\left(\tau - \frac{\tau^2}{2}\right)\left(\frac{1 - \alpha}{\sigma}\right) \tag{2.12}$$

It is possible to show that the terms (2.10) and (2.12) are negative, while (2.11) is equal to 0. Starting with (2.10), we have:

$$-k_{p_i} + (1 - \tau)(\alpha k_{p_i}) = k_{p_i}(\alpha - 1) - \tau \alpha k_{p_i}k_{w_i}$$

where

$$k_{p_i}(\alpha - 1) < 0, \quad \text{for any } \alpha < 1, \text{and}$$

$$-\tau \alpha k_{p_i}k_{w_i} < 0, \quad \text{for } \tau > 0 \text{ and } \alpha > 0$$

From term (2.11), replacing $\tau = \sigma k_{w_i}$, we have:

$$(1 - \alpha)k_{w_i} - \frac{(1 - \alpha)}{\sigma}\sigma k_{w_i} = 0 \tag{2.13}$$

Finally, from the negative term (2.12):

$$\left(\tau - \frac{\tau^2}{2}\right) > 0, \quad \text{and}$$

$$\left(\frac{1 - \alpha}{\sigma}\right) > 0, \quad \text{for any } \alpha < 1$$

It follows that there is one $0 < \tau^* < \sigma k_{w_i}$ ($\sigma k_{w_i} < 1$), for which $LHS = 0$, that maximizes the income of the poor k_{p_i} constrained by the threat of capital flight. This is the level of taxation established by the leftist incumbent once in office.

3

Investors' "Vote" in Presidential Elections

The model introduced in the previous chapter conveys that market discipline works as investors' negative responses to the election of the Left forces left-leaning governments into adopting an economic program closer to markets' preferences than they would otherwise.

It also suggests that market discipline is more effective in "bad times," when poor economic prospects make investors more reactive to unfavorable policies. In "good times," conversely, markets' increased complacency widens governments' room to advance a leftist agenda.

In the long run, the model implies that, as capital mobility increases, market discipline should force the convergence of the Left toward the Right[1] in relatively stable economies but not in those that are highly vulnerable to economic fluctuations. In these countries, leftist governments should instead embrace a neoliberal agenda in bad times but promote radical redistribution in good times.

This chapter and the next examine how these claims about investors' and governments' behavior hold in Latin America. Here, I focus on creditors' response to government ideology, and how it varies between good and bad times. In Chapter 4, I turn to governments.

CREDITORS' RESPONSE TO PARTISANSHIP

Does government ideology matter to creditors of sovereign debt? For this to be true, it is necessary that the policies creditors favor (and disfavor) have different prospects of being enacted depending on the ideology prevailing in office.

---

[1] Recall that, in the model, this means that the Left curbs its redistributive attempts.

45

46   *The Politics of Market Discipline in Latin America*

In the particular case of international bondholders, whose assets are exposed to inflation, currency fluctuations, and the risk of default, returns on investment vary depending not only on governments' macroeconomic decisions, but also on a broader range of supply-side policies that affect their ability to pay debt (Mosley 2003).

It follows that sovereign bondholders should worry about ideology only to the extent that policies advanced by governments of different ideological leanings affect the macroeconomy, as well as creditworthiness, in distinct ways.

Partisan theories suggest they do. They posit that parties promote policies that are consistent with the preferences of their core constituencies, and that governments with different ideological leanings pursue distinct sets of priorities in office (Alesina 1987; Alesina and Rosenthal 1995; Hibbs 1977).

Conservative governments are argued to favor economic growth over income equality and to prioritize monetary and fiscal orthodoxy to maintain price stability (Oatley 1999). They are also more inclined to establish an investor-friendly economic and institutional environment (Block, Vaaler, and Schrage 2006; Santiso 2003), lowering taxation and public expenditures (Wibbels and Arce 2003),[2] favoring the deregulation of the labor market, trade and financial liberalization, and the privatization of state assets.

Progressive governments, conversely, are more likely to protect labor markets (Botero, Djankov, Porta, and Lopez-De-Silanes 2004), accept higher levels of inflation, and expand the public sector to promote employment. They are also less prone to balance budgets, and more inclined to redistribute income (Bobbio 1994) by increasing social expenditures and taxes on businesses and the wealthy (Bartels 2008; Garrett 1998; Hays, Stix, and Freeman 2000; Leblang and Bernhard 2006). In less developed and largely indebted countries, governments on the Left are also associated with higher chances of sovereign defaults (Mosley 2003), with the imposition of capital controls (Mosley and Singer 2008), and with the nationalization of private companies.

If these depictions of left-wing and right-wing governments hold, it is plausible that, other conditions fixed, bondholders favor conservative over leftist governments. Recent findings in the political economy literature support this claim; authors have shown that governments with a higher percentage of left-leaning cabinet members pay

---

[2] It is worth noting that the long-term effect of such policies is disputable. Endogenous growth theorists, for instance, might claim that social expenditures in health and education are likely to increase business profitability in the long run.

Investors' "Vote" in Presidential Elections 47

higher interest rates than those in which right-wing members prevail (Garrett 1998; Leblang and Bernhard 2006; Mosley 2003), and that speculative attacks are more likely to occur after the election of the Left, both in developed (Leblang and Bernhard 2000) and less developed economies (Leblang 2002). Block and Vaaler (2004) further find that risk agencies lower sovereign bond ratings when leftist governments are elected in Latin America.

In this chapter, I examine the behavior of sovereign risk in Latin American emerging economies, to access whether bondholders actually perceive leftist governments as riskier. If this is true, sovereign risk should be higher when leftist governments are in office.

Moreover, assuming that security prices reflect all public information available at a given moment (Malkiel 2003; Moser 2007),[3] bondholders' response to government ideology should be observable already in the course of presidential campaigns, as markets come closer to anticipating the likely winner.

Yet it is necessary to consider the international scenario when comparing investors' response to ideology in Latin America; I have argued that these responses should vary along cycles of currency booms and crises – driven by fluctuations in commodity prices and international interest rates – that characterize the low-savings-commodity-exporting economies of the region. Sovereign risk should be lower during currency booms, when governments' capacity to pay debt improves substantially, regardless of the ideology prevailing in office.

The following hypotheses summarize these expectations:

Hypothesis 1 *Sovereign risk should be higher under a leftist government, compared to a conservative one.*

Hypothesis 2 *Sovereign risk should increase during presidential campaigns in which a leftist president is expected to win, and decrease when the opposite occurs.*

Hypothesis 3 *Sovereign risk should be lower in good times – when commodity prices are high and international interest rates are low – than in bad times, when the opposite occurs.*

---

[3] See Malkiel (2003, p. 60) for a review of the debate about the efficient market hypothesis. In his words, "financial markets are far more efficient and far less predictable than some recent academic papers would have us believe.... Many of us economists who believe in efficiency do so because we view markets as amazingly successful devices for reflecting new information rapidly and, for the most part, accurately."

GOVERNMENT IDEOLOGY AND ECONOMIC POLICYMAKING

Since redemocratization, started in the 1980s, there has been broad variation in governments' ideology and economic policies in Latin America, both across countries and over time.

Following the neoliberal wave of the 1980s and 1990s, in which irrespective of their declared ideology most presidents ended up embracing an orthodox economic agenda, the 2000s brought about a much debated resurgence of the Left in Latin American politics.

Starting with Hugo Chávez in Venezuela in 1998, presidents identified with the Left have been elected in Brazil, Chile, Uruguay, Ecuador, and Argentina, while neoliberal governments remained prevalent in Colombia, Peru, and Mexico.[4] Consistent with partisan theories, governments of distinct ideologies established different economic priorities and advanced alternative economic policies in the region. State-oriented governments, or what has been referred to as the radical, populist, or contentious Left, (Castañeda 2008; Edwards 2010; Flores-Macías 2010; Roberts and Levitsky 2011) adopted economic policies very different from their market-oriented counterparts, be them the so-called moderate or liberal democratic Left, or governments identified with the economic Right (Table 3.1).

The Justicialistas Néstor Kirchner and Cristina Fernández de Kirchner on Argentina are an example of the state-oriented Left that resurged in Latin America during the 2000s.[5] In the macroeconomic realm, they controlled the exchange rate, restricted cross-border capital flows, and adopted protectionist measures. Kirchner and Fernández also intervened in the Central Bank and maintained an expansive monetary policy, accepting high levels of inflation in an effort to boost growth and employment. In the micro level, both governments pursued nationalizations, subsidized energy prices, and fought hard to conclude and sustain a default on the country's public debt.

Rafael Correa advanced similar policies in Ecuador.[6] After losing access to international financial markets following a default on its Brady debt in 1999, most administrations in the country devoted major efforts

---

[4] Note that I restrict the analysis to Latin American financially integrated emerging economies, defined as those that issue sovereign bonds in international markets. Leftist governments were elected in many other Latin American countries such as Bolivia, El Salvador, and Nicaragua, but they are not discussed here because they do not fit the selection criterion.

[5] See Chapter 8.

[6] See Chapter 6.

Investors' "Vote" in Presidential Elections

TABLE 3.1. *Ideology and Economic Policy Making (2007–2011)[a]*

Economic Policies and Indicators	State-oriented Left	Market-oriented	
		Left	Right
Inflation	13.1	5.0	3.9
GDP growth (%)	6.7	4.9	4.8
Primary Balance (% GDP)	1.0	2.0	1.2
External Debt (% GDP)	31	33	25
Interest Payments (% Exports)[b]	4.7	5.8	5.8
Trade (% GDP)	51	53	49
Current Account(% GDP)	2.6	−1.0	−1.8
Exchange Rate policy	Intervention	Free float	Free float
Central Bank	Intervention	Independent	Independent
Trade	Subsidies/ protection	Free	Free
Nationalization	Yes	No	No
Contracts	Renegotiated	Maintained	Maintained

[a] Data for inflation and GDP growth from 2004-2011; inflation in Argentina reported until 2007, inflation in Venezuela reported starting 2009, inflation in Chile reported for 2010–2011, GDP growth reported for Argentina until 2006.
[b] Interest payments on foreign debt.
Source: World Development Indicators, except for Primary Balance from CEPALStats.

toward regaining investors' confidence. This strategy was completely reversed by the leftist Correa since 2006.

Under his leadership, Ecuador renegotiated concessions for explorations of utilities and oil and re-regulated labor markets. Correa also stripped the Central Bank of autonomy, advanced a de facto nationalization of the banking system, and announced a partial default on the country's public debt in December 2008. In the macroeconomic realm, the government converted an average primary surplus of 2.6 percent of GDP between 1999 and 2006 into an average deficit of 0.7 percent between 2007 and 2011, despite an 11 percent increase in public revenues in the period. Social expenditure increased from 5.4 percent of GDP in 2006 to 8.3 percent in 2008 (Conaghan 2011).

President Hugo Chávez went even further in Venezuela.[7] He secured fiscal surpluses in all but two out of his eleven years in office, despite an unprecedented boom in oil prices. In 2003, the president imposed capital controls that severely limited outflows of foreign currency from Venezuelan citizens and business, and maintained the highest rates of inflation in the region. Chávez also renegotiated oil contracts, and nationalized a

---

[7] See Chapter 7.

broad range of industries, including steel, cement, and food distribution, becoming the most conspicuous representative of Latin America's radical Left.

The so-called moderate, or market-oriented Left followed remarkably different strategies, sometimes barely distinct from its neoliberal opponents. Chile under the Socialist governments of Eduardo Lagos and Michele Bachelet, Brazil under Lula da Silva and Dilma Rousseff of the Workers' Party, and Uruguay governed by Tabaré Vázques and José Mujica of the Broad Front, all advanced redistributive policies, but only within the limits imposed by an orthodox macroeconomic agenda.

Brazil maintained consistently high primary fiscal balances that sharply reduced the country's indebtedness between 2005 and 2008, a floating exchange rate regime, and a monetary policy oriented toward inflation control.[8] In the microeconomic realm, though, and particularly after the second Lula administration, the government increased social expenditures, raised the minimum wage, and initiated a credit policy that boosted consumption in the country. Through the Brazilian National Development Bank (Banco Nacional de Desenvolvimento Econômico e Social [BNDES]), the government compensated manufacturers dissatisfied with high interest rates with subsidized loans, and promoted industrial policies.

Uruguay's performance resembles that of Brazil; steady primary balances reduced the country's fiscal deficit, the government allowed the currency to free float, and inflation was kept remarkably low. In the microeconomic realm, the government prioritized the extension of universal rights on education, health and social security, yet Uruguay was the only emerging economy in Latin America in which inequality slightly increased in the 2000s.

At last, Chile represents the other extreme of the left-leaning spectrum. Even though the Socialist administrations of Ricardo Lagos, and especially that of Michele Bachelet advanced the country's social agenda compared to previous governments, the Chilean Left was characterized by a technocratic approach to governance. Efforts to reassure the country's dynamic and powerful business community ended up leading the government to abandon commitments with a more far-reaching change (Roberts 2011).

In the macroeconomic realm the Socialist governments continued the Christian Democratic orthodox agenda, maintaining primary and fiscal surpluses through most of the decade, as well as a free-floating exchange rate system and an independent central bank.

---

[8] See Chapter 5.

Finally, in the neoliberal governments that prevailed in Peru until 2011, as well as in Colombia and Mexico, macroeconomic orthodoxy went in parallel with very timid redistributive efforts. These were the countries with the smallest government transfers to the poor in the region (Lustig and McLeod 2011).

INVESTORS' RESPONSE TO GOVERNMENT IDEOLOGY

Recent scholarly literature suggests that, in emerging economies, sovereign risk depends on countries' economic fundamentals, external liquidity conditions, and political risk.[9]

Yet, because these studies are mostly pursued by economists and oriented toward predicting risk rather than to investigating cause relations, they frequently overlook the fact that besides a direct effect political risk and external conditions also have an *indirect* effect on sovereign risk, which works through their impact on country's economic fundamentals. As a result, by controlling for these fundamentals, models tend to underestimate the total effect of both factors on sovereign risk.

Political risk refers to the potential negative impact of a policy decision on investment returns. As summarized by Ian Bremmer, president of the Eurasia Group,[10]

Political risk is about understanding that governments and businesses have different expectations and goals.

As such, political risk is closely related to government ideology; for the reasons just discussed in this chapter, the expectations and goals of governments on the Left should be less aligned with those of capital holders than is the case of neoliberal administrations.

Investors' response to the Peruvian presidential election of 2011 illustrates the relations between governments' ideology, policymaking, and risk. After a confidence crisis that caused the largest one-day drop in the history of the country stock market,[11] the Economist Intelligence Unit upgraded Peru's political risk as soon as analysts realized that the newly elected leftist president Ollanta Humala would not pursue a radical economic agenda:

Fears that the Humala administration would reverse Peru's pragmatic, business-friendly policy environment have now largely subsided. As a result, and owing to

---

[9] See Bellas, Papaioannou, and Petrova (2010) for an encompassing review of these findings.

[10] Eurasia is a leading firm in political risk research.

[11] Romo, Rafael and DeMoura, Helena, "Left-leaning Humala Wins Peruvian Presidential Election." CNN, June 6, 2011.

52 *The Politics of Market Discipline in Latin America*

TABLE 3.2. *Country Risk Ratings in Latin America*

Country	Rating
Chile	A
Uruguay	BBB
Brazil	BBB
Peru	BBB
Colombia	BB
Mexico	BB
Argentina	B
Venezuela	CCC
Ecuador	CC

Source: "Country Risk Reports," Economist Intelligence Unit, September 2013.

the broadly stable outlook for 2013, we have upgraded our political risk rating to BBB. ("Peru Country Risk Service," Economist Intelligence Unit, February 2013)

It is not surprising, thus, that the state-oriented governments of Ecuador, Argentina, and Venezuela are perceived as riskier (Table 3.2). Neither is that countries like Chile, Uruguay, and Brazil, in which elected leftist governments advanced market-oriented programs very similar to those of their conservative counterparts, are seen as among the least risky in the region.[12]

It follows that, if political risk is associated with economic fundamentals, because they are both in large part determined by the ideology of the government in office, a model that aims to capture the impact of government ideology on sovereign risk needs to take these relations into consideration.

External conditions also have an effect on economic fundamentals, which is independent of government ideology. In the case of commodity-dependent-low-savings Latin American countries, two factors are particularly important: international interest rates and commodity prices.

Low international interest rates reduce debt service, lowering governments' expenses, and foster capital inflows to emerging economies. High export prices also contribute to stronger fiscal results, by increasing

---

[12] Political risk is also related to government ideology because risk increases with policy volatility. The broader is the ideological spectrum in a country, the riskier it is perceived to be. As discussed in Chapter 2, policy volatility is particularly strong in Latin American countries, where power is highly concentrated in the executive branch, and high income inequality fosters polarization.

tax revenue, and strengthen countries' current accounts. These impacts could be easily observed during the "good times" started in the 2000s in Latin America, when most governments reduced their indebtedness and maintained fiscal surpluses. As the scenario reverted momentarily after the 2008 crisis, all countries, including fiscally conservative Chile, either reduced surpluses or reverted to deficits. Moreover, economic growth slowed down throughout the region, as currencies devalued and inflation hiked, irrespective of government ideology.

Finally, some aspects of economic fundamentals are path dependent, that is, affected by past policies and by economic and political institutions that are not related to international conditions or to current governments, but that hold important long-term implications to the economy. For instance, it has been shown that countries with a past history of default pay higher costs of capital (Tomz 2007), and that independent central banks tend to maintain lower levels of inflation (Alesina and Summers 1993; Rogoff 1985). To effectively understand the impact of ideology on bondholders' behavior, these relations also need to be considered.

RESEARCH DESIGN

The causal relations depicted in Figure 3.1 provide the basis for the statistical analyses introduced in this section, which are designed to test hypotheses about the effects of governments' ideology on sovereign risk and how they vary between "good" and "bad" times.

The models presented next reflect the claim that economic fundamentals are a result of world economic conditions, government ideology, and country specificities, and explore the role of these factors on sovereign risk. I use a mix of panel and cross-section analyses, depending on the hypothesis tested and on limitations intrinsic to the data.

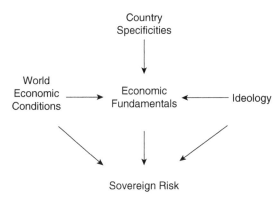

FIGURE 3.1. Causal Model.

54   *The Politics of Market Discipline in Latin America*

Before presenting models and results, the variables included in the analyses are introduced next.

Dependent Variable: Sovereign Risk

BOND SPREADS Sovereign bond spreads, which compute the difference between the yields of a particular bond compared to a standard risk-free Treasury Bond, are widely used as a measure of a country's overall risk premium.

Here I use the monthly spread of countries' Emerging Market Bond Index Global (EMBIg). The EMBIg is a JP Morgan index of dollar-denominated sovereign bonds issued by a selection of emerging market countries. According to the Financial Times, EMBIg indices are the most extensively used and comprehensive emerging market sovereign debt benchmark.[13]

The EMBIg, in particular, extends the coverage of previous indices, to include U.S. dollar–denominated Brady bonds, loans, and Eurobonds with an outstanding face value of at least $500 million. Because the EMBIg's secondary market liquidity constraints are more relaxed than previous versions of the index, and countries are selected acording to World Bank per capita income brackets and debt restructuring history rather than credit-rating level, the EMBIg includes a broader range of countries than previous versions such as the EMBI, or the EMBI[+].

Table 3.3 summarizes the data.

Explanatory Variables

Political Ideology

INCUMBENT IDEOLOGY The dummy *Market-oriented* assumes value 1 whenever a government follows a market-oriented economic program, which includes conservative fiscal and monetary policies, the adoption of inflation targets, de facto central bank independence, trade and financial openness, privatization, and deregulation. The variable assumes value zero under state-oriented governments that prioritize employment and wages over the control of inflation, maintain restrictions to trade and capital flows, and increase the role of the state in the economy, via nationalizations and regulation of the private sector.[14] Specified

---

[13] As stated in the *Financial Times* Lexicon: "In addition to serving as a benchmark to measure the performance of the asset class, the indices define and increase the visibility of the emerging market sovereign debt market and provide a list of the instruments traded along with a compilation of their terms."

[14] See Table 3.9 for classification and the Web Appendix for the criteria used to classify each case.

TABLE 3.3. *Sovereign Bond Spreads: Summary Data*

Country	Start	Min.	Max.	Average	Std. Dev.
Argentina	12/31/1993	186	4,568	1,231	1,258
Mexico	12/31/1993	93	600	229	83
Venezuela	12/31/1993	164	1,902	415	297
Brazil	04/29/1994	139	2,118	529	332
Ecuador	02/28/1995	341	4,961	1,046	628
Colombia	02/28/1997	97	1,066	370	206
Peru	03/31/1997	96	1,050	366	197
Chile	05/28/1999	54	383	148	58
Uruguay	05/31/2001	115	1,701	415	297

Source: Spreads of the JP Morgan EMBIg, obtained from Datastream.

as such, my goal is to distinguish investors' response to the radical Left – state-oriented governments that acted against the preferences of markets – vis-à-vis market-oriented moderates and the Right, which governed within market constraints.

CAMPAIGN IDEOLOGY The model includes three dummies that capture presidential campaigns. *Electoral Period* assumes value 1 starting six months prior to a presidential election, until the end of the current presidency. The other two dummies assume value 1 according to the same criterion, in addition to the ideology of the winning candidate. *Next Campaign State* assumes value 1 when the winner of the election runs on a state-oriented campaign and *Next Campaign Market* if the campaign is market oriented.

International Conditions

The "Good Economic Times" Index Conditions of the international economy are captured by variations in commodity prices and international interest rates. Given the limited size of the sample, and that I am not interested in the particular effects of each variable but rather in establishing a measure of how favorable the international economic scenario is, I adopt the index of Good Economic Times (GET), developed by Campello and Zucco Jr. (2012), to capture their joint effect.

The GET is calculated using a principal components reduction of U.S. 10-Year Treasury Constant Maturity Rate – provided by the Federal Research Bank of Saint Louis (FRED) – and UNCTAD's aggregated free market commodity price index.

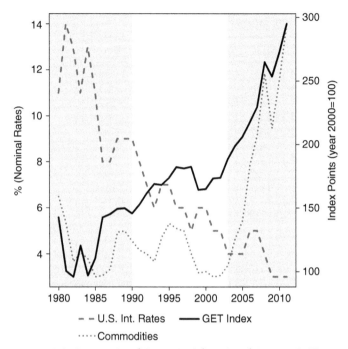

FIGURE 3.2. International Scenario: The "Good Economic Times" Index and Its Components.
Figure shows the evolution of the "Good Economic Times" (GET) index and its two constituent components: U.S. Interest Rates and Commodity Price Index. GET data displayed in reference to 2000 value.

Although GET is measured in a unit-less normalized scale, it has the intuitive property that higher values represent "good times" – when interest rates are low and commodity prices are high – and lower values represent "bad times," when the opposite occurs.

Figure 3.2 shows the variation in the international scenario over the past thirty years, a period in which GET has gone from −1.7 in 1982 to just over 3 in 2011. The GET reflects the hike in U.S. interest rates at the turn of the 1980s, and that helped precipitate the Mexican default and the subsequent debt crisis that ravaged the region, as well as the very favorable period initiated in early 2000, when interest rates were in decline and commodity prices skyrocketed.

The GET index tracks long-term shifts in the economic outlook facing Latin American countries quite accurately, and it is also sensitive enough to capture relatively smaller shifts in economic conditions, such as the Russian and Asian crisis of the late 1990s.

Investors' "Vote" in Presidential Elections   57

TABLE 3.4. *Impact of Ideology on Sovereign Risk (dependent variable: spread of the JP Morgan EMBIg)*

	Model 1	Model 2	Model 3	Model 4
Intercept	981.037	1,216.661	981.037	1,210.947
SE	(149.979)	(160.025)	(149.979)	(160.661)
p value	<0.001	<0.001	<0.001	<0.001
Market-oriented	−459.673	−587.961	−459.673	−586.341
SE	(166.693)	(159.429)	(166.693)	(160.284)
p value	0.009	0.001	0.009	0.001
GET		−198.052		−192.767
SE		(68.390)		(68.364)
p value		0.006		0.008
N	42	42	1,744	1,744
Groups	–	–	42	42
R^2	0.140	0.270	0.150	0.280

Standard errors are shown in parentheses and p values.

Results

How does governments' ideology affect countries' sovereign risk in Latin American emerging economies? A first approximation to test investors' response to the Left (*hypothesis 1*) consists in a simple cross-national comparison of Latin American presidencies. EMBIg data are available only from the mid-1990s (later for some countries), which permits the analysis of 38 presidencies, in 9 countries.

In Table 3.4, the intercept of model 1 shows that the average EMBIg for state-oriented governments, or the radical Left, in the period. The EMBIg was considerably lower under market-oriented presidents. This simple difference in means, however, does not take into consideration that the world economic conditions facing presidents varied dramatically.

To deal with this, I estimate the differences in the EMBIg of state and market-oriented governments controlling for the world economic conditions, which is measured by the GET index (model 2). As the world economy improves (higher values of GET), bond spreads decline significantly. More importantly, when controlled for world economic conditions the impact of government ideology becomes even stronger than before.

These results are quite robust. In the last two columns of Table 3.4 I present analogous "between" models estimated on a time-series cross section of presidencies. This specification amounts to fitting and averaging across a series of cross sections instead of computing average values of

TABLE 3.5. *Impact of Ideology on Sovereign Risk (3-point scale, dependent variable: spread of the JP Morgan EMBIg)*

	Model 5	Model 6	Model 7	Model 8
Moderate	−780.775	−669.745	−780.775	−675.372
SE	(219.575)	(220.167)	(219.575)	(220.885)
p value	0.001	0.004	0.001	0.004
Right	−390.866	−547.155	−390.866	−541.629
SE	(162.992)	(177.505)	(162.992)	(178.445)
p value	0.021	0.004	0.021	0.004
GET		−168.454		−160.641
SE		(87.874)		(87.772)
p value		0.063		0.075
Intercept	981.037	1,181.448	981.037	1,172.631
SE	(143.746)	(173.971)	(143.746)	(174.492)
p value	0.000	0.000	0.000	0.000
N	42	42	1,744	1,744
R^2	0.210	0.260	0.230	0.280

GET for each presidency and then estimating its effect. Results obtained with the two approaches are all but identical.

Table 3.5 presents results for the same models, but separating market-oriented into moderate and right-wing governments. These data suggest that markets do not distinguish the two groups; models 6 and 8 show that, controlling for international conditions, the difference in sovereign risk spreads between right-wing and moderate compared to left-wing governments is about the same.[15]

It is important to note, however, that there is little within-country variation in government ideology in the period when sovereign spreads are available for Latin American emerging markets. This makes it hard to separate the effect of ideology from other country-specific factors that might also affect sovereign risk.

Notwithstanding, the number of presidents elected on a state-oriented campaign exceeds those who effectively implement them in office, as many either govern as moderates or switch to Right once in office. As a result, there is substantially more ideological variation in presidential campaigns than in governments in Latin American emerging economies.

---

[15] Without such control (models 5 and 7), spreads are substantially lower for moderates. This is not surprising, considering that all moderate governments were in office during the economic boom of the 2000s.

Investors' "Vote" in Presidential Elections　　　　　59

This makes the analysis of market responses to the election of the Left a better ground in which to test investors' reactions to ideology.

In contrast with the cross-sectional comparison of governments used to test the basic hypothesis that partisanship of government affects bond spreads, verifying whether markets react to the prospects of ideological change already during elections (*hypothesis 2*) requires the analysis of variables that vary mostly over time, and that are regularly observed in all countries in the sample.

In what follows, I estimate a time-series cross section of nine countries, observed on a monthly basis. The number of monthly observations ranges from 138 to 227 by country. The workhorse model to isolate the effect of time-varying variables in a small number of countries is the fixed effects (i.e., within model) linear regression, and I deal with serial correlation through the inclusion of a lagged dependent variable.

The first two columns in Table 3.6 report results of such an analysis. Model 9 shows that the EMBI increases substantially during electoral periods. Model 10 adds to the picture by partitioning this general election effect according to the ideological content of the winners' campaign. This model reveals that the electoral effect is entirely caused by a strong market reaction to the prospects of a left-wing victory.

Different from expected, there is no change in EMBIg around election time if the winner ran a right-wing electoral campaign. One possible explanation is that there is an intrinsic increase in risk during elections, which is compensated by lower risk when the next winner runs on a market-oriented campaign, and further increased when the opposite occurs. What is clear, though, is that these results reinforce the claim that investors perceive the Left as riskier than its moderate and neoliberal counterparts, and react differently when they expect the next government to advance state-oriented policies.

The EMBIg increase of 65.1 caused by a left-wing victory is substantively large. The average EMBIg in the dataset is 602 and the estimated effect is already net of country-specific characteristics, serial autocorrelation, and the the state of the world economy, which as expected, has a negative association with EMBIg.

Of course, this approach does not allow me to include time-invariant characteristics of countries as predictive models. In principle, a random effects model would allow for simultaneous inclusion of both time-invariant and time-varying variables, but the small number of countries in the data require extremely taxing assumptions to be made, which is why I examined the cross-sectional variation in a separate analysis in the first place.

TABLE 3.6. *Impact of Elections on Sovereign Risk (dependent variable: spreads of JP Morgan EMBIg)*

	Fixed Effects		Random Effects	
	Model 9	Model 10	Model 11	Model 12
Electoral Period	24.566		25.078	
SE	(9.010)		(9.009)	
p value	0.006		0.005	
Next Campaign State		65.100		67.236
SE		(14.442)		(14.206)
p value		0.000		0.000
Next Campaign Market		0.106		−0.728
SE		(11.279)		(11.224)
p value		0.992		0.948
Market-oriented			−7.235	−4.391
SE			(7.723)	(7.729)
p value			0.349	0.570
GET	−4.887	−6.455	−5.365	−6.683
SE	(3.466)	(3.481)	(3.564)	(3.567)
p value	0.159	0.064	0.132	0.061
Lag EMBIg	0.971	0.968	0.978	0.975
SE	(0.006)	(0.006)	(0.005)	(0.005)
p value	0.000	0.000	0.000	0.000
Months	1,737	1,737	1,737	1,737
Countries	9	9	9	9

Note: This table reports coefficients estimated by linear fixed effects and random effects models. Standard errors are shown in parentheses and p values.

With these caveats in mind, I report equivalent random effects specifications in models 11 and 12 in Table 3.6. The estimates of the electoral (time varying) variables are almost identical to the fixed-effects specifications. EMBIg is higher during electoral periods, but this is exclusively the result of market's reactions to the prospects of left-wing electoral victories.

In the random effects specifications, however, the partisanship of current incumbents has no effect, contrasting with the cross-sectional analysis of governments presented earlier. As just explained, this is driven by the lack of enough real-world variation to allow for simultaneous estimation of cross-sectional varying variables and time-varying variables. This can be easily seen by a simple examination of the estimates of country's fixed effects produced by models 9 and 10, and which I report in

Investors' "Vote" in Presidential Elections

TABLE 3.7. *Countries' Fixed-Effects and Sovereign Risk*

	Estimate	Std. Error	Pr(> |t|)
Chile	9.65	10.43	0.35
Mexico	11.62	9.95	0.24
Peru	12.24	9.85	0.21
Brazil	15.40	9.37	0.10
Colombia	16.11	9.89	0.10
Uruguay	18.74	11.68	0.11
Venezuela	23.54	9.72	0.02
Ecuador	25.58	10.92	0.02
Argentina	39.88	11.23	0.00

Table 3.7. Countries such as Argentina, Ecuador, and Venezuela have substantially higher EMBIs than Chile, Mexico, or Peru. These data reinforce the evidence that countries that had mostly left-wing governments in the period exhibit the highest average EMBIs, but are not sufficient to distinguish a "country-effect" from a "partisan effect."

CONCLUSION

The statistical analyses presented in this chapter are consistent with the hypothesis that politics matters for bondholders investing in Latin American emerging economies. They show that state-oriented governments are considered riskier than market-oriented ones, be they moderates or rightist governments. Moreover, results reveal that risk increases during presidential campaigns, whenever investors anticipate the victory of a left-wing candidate. As a result, not only does international funding become more expensive to the Left, but its increase during elections conceivably signals negative prospects to newly elected left-wing governments.

In good times, when foreign currency is abundant, this might not have an important effect on the Left, as spreads tend to be lower. In bad times, however, when countries experience dollar scarcity, this might create strong incentives for left-wing governments to renounce a state-oriented agenda and embrace market-friendly policies aimed at building investor confidence and attracting financial capital to the economy.

Governments' response to investors' behavior and its variation between good and bad times are the object of the next chapter.

62   *The Politics of Market Discipline in Latin America*

APPENDIX

Summary Data

TABLE 3.8. *Coding of Campaigns and Economic Programs*

Election	Candidate	Party	Campaign	Government
ARG95	Menem	Partido Justicialista	1	1
ARG99	De La Rúa	Unión Cívica Radical	1	1
ARG03	Kirchner	Partido Justicialista	0	0
ARG07	Fernández	Partido Justicialista	0	0
ARG11	Fernández	Partido Justicialista	0	0
BRA94	FHC	Partido Socialista Democrático Brasileiro	1	1
BRA98	FHC	Partido Socialista Democrático Brasileiro	1	1
BRA02	Lula	Partido dos Trabalhadores	0	1
BRA06	Lula	Partido dos Trabalhadores	1	1
BRA10	Rousseff	Partido dos Trabalhadores	1	1
CHI99	Lagos	Concertación	1	1
CHI05	Bachelet	Concertación	1	1
CHI09	Piñera	Renovación Nacional	1	1
COL98	Pastrana	Gran Alianza por el Cambio	1	1
COL02	Uribe	Primero Colombia	1	1
COL06	Uribe	Primero Colombia	1	1
COL10	Santos	Partido Social de Unidad Nacional	1	1
ECU96	Bucarám	Partido Roldosista Ecuatoriano	0	1
ECU98	Mahuad	Democracia Popular	1	1
ECU02	Gutiérrez	Partido Sociedad Patriótica 21 de Enero	0	1
ECU06	Correa	Alianza Pais	0	0
ECU09	Correa	Alianza Pais	0	0
ECU13	Correa	Alianza Pais	0	0
MEX94	Zedillo	Partido Revolucionario Institucional	1	1
MEX00	Fox	Partido Acción Nacional	1	1
MEX06	Calderon	Partido Acción Nacional	1	1
MEX12	Peña Nieto	Partido Revolucionario Institucional	1	1
PER01	Toledo	Peru Posible	1	1

TABLE 3.8 (*continued*)

Election	Candidate	Party	Campaign	Government
PER06	García	Alianza Popular Revolucionária Americana	1	1
PER11	Humala	Partido Nacionalista Peruano	1	1
URU99	Battle	Partido Colorado	1	1
URU04	Vázquez	Frente Amplio	1	1
URU09	Mujica	Frente Amplio	1	1
VEN93	Caldera	Convergencia Nacional	0	0
VEN98	Chávez	Movimiento Quinta República	0	1
VEN00	Chávez	Movimiento Quinta República	0	0
VEN06	Chávez	Partido Socialista Unido de Venezuela	0	0
VEN12	Chávez	Partido Socialista Unido de Venezuela	0	0

TABLE 3.9. *Two Lefts in Latin America*

Country	Market-oriented	State-oriented
Argentina		Kirchner (05/03–12/07)
Argentina		Fernández (12/07–)
Brazil	Lula (01/03–12/10)	
Brazil	Rousseff (01/11–)	
Chile	Lagos (03/00–03/06)	
Chile	Bachelet (03/06–03/10)	
Ecuador		Correa (01/07–)
Peru		Humala (07/11–)
Uruguay	Vázquez (03/05–03/10)	
Uruguay	Mujica (03/10–)	
Venezuela		Chávez (08/00–03/13)

4

The Politics of Currency Booms and Crises: Explaining the Influence of Investors' "Vote"

In Chapter 3 we have seen that bondholders perceive the statist left as riskier than their market-oriented counterparts – be they moderate or conservative governments – and react negatively whenever they anticipate a leftist victory in presidential elections.

This chapter focuses on the other side of the confidence game, examining the conditions under which investors' behavior influences the program advanced by newly inaugurated leftist governments.

In principle, there are numerous reasons why this behavior should be influential; a loss of market confidence raises the costs of funding, not only for governments but also for domestic banks and firms that have access to international markets, with trickling down effects that extend even to businesses whose funds are raised domestically.

Depending on its magnitude, a confidence crisis can turn into a speculative attack in which sudden and massive capital flight provokes a quick devaluation of the currency, leading to economic insecurity and inflation, and discouraging investment. For all these reasons, it makes sense that governments, regardless of their ideological leanings, do worry about a sudden loss of investor confidence.

Yet the analysis presented here demonstrates that, in Latin America, leftist governments' concern with a loss of creditor confidence is restricted to periods of dollar scarcity, in which there is a pressing need of attracting capital inflows. Leftist presidents inaugurated during currency crises often renounce their original program in favor of market-oriented policies aimed at restoring confidence.

In the absence of these crises, however, market discipline is less effective. Released from the necessity of attracting external funds, governments are afforded a wider room to deviate from investors' agenda.

The Politics of Currency Booms and Crises   65

Leftist presidents not subjected to currency pressures are those most likely to actually promote a left-wing economic program.

CURRENCY BOOMS, CRISES, AND THE LEFT

As seen in Chapter 2, leftist presidents are different from their conservative counterparts, subject to conflicting incentives to advance their preferred agenda and at the same time attract investors that favor a market-oriented program.

This conflict is especially critical in unequal democracies; because redistributive policies boost the welfare of poor citizens in a way that economic growth alone cannot do, leftist governments are subject to particularly strong electoral pressures to pursue such programs.

These pressures are countered, however, by those created by investors' capacity to redirect resources to countries where policies are deemed more friendly (Boix 2003; Przeworski and Meseguer 2005). The open confrontation of investors can provoke capital flight, depress the economy, and end up making the poor worse off.

In this context, presidents elected promising to promote a leftist program have to decide which policies to advance considering both voters' and capital holders' – in their case opposed – preferences. Currency crises, characterized by sudden and massive capital flight potentially exacerbate this dilemma, as they force governments toward taking urgent measures to reattract capital flows. These measures often involve abandoning a leftist program in favor of an investor-friendly agenda.[1]

Figure 4.1 illustrates this logic. It shows that, in Latin America, leftist presidents that embraced market-oriented policies – policy switchers (Stokes 2001) – are twice more likely to have been inaugurated in the midst of a currency crisis (79 versus 38 percent) than those who maintained a state-oriented agenda.

In addition, and consistent with what we have seen in the previous chapter, the figure reveals that currency crises are more likely to occur during elections won by candidates that campaigned on a leftist, state-oriented agenda (63 versus 37 percent).

The decision to embrace a market-oriented program to attract foreign inflows of capital has been extensively documented in the literature that studies the determinants of capital inflows to the developing world (Calvo, Leiderman, and Reinhart 1993); accordingly, Santiso (2003, p. 27) contends that "Latin America's reform fever of 1990s must be seen in the context of the urgent need for new capital inflows."

---

[1] Currency crises are defined later in this chapter.

		State-oriented (Government)	Market-oriented (Government)
CAMPAIGN	**Market-oriented**		CRI 82 · COL 90 · GUA 85 · CHI 99 · GUA 03 ECU 84 · GUA 90 · PER 95 · ELS 99 · DOM 04 URU 84 · ECU 92 · DOM 96 · GUA 99 · ELS 04 BOL 85 · BOL 93 · ECU 96 · URU 99 · URU 04 HON 85 · CHI 93 · NIC 96 · MEX 00 · CHI 05 MEX 88 · BRA 94 · BOL 97 · HON 01 · HON 05 BRA 89 · DOM 94 · HON 97 · NIC 01 · BRA 06 CHI 89 · ELS 94 · BRA 98 · PER 01 · COL 06 ELS 89 · MEX 94 · COL 98 · BOL 02 · CRI 06 HON 89 · URU 94 · CRI 98 · COL 02 · MEX 06 URU 89 · ARG 95 · ECU 98 · CRI 02 · NIC 06 ARG 99 · PER 06
	State-oriented	CRI 78 · COL 94 COL 82 · VEN 00 ARG 83 · ARG 03 VEN 83 · BOL 05 DOM 86 · ECU 06 VEN 93 · VEN 06 PER 85 COL 86	PER 80 · ARG 89 · VEN 98 DOM 82 · BOL 89 · DOM 00 ELS 84 · CRI 90 · BRA 02 GUA 85 · DOM 90 · ECU 02 CRI 86 · PER 90 ECU 88 · HON 93 VEN 88 · CRI 94

GOVERNMENT

FIGURE 4.1. Policy Switches and Currency Crises in Latin America.
Notes: The figure represents Latin American presidential elections, classified into state-oriented and market-oriented according with the campaign rhetoric of the winning candidate (*y*-axis) and with the policies launched after inauguration (*x*-axis). Elections marked in bold were held during currency crises.

It has also been documented by Drake (1991, p. 36), who asserted that leftist governments' decision to embrace neoliberal programs "reflects the contradiction between the immiseration of the majority of the population and the imperatives of neoliberal economic restructuring to favor market mechanisms and honor the foreign debt."

These claims, made in reference to different periods of time, suggest that the trade-off proposed here is not restricted to the early 1990s, as in Santiso and Martinez or Calvo et al., or to the aftermath of the 1980s debt crisis – the period Drake was referring to. Rather, it is present in periods of dollar scarcity more generally, in which governments are subject to the urgent need of attracting foreign finance.

Before the mid-1990s, it was manifested as leftist governments experienced pressures from a limited number of private banks and multilateral financial institutions to adopt a market-oriented agenda to guarantee a new loan agreement or to roll debt.

With the internationalization and diversification of the creditor base that occurred since then, direct leverage was replaced with market discipline – bond markets' negative responses forcing leftist governments in

The Politics of Currency Booms and Crises 67

need of finance to embrace a market-oriented agenda aimed to gather the confidence of the investor community, and in this way re-attract capital to the economy.

The same rationale implies that presidents elected on a leftist agenda should be less likely to advance market-oriented policies during currency booms, as dollar abundance reduces the need for foreign finance, enhancing their ability to deviate from investors' preferences in favor of their original program. Along these lines, it is worth noting another pattern that emerges in Figure 4.1; most Latin American governments that actually advanced a leftist agenda did so in the first half of the 1980s, and later in the 2000s. Policy switches to neoliberalism were concentrated mostly between the second half of the 1980s and the early 2000s.

Interestingly, presidents who remained on the Left during a currency crisis, as was the case of those elected in the early 1980s, experienced severe economic collapse. Alan García in Peru, Raúl Alfonsín in Argentina, and Jaime Lusinchi in Venezuela are examples of that. Their failure probably informed their successors' decision to embrace neoliberalism, until an unprecedented currency boom allowed leaders like Hugo Chávez in Venezuela and Rafael Correa in Ecuador to reap the electoral benefits of governing on the Left during "good times."

Finally, it follows from the rationale proposed here that, because presidents who campaign on a market-oriented platform receive voters' mandate to adopt the same policies creditors prefer, there are no reasons to expect neither dollar scarcity nor abundance to affect their behavior substantially. It is not unlikely that these presidents advance some level of pro-poor policies in "good times" more than in "bad times," but they should do so without renouncing a market-oriented agenda.

The hypotheses that follow summarize the preceding arguments:

Hypothesis 1 *Currency crises should increase the likelihood that presidents who campaign on leftist policies switch to a market-oriented program in office.*

Hypothesis 2 *Currency booms should decrease the likelihood that presidents who campaign on leftist policies switch to a market-oriented program in office.*

Hypothesis 3 *Neither currency crises nor booms should affect the prospects for policy switches in the case of presidents who campaign on a market-oriented agenda.*

Political Systems and Capacity to Switch

Once a president decides the economic program she intends to pursue, her chances of advancing it increase the less costrained she is by the domestic political system (Corrales 1998; Haggard and Kaufman 1995).

Strong presidents are usually thought of as those who have the capacity to influence legislation, which arguably rests on two categories of powers: partisan and constitutional (Mainwaring and Shugart 1997). Partisan powers reflect the incumbent party's strength in the legislature, and the need to foster alliances. Constitutional powers, inherent in the office of the presidency, allow incumbents to have their preferences taken into consideration in the passage of legislation (Mainwaring and Shugart 1997, p. 40).

In Latin American political systems, the president is elected independently from the legislature, and it is quite common that the incumbent party does not control a majority in Congress. In these cases, the lack of legislative support might significantly limit a president's capacity to influence policymaking. It follows that, other conditions fixed, the larger the proportion of the incumbent's party's seats in the legislature, and therefore the lower the need to foster political alliances with potential opposers, the more capable a president becomes of initiating her preferred policies.

Constitutional powers – mainly veto and decree powers – also affect presidential strength, allowing the executive to shape policy output even without a legislative majority. These powers determine the ability of the incumbent to influence (or even dominate) the lawmaking process that results from the president's standing with respect to the legislature.

Presidents with strong constitutional powers can initiate and veto legislation and should be in a better position to push for their preferred agenda, either by influencing the adoption of policies that represent a change in the status quo or by blocking unfavorable policy changes promoted by the opposition.

Even when a legislative majority can rescind a decree, presidents might still be able to play a major role in shaping legislative outcomes. Unlike a bill passed by a legislature, a presidential decree is already law – not a proposal – before the other branch can react to it. Thus, Latin American presidents frequently resort to the strategy of overwhelming the legislative agenda with a flood of decrees, making it difficult for the Congress to consider measures before they have a possibly irreversible effect. Finally, presidents can always use decree power strategically, attempting to discern a point in the policy space at which a congressional majority is indifferent between the status quo and the decree.

The Politics of Currency Booms and Crises

For all these reasons, presidents with stronger constitutional powers are more likely to switch programs once they decide to, as they are better positioned to shape policy outcomes according to their own preferred agenda. In sum:

Hypothesis 4 *The likelihood of policy switches should increase with the strength of the incumbent party in the legislature.*

Hypothesis 5 *The likelihood of policy switches should increase the more constitutional powers the executive has.*

In addition, an extensive literature has developed since Mainwaring and Scully's (1995) influential analysis of the political implications of party and party system institutionalization. According to this literature, a major consequence of institutionalization should be to foster governments' responsiveness to electoral demands (Jones 2005; Mainwaring and Torcal 2006; Payne, Zovatto G., Florez, and Zavala 2003).

The institutionalization of party systems is conceived as a process by which a practice or organization becomes well established and widely known, and where actors develop expectations, orientations, and behavior, based on the premise that this practice/organization will prevail into the foreseeable future (Mainwaring and Torcal 2006).

In institutionalized party systems, thus, political actors should develop clear and stable expectations about the behavior of other actors. Stable patterns of electoral competition, the presence of party roots in society, citizens' recognition of the legitimacy of party politics, and the institutionalization of party organization, as opposed to parties working as electoral vehicles for personalistic leaders, are all necessary conditions for establishing what is considered "good representation." This notion subsumes representatives who do not work on the basis of leaders' voluntarist will and who are elected and govern in response to voters' programmatic preferences.

For all that, both party and party system institutionalization should lower the incentives leftist presidents face to openly betray campaign promises. First, voters' programmatic preferences should increase presidents' electoral costs of doing so. If these constraints are not sufficient, institutionalized parties should be willing and more capable of vetoing presidents' attempts to switch policies, at the risk of losing support from activists, legislators, and voters otherwise. Therefore,

Hypothesis 6 *The likelihood of policy switches should decrease with the institutionalization of party systems.*

70 *The Politics of Market Discipline in Latin America*

Hypothesis 7 *The likelihood of policy switches should decrease with the institutionalization of the incumbent's party.*

RESEARCH DESIGN AND EMPIRICAL ANALYSIS

I test the impact of currency crises and booms on the probability of policy switches using a probit model in which the dependent variable is *Switch*. The explanatory variables capture currency crises and booms that occurred in the months immediately before and after presidential inauguration (named the "electoral period"), as well as political conditions deemed relevant to explain presidents' probability of switching. The sample includes elections held in a large sample of Latin American countries[2] since their re-democratization in the 1980s.

Dependent Variable: Switch

To examine the effect of currency crises and booms on presidents' decisions to deviate from their original program, it is necessary to identify (1) presidents' original programs and (2) the policies they implemented once in office. I use campaign promises as a proxy for the first and the policies reported in the media during the first year of government as an indicator of the second. There are clear limitations in the use of campaign rhetoric as a signal of future policy choices, but there are also many reasons to believe that in Latin American inchoate party systems candidates' public declarations reveal more of their agenda than party manifestos like those frequently used in comparable studies of European countries.

Candidates who promise to increase the role of the state and regulation in the economy, prioritize employment and wage increases over control of inflation, and commit to maintaining strategic restrictions to trade and to advancing industrial policies, as well as to imposing limitations on cross-border capital movements and on the payment of the external debt were classified as campaigning on a leftist, state-oriented agenda.

Lucio Gutiérrez's campaign in the Ecuadorean 2002 presidential election exemplifies this discourse; Gutiérrez was a harsh critic of the dollarization of the economy, and his rhetoric centered on the condemnation of neoliberalism. Gutiérrez portrayed his candidacy as the hope of the poor, the marginalized, the excluded, and promised to increase social spending to reduce income inequality and poverty. The candidate further

---

[2] Countries studied are Argentina, Bolivia, Brazil, Chile, Colombia, Costa Rica, Dominican Republic, Ecuador, Guatemala, Honduras, Mexico, Nicaragua, Peru, Uruguay, and Venezuela.

The Politics of Currency Booms and Crises

proposed a "Debt Club" aimed at coordinating the restructuring of Latin American foreign debt, and ruled out any prospects of Ecuador joining the Free Trade Area of the Americas (FTAA).

Candidates who commit with reducing the role of the state in the economy through privatization and deregulation, prioritize anti-inflationary shocks and inflation targets, and promise to eliminate subsidies and tariffs and to launch financial liberalization measures and central bank independence were classified as campaigning on a right-wing, or market-oriented, economic agenda.

Álvaro Uribe, elected president of Colombia in the same year as Gutiérrez in Ecuador, campaigned as a typical market-oriented candidate. He ran on the promise of conservative, orthodox economic policies, and was described as a tough right-winger by analysts and the media. His main goal was to restore Colombia's fiscal balance and to keep inflation low. Uribe had a friendly approach to the International Monetary Fund (IMF), and made clear his intentions to renew agreements with the Fund and his priority to relations with the United States.

Information regarding electoral campaigns was obtained from newspaper data available in lexis-nexis academic (all sources in English) released in the six months prior to each presidential election, and extended Stokes' (2001) sample from 44 to 89 cases, including elections held until 2006.

The same criteria and sources were used to classify governments' policy initiatives. The information used to code each government as Left or Right was also obtained from newspaper sources and completed with case studies when data were scarce.[3] Because I am interested in post-electoral switches, I restricted the coding to the first year of a president's term.

As argued in Chapter 3, the limitation of categories into only two groups surely fails to capture a more complex reality where these policies are a matter of degree.[4] Yet the difficulty in determining these degrees counsels against continuous codings and in favor of a dichotomous choice. The two categories adopted capture the basic message of

---

[3] See Conaghan, Malloy, and Abugattas (1990), Cuddington and Carlos (1990), Wilson (1994), Rosario (1995), Mauceri (1995), Hojman (1996), Roberts (1996), Lander and Fierro (1996), Pastor and Wise (1997), Weiss (1997), Blake (1998), Boito Jr. and Randall (1998), Cameron and North (1998), and Robinson (2000).

[4] This is particularly true with respect to the so-called moderate Left, in its majority coded on the right. Despite increased social expenditures and some time higher levels of intervention in the economy, cases were coded as such for their very explicit market-oriented agenda and adoption of orthodox macroeconomic policies.

72 *The Politics of Market Discipline in Latin America*

presidential campaigns, often framed between more (Left-leaning) or less (Right-leaning) state intervention in the economy.

The dependent variable here is the dummy *Switch*, which takes the value of 1 when the program advanced in a government's first year differs from the policies promised during the campaign and 0 otherwise.[5]

Explanatory Variables

CRISIS AND BOOM Currency crises/booms, reflecting dollar scarcity/abundance, are captured by the index of *exchange market pressure* (*EMP*), created by Eichengreen, Rose, Wyplosz, Dumas, and Weber (1995). The index aggregates changes in international reserves and exchange rates for each country included in the sample, weighted by their volatility, which is measured by the standard deviation of the distribution of EMPs.

Exchange market pressures are reflected in falling reserves (r) and/or in a depreciation of the exchange rate (s) (positive *EMP*). The opposite applies to exchange market booms, when international reserves increase and/or the exchange rate appreciates (negative *EMP*):

$$EMP_{i,t} = \frac{\Delta s_{i,t}}{\sigma_{\Delta s_{i,t}}} - \frac{\Delta r_{i,t}}{\sigma_{\Delta r_{i,t}}} \qquad (4.1)$$

Although Eichengreen et al. (1995) use the same standard deviation for the entire sample, and Leblang (2002) uses one value for each country, I adopt one-year moving averages of standard deviations for each country. This is arguably a better measure, as earlier observations of both indicators are highly volatile, with volatility significantly decreasing over the three decades studied. The use of a single standard deviation for the whole period would overestimate crises occurred in the early 1980s, and underestimate those observed in the late 1990s and 2000s.

Still following Eichengreen et al. (1995), I create two dummy variables designed to reflect dollar scarcity/abundance, which occur whenever *EMP* assumes extreme – adopting a cutoff of one standard deviation from the mean – positive/negative values. The inclusion of two dummies increases the flexibility of the analysis, compared to single categorical variable encompassing booms and crises.

$$Scarcity_{i,t} = \begin{cases} 1, & \text{if } EMP_{i,t} > \mu(EMP_{i,t}) + 2\ \sigma(EMP_{i,t}) \\ 0, & \text{otherwise} \end{cases} \qquad (4.2)$$

---

[5] Please consult the Web appendix for a database that includes campaign promises and government initiatives used to justify the coding of each election.

The Politics of Currency Booms and Crises

$$\text{Abundance}_{i,t} = \begin{cases} 1, & \text{if } EMP_{i,t} < \mu(EMP_{i,t}) - 2 \; \sigma(EMP_{i,t}) \\ 0, & \text{otherwise} \end{cases} \tag{4.3}$$

In the empirical model, I test a set of variables that capture episodes of currency crises and booms, calculated as sums of the dummies *Scarcity* and *Abundance*, respectively, during different time periods. *Crisis* sums the values of *Scarcity* in the twelve months that surround an inauguration (plus the month of inauguration), capturing pre- and postelectoral turbulence in currency markets. *Crisis.pre* does the same but only for the preinauguration period (six months prior to inauguration and the month of inauguration) whereas *Crisis.post* sums *Scarcity* only for the postinauguration period (six months after inauguration). These variables apprehend the persistence of pressures governments experience in the periods of interest. Governments under extreme pressure for two months (*Crisis* = 2) should be less likely to switch than those that experienced the same pressures during the full period (*Crisis* = 13). The same was done for periods of dollar abundance, creating the variables *Boom*, *Boom.pre*, and *Boom.post*.

INFLATION Scholars have long studied the influence of inflationary crises on governments' decision to pursue market-oriented policies in Latin America. Arguably, hyperinflation should not only motivate incumbents to advance these many times painful programs (Haggard and Kaufman 1995; Stokes 2001), but it should also make citizens more willing to accept the risks they carry when finding themselves in the "domain of loss" (Weyland 1996). In addition, even though currency and inflationary crises do not always coincide, it is noteworthy that largest currency crashes "are similar in timing and order of magnitude to the profile of inflationary crises"(Reinhart and Rogoff 2009, p. 6). It is necessary, thus, to separate these effects in the empirical analysis; I do so by including a variable *Inflation* (the log of the average annualized inflation rate in the twelve months that surround presidents' inauguration) as a control in the model.

Political Factors

Presidents' capacity to switch policies depends on conditions specific to the political system in which they operate. For this reason, variables likely to reflect these institutional and political incentives/barriers are also included in the model.

EXECUTIVE This variable reflects the constitutional powers of the executive and was obtained from the Inter-American Development Bank

74 *The Politics of Market Discipline in Latin America*

and International Institute for Democracy and Electoral Assistance (IDB/IDEA) database (Payne, Zovatto G., Florez, and Zavala 2002). The index ranges from 3 to 15 and includes measures of package veto, partial veto, decree power, exclusive initiative, convocation of referendum/plebiscite, and power to define budget and to default budget.

LEGISLATURE The share of seats controlled by the incumbent's party in the lower house is the measure of government strength in the legislature. Sources were also IDB/IDEA, the Political Database of the Americas (PDBA), and Psephos electoral database.[6]

VOLATILITY Electoral volatility is the easiest variable to measure and possibly the most important dimension of party system institutionalization, as institutionalization is conceptually very closely linked to stability (Mainwaring and Torcal 2006). Although party system institutionalization encompasses at least three other dimensions besides the stable intraparty competition captured by volatility, the latter is still the most widely used proxy for institutionalization. Electoral volatility (votes for the lower house) is calculated, for the sample used in this article, using data obtained from the PDBA and Psephos databases.

PARTY Party age is used here as proxy for party institutionalization (Mainwaring and Torcal 2006). Despite the fact that old parties might not be institutionalized, age is arguably a necessary condition for institutionalization, and therefore strongly associated with it. Ease to measure is an additional motivation for using age to capture the effects of party institutionalization. Information on party age was obtained from the Database of Political Institutions (DBPI), as well as from political dictionaries of Latin America (Ameringer 1992; Gunson, Chamberlain, and Thompson 1989).

Descriptive statistics are presented in Table 4.1.

Results

How do currency crises and booms affect the likelihood that Latin American presidents switch programs after inauguration?

Because currency crises and booms are expected to affect left- and right-leaning presidents in different ways, I analyze these cases separately. This strategy has the additional advantage of controlling for

---

[6] Data restricted to presidents' party only, not including governing coalitions.

The Politics of Currency Booms and Crises

TABLE 4.1. *Summary Statistics of Explanatory Variables: All Campaigns*

	Min.	Median	Mean	Max.	SD
Executive	3.00	7.00	7.97	15.00	3.68
Legislature	0.00	41.40	36.05	96.00	19.06
Volatility	3.30	18.70	22.67	62.80	14.04
Party	1.00	24.00	42.35	165.00	46.69
Crisis	0.00	4.00	4.29	13.00	3.61
Boom	0.00	0.00	2.04	13.00	3.16
Inflation	−0.19	2.49	2.85	9.26	1.73

Note: Summary statistics of explanatory variables including the whole sample.

TABLE 4.2. *Summary Statistics: Market-Oriented Campaigns*

	Min.	Median	Mean	Max.	St. Dev.
Crisis	0.00	3.00	3.60	12.00	3.57
Boom	0.00	1.00	2.37	13.00	3.25

Note: Summary statistics for currency crises and booms, restricted to elections of candidates who promised a market-oriented platform.

potential endogeneity in the results, driven by the fact that a component of the dependent variable (*Campaign*) might influence the values of the most important independent variable (*Crisis*). As previously pointed out (Figure 4.1), currency crises are more likely to occur when a state-oriented, rather than a market-oriented candidate is elected.

Market-oriented Campaigns
The null impact of currency crises and booms on policy switches from right to left becomes evident as we observe that, although the treatment varies (as evidenced in Figure 4.2), the effects remain constant (candidates elected on a market-oriented platform *never* switch).

In case neither the treatment nor effects varied, it would be impossible to determine the influence of currency crises and booms on market-oriented candidates' propensity to switch. As it stands, the evidence supports the claim that neither currency crises nor booms have any effect in this group.

Leftist Campaigns
Empirical analysis offers strong support for the hypothesis that leftist presidential candidates elected in the midst of currency crises are more likely to switch to a market-oriented program soon after inauguration. Table 4.3 displays the effect of changes in the main explanatory variables

TABLE 4.3. *Impact of Explanatory Variables on the Probability of a Policy Switch (dependent variable: switch)*

	Model 1	Model 2	Model 3	Model 4	Model 5
Crisis	0.480	0.465		0.617	0.588
SE	0.178	0.200		0.219	0.241
p value	0.007	0.034		0.005	0.015
Boom		−0.034		0.295	0.265
SE		0.213		0.306	0.325
p value		0.874		0.334	0.415
Executive			0.436	0.618	0.617
SE			0.265	0.268	0.251
p value			0.100	0.021	0.014
Legislature			0.210	0.303	0.297
SE			0.256	0.284	0.294
p value			0.413	0.287	0.312
Volatility			−0.736	−0.810	−0.820
SE			0.198	0.189	0.197
p value			0.000	0.000	0.000
Party			−0.711	−0.772	−0.772
SE			0.194	0.220	0.218
p value			0.000	0.000	0.000
Inflation					0.176
SE					0.245
p value					0.473

Note: Effect of changing one standard deviation around the mean in the variables of interest on the probability of switches from state-oriented to market-oriented programs, based on models presented in Table 4.4 in the Appendix. All other variables remain fixed in their mean values.

(first differences) on the likelihood of switches from left- to right-wing programs, and shows that the effects of *Crisis* are positive, substantial, and consistent across different model specifications.[7]

Holding all other variables in their mean values, a 1 standard deviation change around the mean in the variable *Crisis* leads to a 59 percentage point increase in the likelihood that a president elected on a leftist campaign switches to a market-oriented program in office, significant at a lower than 1 percent level (model 5). This effect can be better appreciated in Figure 4.2.

According to these results, if President Hugo Chávez had been elected in 1998 subject to the exact same institutional conditions but under the

---

[7] Regression coefficients are available in Table 4.4 in the Appendix, which also presents models 6 and 7, where *Crisis.pre*, *Boom.pre* and *Crisis.post*, *Boom.post* are included.

The Politics of Currency Booms and Crises 77

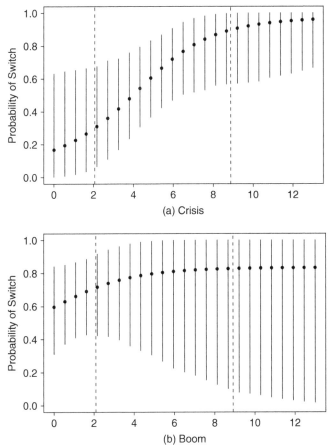

FIGURE 4.2. Impact of Crises and Booms on Policy Switches.
Note: Impact of *Crisis* and *Boom* on the probability that presidents elected on a state-oriented agenda switch to an efficiency-oriented program in office. Simulation in Zelig-R, draws = 20, includes a 95 percent confidence interval. Vertical lines denote a 1 standard deviation interval around the mean value of the explanatory variable.

economic scenario observed in his 2006 election, his chances of switching to a conservative economic program would have been 43 percentage points lower, with 95 percent confidence. Peruvian president Alberto Fujimori, if inaugurated in 1990 under the circumstances of Alan García in 2006, would present 82 percentage points lower chances of switching, with 95 percent confidence.

Interestingly, booms do not seem to reduce the likelihood of Left to Right switches; effects never reach acceptable levels of statistical significance. This implies that, in the absence of crises ("normal" and

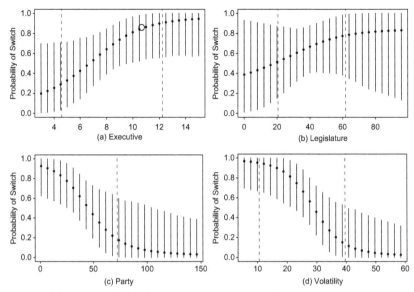

FIGURE 4.3. Impact of Political Factors on Policy Switches.
Note: Effect of executive powers (*Executive*), share of the incumbent party in the legislature (*Legislature*), incumbent party institutionalization (*Party*), and party system institutionalization (*Volatility*) on the probability that presidents switch from state-oriented campaigns to market-oriented programs in office. Simulation in Zelig-R, draws = 20, includes a 95 percent confidence interval. Vertical lines denote a 1 standard deviation interval around the mean value of the explanatory variable.

"booming" periods), leftist presidents pursue their original agenda. Although this could suggest that the need to attract short-term financial is not very constraining in Latin America, it is important to note that almost half of the elections included in the sample occur under currency crises, rising to 62 percent when the winner is a leftist candidate.

Table 4.3 also shows the effects of political variables on the probability of switches, which can be observed further in Figure 4.3. It reveals that a 1 standard deviation change around the mean in the variable *Executive* increases by 62 percentage points the chances that a left-wing president switches to a market-oriented program, significant at a 5 percent level (model 5). I find no evidence that incumbent party's presence in Congress (*Legislature*) affects the likelihood of switches. The coefficient for party age (*Party*) is negative and significant, confirming that it is harder for a president from an institutionalized party to switch.

Surprisingly, *Volatility* has a negative and significant impact on the likelihood of Left to Right switches, conveying that policy switches are more likely to occur in institutionalized party systems. In theory,

The Politics of Currency Booms and Crises

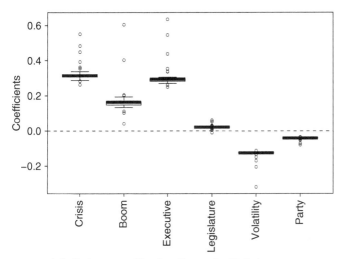

FIGURE 4.4. Robustness Check – Case-wise Deletion.
Note: Results indicate how coefficients of each of the main variables included in model 4 vary with the deletion of each election included in the sample.

electoral volatility could be capturing the negative effects of party system fragmentation on policy switches, but the low correlation between these two variables in the sample (0.14) and the fact that the inclusion of fragmentation in the model does not produce any change either in the effect of volatility on the likelihood of switches or in the probability of switches themselves suggests this is not the case.

It is also possible that voters punish switchers more strictly than nonswitchers for bad economic results (Stokes 2001). If so, politicians might only dare to openly betray campaign promises when they know they can count on voters' loyalty – consistent parties would have more legitimacy to switch, in a sort of "Nixon goes to China" effect.

It is important to note, however, that *Volatility* should capture the effects of party system institutionalization only when the stability of electoral competition is associated with the development of parties' stable and programmatic roots in society. Whenever this association does not hold, as Luna (2008) convincingly argues is the case in Latin America, volatility might not be an appropriate measure of party system institutionalization. In the absence of stable programmatic linkages between parties and electorate, it should be less surprising that volatility has not the expected effect on presidents' likelihood to switch.

To verify the robustness of results, I performed a case-wise deletion in the sample, still based on model 5 of Table 4.3. Figure 4.4 conveys that coefficients are resistant to the deletion of each of the cases included in the sample.

Conclusion

After having shown that sovereign bondholders react negatively to the election of the Left in Chapter 3, this chapter examined the other side of market discipline – the economic and political conditions under which investors' behavior is capable of constraining leftist governments.

The analysis presented supports the claim that the need to attract financial capital during currency crises pushes governments on the Left toward abandoning their original agenda in favor of orthodox economic policies they expect will build confidence in the investment community. Statistical results have shown that strong leftist presidents inaugurated in the midst of severe currency pressures are the ones most likely to advance market-oriented policies.

These two pieces of evidence reveal one important mechanism through which investors "discipline" governments in Latin American emerging economies, and that contributes to explain the long-lasting persistence of neoliberalism in the region despite the frustrating record observed in terms of economic growth and reduction of income inequality.

During the bad times – dollar scarcity associated with low commodity prices and high interest rates – that characterized most years since Latin American re-democratization, leftist governments adopted policies driven by the immediate need to build confidence among financial investors and attract inflows of capital to their domestic economies.

Conversely, as international conditions improved in the early 2000s as a result of an extraordinary rise in commodity prices coupled with a substantial decrease of international interest rates, presidents on the Left were released from the urgent need of attracting capital inflows, and afforded a wider room to advance their original agenda (Castañeda 2006, 2008; Edwards 2010; Roberts and Levitsky 2011; Weyland, Madrid, and Hunter 2010).

Research Design: Case Studies

So far, I have looked at each side of the confidence game played by creditors and politicians during elections separately: how bondholders respond to left-leaning governments, and under which circumstances these reactions force leftist governments to switch to an investor-oriented economic agenda.

The next chapters present case studies of Brazil, Argentina, Ecuador, and Venezuela that focus on the *interactions* between investors and governments, and address two main goals. The first is to trace the mechanisms that connect a move to the Left in government, market panic,

The Politics of Currency Booms and Crises 81

and policy switches. In doing so, they evidence causal relations claimed in the book and that cannot be tested directly through statistical analyses. The second goal is to tease out how exogenously driven cycles of currency booms and crises affect the effectiveness of market discipline over time, and how prospects of long-term convergence vary depending on countries' exposure to these cycles.

The cases chosen offer opportunities for within and between-country comparisons. Brazil serves as an example of a more stable economy, in contrast with Ecuador and Venezuela, countries highly vulnerable to cycles of currency booms and crises. The chapter on Brazil shows that market discipline does not vary significantly in more stable economies, and how this contributes to explain the long-term moderation of the Left in these countries. After Lula's move rightward in 2003 no other PT government returned to the party's state-oriented leftist agenda that prevailed until 2001.

Conversely, the chapters on Ecuador and Venezuela show how the effectiveness of market discipline varies with cycles of currency booms and crises in countries where these cycles are very pronounced. In the first, voters elected two leftist presidents with a relatively similar political discourse and political constituency, but under very distinct economic conditions – Lucio Gutiérrez during a currency crisis, and Rafael Correa under a boom. This means that whereas institutional and political variables were held constant, the economic factor of interest varied, making it easier to observe its effect. In Venezuela, the effect of currency boom and crisis is even clearer considered that it is possible to "control for incumbency effects," as economic conditions varied markedly under a single president, that is, Hugo Chávez.

As a result, contrasting with the Brazilian case the experiences of Ecuador and Venezuela illustrate how over time variation in the effectiveness of market discipline prevents a long-term moderation of the Left.

Finally, the chapter on Argentina explores how governments' room to maneuver can be widened not only by a relatively sudden increase in inflows of foreign currency, as happened in the other three countries, but also by a decrease in dollar outflows, prompted by a default on a very high public external debt. The default reduced the government's external financing needs, and therefore the urgency to tap into international financial markets, while also limiting the access of the private sector to international finance. The commodity boom that followed consolidated the high autonomy from financial markets' policy preferences enjoyed by the administrations of Kirchner and Fernández.

APPENDIX

TABLE 4.4. *Impact of Explanatory Variables on Left to Right Policy Switches (dependent variable: switch)*

Variable	Model 1	Model 2	Model 3	Model 4	Model 5	Model 6	Model 7
Crisis	0.21	0.21		0.32	0.31		
SE	0.08	0.08		0.14	0.15		
p value	0.01	0.02		0.02	0.03		
Crisis.pre						0.22	
SE						0.14	
p value						0.13	
Crisis.post							0.23
SE							0.15
p value							0.12
Boom		−0.02		0.16	0.16		
SE		0.10		0.18	0.18		
p value		0.87		0.37	0.40		
Boom.pre						0.33	
SE						0.35	
p value						0.34	
Boom.post							0.07
SE							0.20
p value							0.73
Executive			0.18	0.30	0.30	0.23	0.22
SE			0.12	0.15	0.15	0.14	0.12
p value			0.13	0.04	0.05	0.10	0.08
Legislature			0.01	0.02	0.02	0.02	0.02
SE			0.02	0.02	0.02	0.02	0.02
p value			0.42	0.28	0.35	0.34	0.46
Party			−0.03	−0.04	−0.04	−0.05	−0.03
SE			0.01	0.02	0.02	0.02	0.01
p value			0.01	0.02	0.02	0.03	0.02
Volatility			−0.09	−0.12	−0.13	−0.11	−0.11
SE			0.01	0.02	0.02	0.02	0.01
p value			0.01	0.01	0.01	0.03	0.01
Inflation					0.18	0.25	0.23
SE					0.24	0.23	0.23
p value					0.46	0.28	0.58
Intercept	−0.87	−0.81	1.62	−0.75	−0.90	0.42	0.59
SE	0.49	0.61	1.14	1.64	1.67	1.40	1.40
p value	0.07	0.19	0.15	0.65	0.59	0.76	0.67
Chi-squared	7.58	7.61	14.99	21.96	22.56	18.63	19.19
p value	0.00	0.01	0.06	0.00	0.00	0.02	0.03
%Correct	0.69	0.69	0.72	0.84	0.84	0.84	0.78
log.Likelihood	−17.83	−17.81	−14.20	−10.63	−10.33	−12.30	−12.02
N	32	32	32	32	32	32	32

TABLE 4.5. Coding of Campaigns and Economic Programs

Election	Inauguration	Candidate	Party	Campaign	Government	Switch
ARG83	Dec-83	Alfonsín	Unión Cívica Radical	0	0	0
ARG89	Jul-89	Menem	Partido Justicialista	0	1	1
ARG95	Jul-95	Menem	Partido Justicialista	1	1	0
ARG99	Dec-99	De La Rúa	Unión Cívica Radical	1	1	0
ARG03	May-03	Kirchner	Partido Justicialista	0	0	0
BOL85	Aug-85	Estenssoro	Movimiento Nacionalista Revolucionario	1	1	0
BOL89	Aug-89	Zamora	Movimiento de Izquierda Revolucionaria	0	1	1
BOL93	Aug-93	Lozada	Movimiento Nacionalista Revolucionario	1	1	0
BOL97	Aug-97	Banzer	Acción Democrática Nacionalista	1	1	0
BOL02	Jun-02	Lozada	Movimiento Nacionalista Revolucionario	1	1	0
BOL05	Jan-06	Morales	Movimiento al Socialismo	0	0	0
BRA89	Mar-90	Collor	Partido da Renovação Nacional	1	1	0
BRA94	Jan-95	FHC	Partido Socialista Democrático Brasileiro	1	1	0
BRA98	Jan-99	FHC	Partido Socialista Democrático Brasileiro	1	1	0
BRA02	Jan-03	Lula	Partido dos Trabalhadores	0	1	1
BRA06	Jan-07	Lula	Partido dos Trabalhadores	1	1	0
CHI89	Mar-90	Aylwin	Concertación de Partidos por la Democracia	1	1	0
CHI93	Mar-94	Frei	Concertación de Partidos por la Democracia	1	1	0
CHI99	Mar-00	Lagos	Concertación de Partidos por la Democracia	1	1	0
CHI05	Mar-06	Bachelet	Concertación de Partidos por la Democracia	1	1	0
COL82	Aug-82	Betancur	Partido Conservador Colombiano	0	0	0

TABLE 4.5 *(continued)*

Election	Inauguration	Candidate	Party	Campaign	Government	Switch
COL86	Aug-86	Barco	Partido Liberal Colombiano	0	0	0
COL90	Aug-90	Gaviria	Partido Liberal Colombiano	1	1	0
COL94	Aug-94	Samper	Partido Liberal Colombiano	0	0	0
COL98	Aug-98	Pastrana	Gran Alianza por el Cambio	1	1	0
COL02	Aug-02	Uribe	Primero Colombia	1	1	0
COL06	Aug-06	Uribe	Primero Colombia	1	1	0
CRI78	May-78	Odio	Partido de Unidad Socialcristiana	0	0	0
CRI82	May-82	Monge	Partido Liberación Nacional	1	1	0
CRI86	May-86	Arias	Partido Liberación Nacional	0	1	1
CRI90	May-90	Calderón	Partido de Unidad Socialcristiana	0	1	1
CRI94	May-94	Figueres	Partido Liberación Nacional	0	1	1
CRI98	May-98	Rodriguez	Partido de Unidad Socialcristiana	1	1	0
CRI02	May-2	Pacheco	Partido de Unidad Socialcristiana	1	1	0
CRI06	May-06	Arias	Partido Liberación Nacional	1	1	0
DOM82	Aug-82	Blanco	Partido Revolucionário Dominicano	0	1	1
DOM86	Aug-86	Balaguer	Partido Reformista Social Dominicano	1	1	0
DOM90	Aug-90	Balaguer	Partido Reformista Social Dominicano	0	1	1
DOM94	Aug-94	Balaguer	Partido Reformista Social Dominicano	1	1	0
DOM96	Aug-96	Fernández	Partido de la Liberación Dominicana	1	1	0
DOM00	Aug-00	Mejia	Partido Revolucionário Dominicano	0	1	1
DOM04	Aug-04	Fernández	Partido de la Liberación Dominicana	1	1	0
ECU84	Aug-84	Cordero	Partido Social Cristiano	1	1	0
ECU88	Aug-88	Borja	Izquierda Democrática	0	1	1

ECU92	Aug-92	Durán Ballén	Unión Republicana/Partido Conservador	1	1	0
ECU96	Aug-96	Bucarám	Partido Roldosista Ecuatoriano	0	1	1
ECU98	Sep-98	Mahuad	Democracia Popular	1	1	0
ECU02	Jan-03	Gutiérrez	Partido Sociedad Patriotica 21 de Enero	0	1	1
ECU06	Jan-07	Correa	Alianza Pais	0	0	0
ELS84	Jun-84	Duarte	Alianza Pais	0	1	1
ELS89	Jun-89	Cristiani	Alianza Republicana Nacionalista	1	1	0
ELS94	Jun-94	Calderón Sol	Alianza Republicana Nacionalista	1	1	0
ELS99	Jun-99	Flores	Alianza Republicana Nacionalista	1	1	0
ELS04	May-04	Saca	Alianza Republicana Nacionalista	1	1	0
GUA85	Jan-86	Arevalo	Democracia Cristiana Guatemalteca	0	1	1
GUA90	Jan-91	Serrano	Movimiento de Acción Solidaria	1	1	0
GUA95	Jan-96	Irigoyen	Partido de Avanzada Nacional	1	1	0
GUA99	Jan-00	Portillo	Frente Republicano Guatemalteco	1	1	0
GUA03	Dec-03	Berger	Partido de Avanzada Nacional	1	1	0
HON85	Jan-86	Azcona Hoyo	Partido Liberal de Honduras	1	1	0
HON89	Jan-90	Callejas	Partido Nacional de Honduras	1	1	0
HON93	Jan-94	Reina	Partido Liberal de Honduras	0	1	1
HON97	Mar-98	Flores	Partido Liberal de Honduras	1	1	0
HON01	Mar-02	Maduro	Partido Nacional de Honduras	1	1	0
HON05	Jan-06	Zelaya	Partido Liberal de Honduras	1	1	0

TABLE 4.5 (*continued*)

Election	Inauguration	Candidate	Party	Campaign	Government	Switch
MEX88	Dec-88	Salinas	Partido Revolucionario Institucional	1	1	0
MEX94	Dec-94	Zedillo	Partido Revolucionario Institucional	1	1	0
MEX00	Dec-00	Fox	Partido Acción Nacional	1	1	0
MEX06	Dec-06	Calderón	Partido Acción Nacional	1	1	0
NIC96	Jan-97	Aleman	Alianza Liberal	1	1	0
NIC01	Jan-02	Bolaños	Partido Liberal Constitucionalista	1	1	0
NIC06	Jan-07	Ortega	Frente Sandinista de Liberación Nacional	1	1	0
PER80	Jul-80	Belaúnde	Acción Popular	0	1	1
PER85	Jul-85	García	Alianza Popular Revolucionária Americana	0	0	0
PER90	Jul-90	Fujimori	Cambio 90	0	1	1
PER95	Jul-95	Fujimori	Cambio 90	1	1	0
PER01	Jul01	Toledo	Peru Posible	1	1	0
PER06	Jul-06	García	Alianza Popular Revolucionária Americana	1	1	0
URU84	Mar-85	Sanguinetti	Partido Colorado	1	1	0
URU89	Mar-90	Lacalle	Partido Nacional	1	1	0
URU94	Mar-95	Sanguinetti	Partido Colorado	1	1	0
URU99	Mar-00	Battle	Partido Colorado	1	1	0
URU04	Mar-05	Vázquez	Frente Amplio	1	1	0
VEN83	Feb-84	Lusinchi	AD	0	0	0
VEN88	Feb-89	Pérez	Acción Democrática	0	1	1
VEN93	Feb-94	Caldera	Convergencia Nacional	0	0	0
VEN98	Feb-99	Chávez	Movimiento Quinta República	0	1	1
VEN00	May-00	Chávez	Movimiento Quinta República	0	0	0
VEN06	Jan-07	Chávez	Partido Socialista Unido de Venezuela	0	0	0

5

Currency Crisis, Policy Switch, and Ideological Convergence in Brazil

After eight years under a conservative government that promoted a widespread liberalization of the Brazilian economy, investors' fears that the Workers' Party (PT) would revert these policies in case it won the presidency provoked a collapse in financial markets during the 2002 campaign (Barbosa and Pereira de Souza 2010; Santiso 2003).

The crisis transcended the financial sector. It caused a sharp devaluation of the Brazilian real, accelerated inflation rates, and provoked recession, severely affecting the real economy. It also had a fundamental impact on the newly elected administration. The urgency to gain market confidence to re-attract capital flows subjected the government to investors' influence, resulting not only in the adoption of an unexpectedly orthodox economic program, but also in the appointments of conservative leaders as heads of the Central Bank and the Finance ministry (Carcanholo 2006). In the words of a member of Lula's team, it was a matter of "giving up the rings to keep the fingers."[1]

Lula's move rightward had long-term implications to Brazilian politics. Studies show that the similarities between the program advanced by the PT and those implemented under the previous administration, particularly in the economic realm, contributed to dilute ideological differences voters perceive among Brazilian parties (Carreirão 2007).[2]

The influence of Lula's U-turn on the trajectory of the Left in other emerging economies was also tremendous. It was comparable to the

---

[1] Author's interview with member of the Lula 2002 campaign's team, September 2008.

[2] Carreirão (2007) shows that the percentage of the electorate uncapable of placing itself in an ideological scale increased from 23 percent to 42 percent between 2002 and 2006. This movement was particularly strong in the Left, where only 9 percent of the electorate placed in 2006, compared to 26 percent in 2002.

impact François Mitterrand had on the European Left in the early eighties when, after a persisting speculative attack, the French president was forced to abandon a socialist program in favor of a conservative economic agenda, burying what Helleiner (1994) referred to as "keynesianism of one country."

Lula's orthodox shift turned him into the poster child of a "responsible Left" in Latin America (Castañeda 2006; Roberts and Levitsky 2011; Weyland, Madrid, and Hunter 2010), one that "pursues the twin goals of growth and equality within the confines of a responsible economic policy,"[3] frequently contrasted with the "radical Left" epitomized by Hugo Chávez in Venezuela.

Since 2002, this rather simplistic but widely accepted dichotomy has framed political analysis in Latin America and in other emerging economies. Analysts have recurrently speculated whether presidential candidates on the Left belong to "Lula's" or "Chávez's" type. This happened, among others, with Tabaré Vázquez in Uruguay, Rafael Correa in Ecuador, Manuel López Obrador in Mexico, and Alan García in Peru.

In another evidence of the influence of Lula's U-turn, a decade after the PT election in Brazil the presidential candidate Ollanta Humala reacted to a confidence crisis in Peru by releasing a "Letter to the Peruvian People." The letter was explicitly drawn from the "Letter to the Brazilian People" that Lula had announced in 2002, and that was dubbed "letter to calm bankers" by frustrated members of the Workers' Party.

This chapter traces the mechanisms through which market discipline was imposed on the Brazilian Workers' Party. I examine Lula's electoral discourse in the 1989, 1994, 1998, and 2002 presidential races, using primary evidence from videos of the PT electoral programs broadcast in Brazil's open television channels. I argue that, despite the changes in the party's internal organization and electoral strategies, extensively documented in the literature (Amaral 2012; Hunter 2008, 2011; Meneguello and Amaral 2006; Samuels 2004), the PT program remained quite consistent until 2001. It was only during the 2002 campaign that it moved radically toward the Right.

In conjunction with these videos, extracts from financial reports released throughout the 2002 campaign reveal the confidence game played by the party leadership and financial markets, and how the

---

[3] "Contentment and complacency: Lula is coasting towards a second term," *The Economist*, August 31, 2006.

Currency Crisis, Policy Switch, and Ideological Convergence 89

effort to reestablish investors' confidence was determinant to Lula's shift rightward.

Next, I show that a release of financial market constraints after the commodity boom initiated in 2004 did not trigger PT's return to its historical agenda, or forestalled the consolidation of the party's move to the center. I contend that the size and complexity of the Brazilian economy limit the country's exposure to cycles of currency booms and crises, and for this reason the intensity of market constraints do not change substantially overtime. Once the PT learned and adapted to these constraints after 2002, conditions did not vary enough, with the boom, to grant a return to the party's original agenda, allowing for the consolidation of its change.

Ultimately, there is no way to understand either the Lula presidency or its consequences to the Brazilian Left without reference to financial globalization and market discipline. The Workers' Party's experience, for its relevance, sheds light on how the centrality of building market confidence has contributed to the persistence of neoliberalism in Latin America.

Background

The election of 2002 was Lula da Silva's fourth attempt to become president of Brazil. The first time he ran was in 1989, in the first presidential contest held in the country after twenty-one years of authoritarian regime. The race took place in the midst of a debt crisis that had started with the Mexican default of 1982 and that lasted throughout the 1980s, the Latin American "lost decade."

Three candidates received most of the votes in the first round of the election. Fernando Collor de Mello, the former governor of the small state of Alagoas, ran with the support of Brazilian right-wing parties. Leonel Brizola, a left-wing politician who had played a central role in the democratic government deposed by the military coup of 1964, split the leftist vote with Lula, formerly an important labor leader in the steel industry and founder of the still electorally marginal Workers' Party. After edging Brizola for a spot in the second round, Lula received support against Collor de Mello from most of the defeated parties.

The PT's 1989 campaign framed the presidential race as a struggle in which "the people" confronted the "dominant class." Politics was portrayed as a zero-sum game in which peasants and landowners, workers and employers, citizens and bankers belonged to opposite sides. In this struggle, Lula was presented as the representative of the working class, peasants, and small businesses, and Collor as the candidate of the

90   *The Politics of Market Discipline in Latin America*

Brazilian century-old elites and big business.[4] Lula affirmed, in a spot broadcast on television in November 3, 1989:

> We can change this, the majority of the oppressed can change this [social injustice]. It is just necessary that the peasant not believe that the landowner will pursue an agrarian reform. It is necessary that the banking employee not believe that the banker will pursue a banking reform, that the worker not believe that his employer will write the law that favors him.

Also,

> The only possibility of feeding the Brazilian worker is to end the privileges of those who eat in excess. We will only have a fair society when there aren't those who eat five times a day, at the expense of others that spend five days without eating.... Our hands should not be used solely to produce the bread they eat, but they should be used by all of us to vote on ourselves, that is why you should vote for the Popular Front.

The main priorities of Lula's 1989 program were a land reform and the default on the Brazilian foreign debt. Both initiatives were deemed necessary to overcome a severe inflationary crisis and to construct an egalitarian, socialist society. The program contended that Brazil had been tricked into a never-ending, illegitimate debt, which the government had no moral obligation to pay. Lula proposed to divert funds allocated to the payment of public debt into a "development fund" to be spent on the creation of new jobs, high-tech research, and other projects considered conducive to economic development.

Lula lost the 1989 election by six percentage points, and Collor de Mello launched the market-friendly program announced during his campaign. On the domestic front, he enacted the deregulation of several sectors of the economy and initiated the process of privatization of public companies, at the same time that he astonished the country with a freezing of banking assets. At the international level, Collor abandoned the promise of limiting debt payments, and instead oriented his agenda toward building confidence among international creditors to attract foreign investment. After being impeached on corruption charges, Collor de Mello was replaced by vice president Itamar Franco, who maintained economic liberalization and the control of inflation as top priorities.

It was during the Franco government that Brazil finally curbed hyperinflation, after the adoption of the "Plano Real." The leading figure in this process was Franco's minister of the economy, Fernando Henrique Cardoso, from the Brazilian Social Democratic Party (Partido

---

[4] Quotes in this section were extracted from candidates' TV programs, released in prime time months before the presidential elections. *Source:* DOXA – Laboratório de Pesquisa em Opinião Pública, IESP.

Social Democrata Brasileira [PSDB]), which had joined Franco's grand-coalition cabinet. In 1994, when Lula competed for the presidency for the second time, Cardoso was the incumbent candidate and his main opponent.

Running as the "father of the Real," Cardoso won the contest already in the first round, in a campaign that avoided confrontation and vaguely promised to prioritize employment, health, education, safety, and agriculture. His government furthered the neoliberal agenda initiated under Collor, promoting economic deregulation and privatization, as well as trade and financial liberalization.

After a period of exuberance, the euphoria that followed price stabilization started to fade with the severe consequences imposed by the Mexican, Asian, and Russian financial crises of the mid-1990s on the Brazilian economy. Economic crisis, unemployment, and the future of the neoliberal agenda in Brazil were the main themes around which the presidential race revolved. The 1998 campaign was waged against the backdrop of mounting financial pressures, and amidst speculation over the collapse of the Brazilian currency.

Cardoso attributed the deterioration of the economy to an international crisis, and claimed to be the only one capable of leading Brazil through tough times (Singer 2009). The PT, not surprisingly, blamed the crisis on the incumbent government's neoliberal policies.

Lula's 1998 campaign, thus, resumed the confrontational discourse observed in 1989. He claimed that the economic policies advanced under Cardoso protected bankers and international loan sharks at the expense of the real economy, and promised to reestablish Brazil's economic sovereignty. For the PT, the solution for the crisis depended on imposing exchange controls to protect the value of the Real, drastically reducing what the party identified as "predatory imports," subsidizing interest rates for production, and launching an emergency job creation plan. The differences between Lula and Cardoso were emphasized in the electoral programs broadcasted on television:

The Brazilian government secretly negotiates a monstrous package with the IMF to be advanced immediately after the elections. Cuts in social expenditures and inhuman taxes. If you allow it, Brazil will sink into recession and unemployment. Betrayal. Lie. Those who threw us into the crisis cannot save us from it. Those who caused unemployment cannot overcome unemployment. In the air, program Brazilian Heart. Lula president, Brizola vice-president. The incumbent government, in order to pay interests to international "loan-sharks" took money away even from retired workers. People that gave their life to see the country grow and now receive a starving-wage (September 9, 1998).

92 *The Politics of Market Discipline in Latin America*

The programs insisted on the impossibility of simultaneously governing for creditors and citizens, and the necessity of choosing between servicing the country's debt or promoting policies oriented toward development and social justice. Lula affirmed:

> The president has not the courage to say the truth because he is on his knees in front of the bankers. He has already committed with the IMF. The IMF, which has run Thailand, Indonesia and Russia into the ground. This recipe can also do it with Brazil. Only this year, this government will pay R$65 billion of interests. This would be enough to build more than four billion popular houses. This would be enough to place all landless peasants in Brazil. This is more than we spend with social security, more than total wages paid in Brazil this year. If the president does not have the courage to say where these policies lead, I will do it. Industrial and agricultural collapses, higher unemployment. What we have to do is to lower interest rates, invest in production and limit imports. The president does not do that because his commitment is not with the people. His commitment is with international loan-sharks. On October 4 you can change that. I need your vote (September 24, 1998).

Like in previous races, Lula defended the priority of land reform, whereby a million peasant families would gain access to their own property in the Brazilian countryside. The problem of massive foreign and domestic debt reentered the PT's agenda.

As the financial crisis escalated, the IMF, the World Bank, and the Inter-American Development Bank offered support packages to the Brazilian government, in an effort to avoid a devaluation of the Real and to reassure investors of the country's financial stability. This backing was enough to prop the economy and secure Cardoso's relatively easy reelection. Yet almost immediately after winning the government abandoned the fixed exchange rate regime, which triggered a 50 percent devaluation of the Real.

Cardoso hung on to advance his liberalizing agenda for four more years, but his popularity plummeted on a lackluster track-record of 2.2 percent average GDP growth during the eight years of his presidency, along with fading memories of his success against inflation.

The 2002 Presidential Election

At the beginning of 2002, despite concerns over high indebtedness and persistent current account deficits, Brazil's long-term prospects seemed promising to analysts and investors alike; optimism was reinforced by the absence of spillover effects after Argentina declared a default on its foreign debt in December 2001. Brazil was regarded as an example of a

Currency Crisis, Policy Switch, and Ideological Convergence 93

successful emerging economy, and its sound economic conditions were praised in the international financial community.

Financial reports largely downplayed Cardoso's decreasing popularity; the PSDB was expected to win the presidential election and to maintain a neoliberal agenda for four more years. In late April, however, markets began acting nervously after the first electoral surveys were released indicating lower-than-expected support to the incumbent candidate José Serra. According to a report from the investment bank UBS Warburg, investors feared "all the candidates except Serra."[5]

In May, BCP Securities issued a report entitled *Da Lula Monster*, describing the sense of panic spreading among economic agents as they realized that Lula could be the next Brazilian president (Santiso and Martínez 2003). Investors feared that the leftist candidate would discontinue Cardoso's economic policies, increase government's social expenditures, and accept higher levels of inflation. In the worst-case scenario, Lula was expected to re-nationalize privatized companies and to default on the country's massive foreign debt. Goldman Sachs even developed a *Lulameter* – a mathematical model designed to quantify the likelihood of Lula's victory through the behavior of prices in currency markets.[6]

The fears were not unjustified. At the conclusion of its 2001 annual meeting, the PT released a document titled "Another Brazil Is Possible,"[7] which established the guidelines of its 2002 electoral program; in a section titled "The Necessary Rupture," the party called for a rupture with the IMF and promised to reconsider privatizations, democratize property, and promote land reform, an agenda by no means to the right of previous presidential campaigns. The PT explicitly affirmed that a democratic and popular government would need to *effectively break* with the current model:

The centrality of social justice demands the democratization of property, with a profound urban reform that guarantees property and access to public services, an encompassing agrarian reform, and policies that support family agriculture. In the countryside, our government is committed to ending violence and to redistributing large unproductive properties.

Privatizations will be suspended and reconsidered; all the privatizations already in place will be audited, specially those where there is evidence of misuse of public funds or negligence in preserving national strategic interests.

---

[5] "Latin American Economic & Strategy Perspectives," UBS Warburg LLC, June/July 2002.

[6] The "Lulameter," Emerging Markets Strategy, Goldman Sachs, June 6, 2002.

[7] The document "Another Brazil Is Possible" (Um Outro Brazil é Possível), written by the coordinator-to-be of the 2002 presidential campaign Celso Daniel, was approved at the XIIth National Meeting of the PT, in December 2001.

94 *The Politics of Market Discipline in Latin America*

Regarding the foreign debt, now predominantly private, it will be necessary to denounce the agreement with the IMF, in order to free the economic policy from the restrictions imposed on growth and on the defense of Brazilian commercial interests. We will establish transparent mechanisms to control inflows and outflows of capital, stimulate the reinvestment of foreign direct investment through taxation of profit remittances, and block any initiative to renationalize the foreign debt, reducing the issuance of dollar-denominated domestic debt. Brazil needs to have an active international position on topics related to foreign debt, articulating allies in the process of auditing and renegotiating the foreign public debt.

Even considering that party manifestos are not binding, and are often more "radical" than the message parties transmit to wider audiences, including voters, it is significant that this document was cited in interviews both by a former PT member who left the party after 2002, and by a director of the Brazilian Central Bank (BACEN) who witnessed the transition between the Cardoso and Lula administrations, as evidence of the policies expected to be advanced under Lula.[8]

By June, optimism had fully deteriorated. The Brazilian stock market had dropped sharply, and interest rate futures had risen. The Real depreciated by more than 12 percent in that month, accumulating a depreciation of 23 percent in the first half of the year. The risk premium on Brazilian sovereign bonds rose to Nigerian levels, among the highest in the world.

PT's initial reaction was to downplay the crisis, insisting that markets were fueled by exaggerations. As the situation aggravated, however, the party was publicly called upon by Cardoso's economic team to clarify its commitment to market-friendly policies and fiscal discipline (Goldfrank and Wampler 2008). Lula responded with a "Letter to the Brazilian People," in which this commitment was explicitly made:

The PT and its allies are clear that overcoming the current model, which has been emphatically claimed by society, will not happen as magic, in a few days. There are no miracles in the life of a people and a country. We need a careful transition between what we have now and what society demands.... Naturally, underlying this transition will be the respect of contracts and obligations of the country.[9]

The letter addressed financial market fears, blaming the confidence crisis on the fragility of the economic model advanced under Cardoso, and promised to bring stability. Lula boldly guaranteed he would maintain fiscal discipline and make low inflation a priority, and that a PT government would not make unilateral or voluntaristic decisions. It would, first

---

[8] The former party member emphasized that these policies were part of a document signed by Celso Daniel, who was considered a "moderate" in the PT.

[9] "Letter to the Brazilian People" (Carta ao Povo Brasileiro), Lula da Silva, June 22, 2002.

Currency Crisis, Policy Switch, and Ideological Convergence   95

and foremost, "respect contracts," a euphemism for paying the country's massive public debt and maintaining privatizations. The agrarian reform was reframed as a means to bringing peace to the countryside.

Some party members ironically dubbed the document "Letter to Calm Bankers," and interpreted it as a necessary evil to prevent the escalation of financial market panic. They expected that, after the election, Lula would return to the PT's original agenda.

Investors seemed to agree, as the letter was met with plain indifference; as suggested by the findings presented in the previous chapter, the party's ideological consistency over the years established a very strong prior, not only among voters but in the business and financial communities, about what a Lula presidency would entail. Skepticism about his conversion to a market-friendly agenda was widespread.

Markets' fears turned into outright panic as Lula's leadership in the presidential race consolidated. This panic was reflected in stock and bond markets alike, and brought foreign capital flows to a halt, causing a sharp cut in credit lines for the Brazilian government and private companies. Figure 5.1 contrasts stock markets' pessimism with respect to Lula's victory, with the optimism that prevailed in 1994 when Cardoso was expected to win.

In July, the risk-rating agency Standard and Poor's (S&P) downgraded Brazilian sovereign bonds, alleging concerns about political uncertainties, and outflows reached U.S.$ 1.1 billion, twice as much as in the previous month. The devaluation of the Brazilian real led to a significant rise in the country's foreign debt service of U.S.$ 335 billion, 80 percent of which was denominated in dollars or accumulated interest at floating exchange rates. The monthly inflation reached 1.7 percent, compared to 0.4 percent in June, spreading the belief that the economic stabilization was in jeopardy.

When the PT started its television campaign in August, the contrast with previous races was startling; opposite to the confrontational tone of the 1989, 1994, and 1998 campaigns, Lula promised to "unite, instead of divide" the country. Previously portrayed as representing workers and small business and confronting loan sharks, landowners, and big business, Lula depoliticized his discourse by claiming to be the representative of *all Brazilians*:

"This is a good example that when businessmen and workers collaborate, the result is better for *all*";"This is why my proposal of a social pact between government, business and workers has been increasingly accepted by *all*";"We have to foster development in *all* areas, *all* sectors and *all* social groups."[10]

---

[10] Quotes extracted from PT's 2002 electoral program on TV.

96   *The Politics of Market Discipline in Latin America*

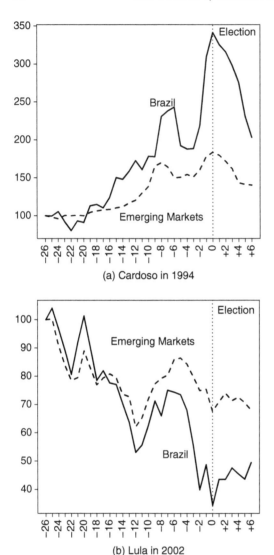

FIGURE 5.1. Stock Market Behavior: 1994 and 2002 Presidential Elections.
Notes: Standard and Poor's (S&P) stock market indices for Brazil and emerging markets in the period that surrounds Brazilian elections (denoted by the vertical line in the graphs).
Source: Datastream.

All of a sudden, policies historically defended by the PT and that were still present in the 2001 resolutions vanished from the party's electoral agenda. Even though high indebtedness remained a major problem in the Brazilian economy, no reference was made to debt renegotiation or

Currency Crisis, Policy Switch, and Ideological Convergence

default, or even to the unfairness of prioritizing debt payments over social expenditures.

The agrarian reform was no longer justified as a means to social justice but was presented as one developmental policy among many others. All references to agrarian reform in 2002 were accompanied by terms like "peaceful, organized, well planned," downplaying its potentially redistributive (and therefore conflictive) nature:

It is a question of honor to bring peace to the countryside, with an organized and pacific land reform, perpetrated in unused land, as regulated by the Constitution. If you have your own land and produce, the government will provide you with incentives to produce even more because, of course, Brazil needs that (September 21, 2002).

A program broadcast in September 2002 illustrates the change; in the video, an important Brazilian cattle rancher explains that when a PT governor was elected in his state, cattle ranchers were all very concerned. Four years later, he added, "they find themselves having the governor as an ally, always attentive to the problems of the industry." Knowing him then, he was "sure that Lula as president will represent a significant advance to the Brazilian cattle industry and will bring peace to the countryside."[11]

As the confidence crisis persisted, the IMF offered a rescue package that was aimed at "calming down markets" but had a clear political agenda – to bind the new administration into maintaining the PSDB's economic policies. In return for the loan, the incoming government should target a fiscal surplus of at least 3.75 percent of the GDP until 2005, accept the IMF's quarterly surveillance of budget data, and keep the "set of current free market policies."[12] All potential winners of the presidential race were publicly asked to commit to the IMF's terms, and so they did. Notwithstanding, not even the agreement was enough to revert financial markets' behavior, which provides an additional measure of investors' priors with respect to the PT's economic agenda:

Of course, it remains to be seen whether or not a party (or leader, for that matter) that has functioned as the opposition can change its ideology so quickly. The current market turbulence reflects that concern.[13]

---

[11] Program broadcast in September 21, 2002.
[12] Global News Wire, October 2, 2002.
[13] "Latin American Economic & Strategic Perspectives," UBS Warburg LLC, October 4, 2002.

98   *The Politics of Market Discipline in Latin America*

As victory became inevitable, investors started to speculate about the early decisions of the new government, their focus turning to appointments to key positions in the Finance Ministry and the central bank that could credibly signal government's resolve to "change":

> While it isn't over until it's over, [the new president] is quite likely to be Luiz Inácio Lula da Silva. But knowing the name of the new president is very different from knowing who the incoming government will be, much less what the government will do. This is because, broad-brush political positioning aside, Lula has yet to define himself and his government's policies, and investors will not receive meaningful clues here until the new government announces its economic cabinet, political partners, and policy agenda. What this means is that there is no magic incantation that the new government can utter to transform market skepticism into trust.[14]

Markets demanded information on the team that would lead the government:

> We think that, in the event that Lula wins the election, in whatever round, he will be called upon to present a market-friendly economic team, and in a relatively short period of time. This would help reassure investors that his move to the center is sincere, and that he is committed to the orthodox fiscal principles that guided the country through crises over the past few years.[15]

Reports from financial institutions listed the measures deemed necessary to win markets' confidence: a strong economic cabinet, with the "correct" policy orientation and experience, and with a strong voice within the government; the early announcement of a restrained policy toward minimum wages and public-sector wages, and guarantees that the primary fiscal surplus would be adjusted upward to ensure debt sustainability; and the early establishment of constructive working relations with the IMF.

The PT government should also implement a "coherent institutional framework" that included an independent central bank, inflation targets, and a floating exchange rate.

Despite the crisis, and José Serra's strategy to blame it on the "PT threat," Lula was elected by a landslide in the second round of the presidential race. Yet the process of understanding and communicating with market players, which was key to the party throughout the campaign, strengthened the relative power of its more conservative members.

---

[14] "Brazil Scenarios," UBS Warburg LLC, October 5, 2002.
[15] "Latin American Economic & Strategic Perspectives," UBS Warburg LLC, October 4, 2002.

Currency Crisis, Policy Switch, and Ideological Convergence

Most importantly, it consolidated the leadership of Antonio Palocci, PT's main interlocutor with the financial community, and whose economic policies barely differed from those of Cardoso's team. In the words of the former director of the BACEN previously mentioned, Palocci "hardly looked like a *petista*, and spoke markets' language."

The confidence crisis left the Brazilian economy nowhere close to where it was in early 2002 (Comesaña 2004). In April 2003, annualized inflation was over the 15 percent mark, twice the rate of the same month in the previous year. Interest rates stood at 26.5 percent, compared to 18 percent. Important sectors of the economy that had debt pegged to the dollar, such as the electric power companies, were left in dire straits. Also, owing to a high share of dollar denominated debt, public accounts deteriorated severely in the period.

After an average annual growth of 0.7 percent in the previous four years, the Brazilian income per capita fell 0.3 percent in 2003, while the share of the poor in the population rose 1.2 percentage points, to its highest level in a decade. Unemployment, which had averaged 8 percent between 1999 and 2002, reached 9.2 percent.[16]

Once in office, the new government immediately rushed to rebuild market confidence; it started by appointing Palocci, rather than a leading PT economist, to the Finance ministry. During the campaign, Palocci had consolidated a reputation of being moderate and market-friendly in the financial community, and was seen as a far preferable option than names such as Aloízio Mercadante or Guido Mantega, considered "too heterodox" and too close to PT's traditional economic agenda.

The economists invited to join Palocci's team put an end on any remaining doubts about the content of the government's economic program. Joaquim Levy and Marcos Lisboa, respectively secretary of the Treasury and secretary of Economic Policy, had unquestionable orthodox credentials, including Ph.D.s from American universities, and professional experience in the private sector and in multilateral institutions. Bernard Appy, the new executive secretary, despite having long-time connections in the PT, was seen as a "moderate" within the party, not likely to question the guidelines of economic policymaking.

Henrique Meirelles, the former president of BankBoston and then recently elected PSDB congressman, was the final choice for the presidency of the central bank. As financial reports had insisted throughout the campaign, Meirelles received full independence to choose his team. He kept many of the former directors of the institution, such as Beny Parnes, Alexandre Schwartsman, and Ilan Goldfajn. All of them

---

[16] ECLAC, Base de Datos Estadísticos.

100 The Politics of Market Discipline in Latin America

were well-regarded orthodox economists, with close ties with the financial industry, which assured investors of the continuity of Cardoso's macroeconomic policies.

In an interview, when asked about the conservative orientation of the government's economic policies, the top political advisor Marco Aurélio Garcia, explained:

We have the problem that the people taking day-to-day decisions about economic policy are almost exclusively conservatives. They are people with historical links to financial circles, to the economic apparatus of previous governments. Very few left-wing economists entered the government, so it was hard to build up pressure within the government. (...) It was the decision of the government's economic team to appoint conservatives to key positions. It was done in the name of credibility.[17]

The economist Leda Paulani reiforces Garcia's claims:

There was a group of left-wing economists who had worked with the PT in the build-up to the election and had contributed to the election victory. They had clear proposals and they could have worked with the economic ministers to carry out these reforms. But they were completely ignored. The ministry of finance and the presidency of the central bank were given to orthodox economists who had worked with Cardoso.[18]

To bring the economy back to its conditions in the beginning of 2002, the first year of Lula's presidency was dedicated to convincing investors about the government's "responsibility," respect to contracts and commitment with the payment of the public debt (Castro and Carvalho 2003; Fleury 2004; Mollo and Saad-Filho 2006).

Toward this end, Lula conserved the main pillars of PSDB's macroeconomic policy: floating exchange rates, inflation targets, and fiscal surpluses. Despite the systematic critique of Cardoso's orthodoxy, the PT administration maintained Brazilian interest rates among the highest in the world, to keep inflation within the targets set in the IMF agreement.

Surprising markets and party members alike, the government actually exceeded the previous orthodoxy by establishing a fiscal surplus of 4.25 percent of the GDP until 2006 (Diniz 2004; Mollo and Saad-Filho 2006). The target, substantially higher than the IMF's goal of 3.75, was intended to "signal to financial agents the PT's commitment of the Lula government with fiscal conservatism, and therefore dissipate concerns with an

---

[17] Wainwright, Hilary; Branford, Sue (Eds.). In the Eye of the Storm: Left-Wing Activists Discuss the Political Crisis in Brazil, p. 29. Transnational Institute. Available at: http://www.tni.org/sites/www.tni.org/files/download/brazildossier.pdf.

[18] Wainwright, Hilary; Branford, Sue (Eds.). In the Eye of the Storm: Left-Wing Activists Discuss the Political Crisis in Brazil, p. 31. Transnational Institute. Available at: http://www.tni.org/sites/www.tni.org/files/download/brazildossier.pdf.

Currency Crisis, Policy Switch, and Ideological Convergence 101

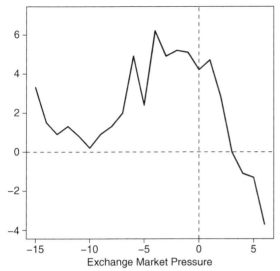

FIGURE 5.2. Currency Pressures in the Brazilian 2002 Election.
Notes: Evolution of currency pressures, as calculated in Chapter 4, in the period around Lula's 2002 inauguration, denoted by the vertical line. The horizontal line marks $EMP = 0$.

explosive increase in public debt" (Barbosa and Pereira de Souza 2010, p. 3).

In addition, Lula's first legislative initiatives addressed the measures investors deemed priorities: pension and tax reform, and the independence of the central bank. As reported by the Economist Intelligence Unit:

Three important economic reforms are before Congress: pension reform, tax reform and the granting of autonomy to the Banco Central do Brasil [Bacen, Brazilian Central Bank]. Progress in these areas will strengthen confidence in the government's ability to ensure macroeconomic stability.[19]

The effort finally seemed to work, as markets boomed early in 2003 and exchange market pressures were released (Figure 5.2).[20]

Table 5.1 illustrates the other end of the "confidence-building" process – the way the new government managed to improve its stand with investors by implementing the demanded reforms immediately after taking office. The table displays "reform scorecards" for the Brazilian

---

[19] "Brazil Country Risk," Economist Intelligence Unit, October 2003.
[20] Exchange market pressures are calculated as detailed in Chapter 4, based on monthly relative changes in international reserves and exchange rates. They rise whenever reserves fall and/or the currency depreciates, and decrease when the currency appreciates and/or international reserves accumulate.

102　　　　　*The Politics of Market Discipline in Latin America*

TABLE 5.1. *Brazil Reform Scorecard – Merrill Lynch*

(a) April 2003					
Reform	Change	Recent Development	Quality	Progress	Total
Social Security	Neutral	Presented April 16–17	2.5	2.5	5.0
Tax Reform	Neutral	Presented April 16–17	2.5	2.5	5.0
Central Bank Autonomy	Positive	Final vote in mid-April	4.0	1.5	5.5
Banking Law	Neutral	Already in Congress	3.0	3.0	6.0
Composite Score			2.5	2.5	**5.2**
(b) December 2003					
Reform	Change	Recent Development	Quality	Progress	Total
Social Security	Positive	Approved in Senate 2nd round	3.5	5.0	8.5
Tax Reform	Positive	Approved in Senate 1st round	2.0	4.8	6.8
Central Bank Autonomy	Neutral	Complementary Law exp. 2004	4.0	2.0	6.0
Banking Law	Neutral	Approved in Lower House	3.0	4.0	7.0
Composite Score			3.1	4.5	**7.6**

Note: The scorecard summarizes the progress score, which ranges from 0 to 5, 5 being the closer a reform is to being approved. The quality score, also ranging from 0 to 5, measures the closer a reform's "current form" is to its considered "best form." The composite score gives the weighted score of the reforms as per the following weights: social security 50 percent, tax 25 percent, banking 15 percent, and central bank autonomy 10 percent.
Source: Merrill Lynch, referred to in Santiso (2006, pp. 43–44).

economy, created by Merrill Lynch, in which the country was assigned a score based on the progress and quality of reforms analysts considered a priority (i.e., how close the current state of a particular reform is from its "ideal" form). The improvement of Brazil's scores between April 2003 (Table 5.1a) and December 2003 (Table 5.1b) helps explain markets' quick recovery during Lula's first months in office.

Currency Crisis, Policy Switch, and Ideological Convergence   103

Among all these measures, the social security reform was considered indisputable evidence of the government's new trajectory; Cardoso had tried to pass this reform for eight years with no success, thanks to the systematic opposition led by the Workers' Party. Making this the first initiative of his government, Lula sent a costly signal to markets, one that not surprisingly triggered a major crisis within the PT.

In the process of approving the reform, which among other measures taxed retired employees, created stricter rules for retirement and cut the amount received by widowers, PT congressmen expressed their discontent by voting against the government. After harsh negotiations, the leadership finally opted for expelling dissidents, leading to a schism that originated the Party of Socialism and Liberty (Partido Socialismo e Liberdade [PSOL]), and further bending the party's control toward its conservative members.

Plínio de Arruda Sampaio, a historical party member and former congressman who later joined the PSOL, summarizes the discontent:[21]

Despite the denials of party leaders, the truth is the PT surrendered to neoliberalism. It was not, as alleged, a transition strategy. Lula and the party leadership were convinced that the neoliberal receipt of market stability at any cost, trade openness, and privileges assigned to foreign investors is the best that can be done for Brazil. The concrete interests of the people had to concede to the demands of the financial capital.

LULA'S FIRST PRESIDENCY: NO PLAN B

Rumors of a "plan B" in 2003, according to which the PT would return to its original agenda once the crisis was over, faded as the government maintained the direction set early on.

After the sharp drop observed in 2002, the real reappreciated 25 percent in 2003, in large part as a result of the positive sentiment shock stemming from the new government's commitment to orthodox macroeconomic policies.[22] Interest rates among the highest in the world attracted short-time financial flows, further contributing to the appreciation of the currency.

Even though the central bank is not legally independent in Brazil, it was de facto under Lula. Not only did the president of the institution have full autonomy to appoint his team, but the Committee of Monetary

---

[21] Plínio de Arruda Sampaio. "Por que não mais PT?" Folha de São Paulo, September 27, 2005.

[22] "Brazil Country Risk," Economist Intelligence Unit, October 2003.

Policy (Comitê de Política Monetária, [Copom]) also established interest rates without any interference from the executive.

In the fiscal realm, the government exceeded its targets in 2003 despite economic stagnation, the same happening in 2004 when the nonfinancial public sector surplus reached 5.8 percent of the GDP.

The reaction of PT congressmen to the government's orthodox economic agenda was not an isolated event; the confidence of financial markets and the IMF came at the cost of disappointing many of PT's traditional supporters among organized labor movements, the poor, and the radical Left.[23]

As support for the government waned in the first years of the new administration, the PT obtained mixed results in the municipal elections of 2004, losing in important cities such as São Paulo and Porto Alegre. The party's candidate in Ribeirão Preto finished third, despite being endorsed by the town's former mayor and minister of Finance, Antonio Palocci. The loss of several state capitals pushed the PT into second place, in terms of electorate governed, behind its main opposer, the PSDB.

As expectations of social improvements were frustrated, criticism of the government's adherence to strict fiscal discipline at the expense of more rapid employment creation escalated among traditional PT's supporters. Business groups also felt alienated by a tight monetary policy that discouraged investment.

Pressures also mounted from organized civil society, particularly from the country's movement of landless peasants (Movimento Sem Terra [MST]), which had historically strong connections with the PT. Targets set at the beginning of the presidential term were not met, and the pace of land redistribution slowed down compared with the former Cardoso administration.

Attempts to pass a labor reform strained the relationship between the government and labor organizations. In an effort to build consensus for reform, in early 2003 the government established a National Labor Forum, which included representatives from labor unions, employers, and the administration. The forum produced a plan, expected to be presented to the legislature after the 2004 elections, but ended up shelved. Prospects of a far-reaching reform stalled as all main trade union federations, with the exception of the Central Única dos Trabalhadores (CUT), left the forum.[24]

---

[23] "Brazil Country Report," Economist Intelligence Unit, December 2004.
[24] "Brazil Country Report," Economist Intelligence Unit, December 2004.

Commodities Boom and Redistribution

After a year marked by strong market discipline, a sharp rise in commodity prices in 2004 significantly widened the government's room to accommodate the opposition and to advance a more interventionist and redistributive microeconomic agenda.

Increased export revenues led to the almost tripling of the country's current account between 2003 and 2004, despite the appreciation of the currency. Corporate profits, strong growth of services (especially electricity and telecommunications), revenue from exporters, and royalties from oil and gas exploration and production boosted fiscal revenues, easing the government's budget constraints and reducing the public debt. Economic growth helped lowering unemployment rates from 2005 onward.

The favorable economic scenario was boosted further by a rise in investors' appetite for Brazilian assets. A net outflow of U.S.$4.2 billion in the first nine months of 2004 shifted to a net inflow of U.S.$4.3 billion in 2005. Net foreign direct investment (FDI) inflows more than doubled to U.S.$6.8 billions in that year.

Abundant inflows of foreign currency eased the trade-off between attracting investors and promoting redistribution. The PT government found itself in a position in which it could maintain market confidence with an orthodox macroeconomic agenda and at the same time raise social expenditures that gathered political support among poor citizens; increased government revenues allowed the maintenance of primary fiscal surpluses and a reduction of the public debt, concurrent with growing transfers to the poorest families (Barbosa and Pereira de Souza 2010, p. 6).

The most important social initiative consolidated after the currency boom was an ambitious social program that would later prove decisive for Lula's reelection in 2006 – the Bolsa Família.

Soon after elected, Lula established eliminating hunger as the social priority of his mandate. During his inauguration, the president declared that his mission would only be accomplished if, at the end of his term, "all Brazilians had three meals a day." The program that consolidated these efforts was denominated "Fome Zero" (No Hunger), and involved not only cash transfers and food donation, but also the creation of urban and countryside jobs, the latter through an encompassing land reform.

According to one of its creators, Fome Zero was originally conceived as an "emancipatory" rather than an "assistentialist" program, and for this reason cash and food benefits would be dispensed for a limited number of years.[25] After that, participants should be able to find a job and make their own living without the government's assistance. Moreover,

---

[25] Interview conducted by the author in August 2011.

106   *The Politics of Market Discipline in Latin America*

local governments would not have any discretion to include or exclude beneficiaries, in an attempt to prevent the program from serving political motivations.

For a number of reasons, among them the resistance of land owners, budget constraints, and little support from the presidency, the original design of the Fome Zero was abandoned. Instead, the government progressively turned its focus to the Bolsa Família, originally one program among other initiatives included in the Fome Zero. The Bolsa Família aimed at consolidating all the social initiatives that were advanced by different areas of previous administration. The most important amongst these policies, however, were cash transfers to families conditional on keeping children at school and with up-to-date vaccination. This policy was not new; Cardoso implemented it with the name of "Bolsa Escola." The major difference under Lula was quantitative – with increased revenues brought by an overly favorable international scenario, the number of families benefited rose dramatically in the PT administration.

Between 2003 and 2006, the budget for the program Bolsa Família increased thirteen times, from R$ 570 million to 7.5 billion, reaching 11.4 million families by the time of the 2006 election.

Increased government revenues and the consolidation of economic growth after 2004 also allowed a 24.2 percent real increase in the minimum wage during Lula's first term,[26] which guaranteed the support of formerly critical labor unions. In addition, the government boosted funding available to formal workers ("crédito consignado"), which grew 80 percent from 2003 to 2005 (Singer 2009).

Industrialists, dissatisfied with monetary orthodoxy and low growth rates that marked the first years of the PT government,[27] were compensated with subsidized loans from the Brazilian development bank (Banco Nacional de Desenvolvimento Econômico e Social [BNDES]).

Disbursements made by the BNDES increased 12.3 percent year on year in the first nine months of 2005. Credits to industry, including machinery, automotive, and aeronautics, rose by 53.3 percent in the same period.

Finally, any opposition the government might have experienced from within the PT also faded as the boom consolidated, and the party anticipated real chances of reelection. According to Marco Aurélio Garcia,

---

[26] Most of the impact of the minimum wage incurs in public jobs and pensions.
[27] The Brazilian economy improved in Lula's first presidency when compared to the 2.1 percent average growth of the second Cardoso presidency. However, it is worth noting that, relative to other middle income countries, Brazil did not fare better under Lula: it went from 57 percent of the average growth between 1999 and 2002 to 60 percent between 2003 and 2006.

Currency Crisis, Policy Switch, and Ideological Convergence 107

"Instead of the party applying political pressure on the government, it gradually became a conveyor belt for the government."[28]

Among the main losers of the Lula administration were social movements, shut out of the administration (Baiocchi 2006, p. 678), particularly the Brazilian movement of landless peasants (Movimento Sem Terra [MST]). After the initial shock of the first year, when Lula did for the landless peasants less than the previous conservative government, it became clear that the agrarian reform long time defended by the PT was no longer a priority, which caused widespread frustration.

In 2005 the government was caught in the middle of a serious corruption scandal involving high-ranking figures of the party, in which the executive was accused of making monthly payments ("mensalão") to congressmen in exchange for support in the legislature. The scandal, on top of a still fragile record of achievements in social policies, pushed government and presidential popularity to an all-time low, raising speculations about Lula's prospects in the upcoming presidential election of 2006. According to a report issued by the EIU in December 2005, the confidence in the president fell from 75 percent in March 2003 to 45 percent in September 2005, with the percentage expressing "no confidence" in the president beginning to run higher than the confidence ratings. The same report noted that:

In its election campaign in 2002 the PT promised to assist the poor by expanding welfare programmes and implementing redistributive policies, but progress on meeting these objectives has been disappointing. Some of the underperformance can be explained by fiscal constraints and the need for compromise and horse-trading to win congressional votes, but the government has also shown weaknesses in administrative capacity. As the election approaches, we expect it to make renewed efforts on social programmes, but the same constraints will limit progress.

Despite the government's emphasis on its social record, with the Bolsa Família benefitting more than 11 million families and boosting the local economy in poor areas of the country, the first Lula presidency made little progress toward reducing Brazilian historically high levels of income inequality. A World Bank report published in September 2005 listed Brazil as the most unequal country in Latin America and the fifth-worst in the world, after Namibia, Botswana, the Central African Republic, and Swaziland.

---

[28] Wainwright, Hilary; Branford, Sue (Eds.). In the Eye of the Storm: Left-Wing Activists Discuss the Political Crisis in Brazil, p. 29. Transnational Institute. Available at: http://www.tni.org/sites/www.tni.org/files/download/brazildossier.pdf.

108 *The Politics of Market Discipline in Latin America*

LONG-TERM CONVERGENCE: POLITICAL DISCOURSE IN 2006 AND 2010

In striking contrast with the crisis of 2002, the presidential election of 2006 produced no reaction whatsoever in financial markets. Topics central to the PT discourse prior to 2002 such as debt renegotiation, capital controls, limitations on imports or agrarian reform were completely abandoned by Lula in his run for reelection. A comparison of Brazilian sovereign bond spreads in 2002 and 2006 offers a good measure of investors' indifference (Figure 5.3).

Lula's main opponent in 2006 was the former governor of São Paulo, the conservative Geraldo Alckmin. Yet the rhetoric of the two leading candidates diverged only marginally on the recipe for the next four years – the "quality" of fiscal discipline, and levels of investment and of interest rates. For the most part, Lula defended macroeconomic orthodoxy and social compensation, and the same did Alckmin, who promised to maintain and even improve the Bolsa Família program. Convergence was evident, as noted by the Economist Intelligence Unit in the Brazilian Country Report of March 2006: "Election uncertainties entail few risks to the overall policy stance. Mr. da Silva's shift of the ruling PT to the political centre underpins broad consensus around the need for prudent policies."

Analysts credit the acceleration of GDP growth, improvements in the minimum wage and the reach of the Bolsa Família program for Lula's victory with a margin of 20 million votes over Alckmin (Hunter and Sugiyama 2009; Licio 2009; Nicolau and Peixoto 2007; Zucco Jr. 2008). This result consolidated the president's comeback and provided him with a strong mandate. Lula managed to detach his own figure from the Workers' Party, which took the entire blame for the corruption scandals of 2005.

The policies enacted during Lula's second term were clearly to the left of his first term, reflecting the wider room to maneuver propitiated by the currency boom.[29] Figure 5.4 shows the favorable conditions under which the 2006 election was held. Compared to 2002 when exchange market pressures were severe, in 2006 these pressures had been substantially released by capital inflows and increased export revenues (Figure 5.4).

Different from the focus on building market confidence that characterized 2003, the second presidency started with a pledge to raise GDP

---

[29] See Barbosa and Pereira de Souza (2010) for a depiction of the conflicts between neoliberals and developmentalists within PT, and how the former started to lose predominance after 2005.

Currency Crisis, Policy Switch, and Ideological Convergence

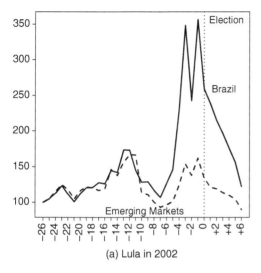

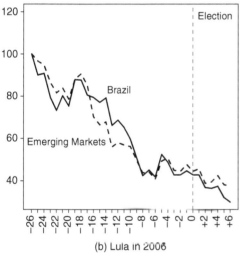

FIGURE 5.3. Brazilian Sovereign Spread: 2002 and 2006 Presidential Elections.
Notes: Spread of the JP Morgan Emerging Markets Bonds Index (EMBI+), for Brazil and Emerging Markets in the period that surrounded the Brazilian 2002 and 2006 presidential elections (denoted by the vertical dashed lines).
Source: Global Financial Data.

growth to around 5 percent per year, almost doubling the average annual growth rate of his first term.

Early in 2007, the government launched a program designed to speed up economic growth (Programa de Aceleração do Crescimento [PAC]) through increases in public and private investment in infrastructure, the latter to be fostered in part through targeted tax breaks.

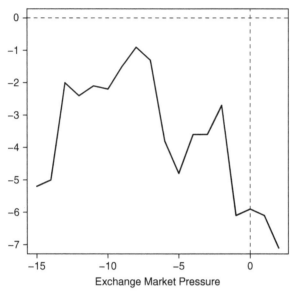

FIGURE 5.4. Currency Pressures in the Brazilian 2006 Election.
Notes: Evolution of currency pressures, as calculated in Chapter 4, in the period around Lula's inauguration in 2006. Month of inauguration denoted by the vertical dashed line. The horizontal dashed line marks $EMP = 0$.

Initially, the PAC budgeted public investments of R$ 504 billion between 2007 and 2010, divided into transportation and logistics, energy and social infrastructure, to be revised and upgraded in the following years. As a result of this initiative, public investment increased from 0.4 percent of GDP between 2003 and 2005 to 0.7 percent between 2006 and 2008, while investment in fixed capital improved from 15.9 to 19 percent of GDP (Barbosa and Pereira de Souza 2010).

The role of the BNDES was increased further in this period. From 2003 to 2010, the bank would disburse R$ 709.2 billion to Brazilian companies, R$ 168.4 billion only in 2010, close to three times the R$ 59.86 billions disbursed in 2002.[30]

Strong corporate profitability and household income growth, combined with a rise in the formalization of business and increased imports, underpinned the public finances. This compensated an acceleration of expenditure growth with the implementation of the PAC and the expansion of public payroll after a decade of restraint, sustaining the growth

---

[30] Batista, Henrique Gomes e Rodrigues, Lino."BNDES triplica na Era Lula e retoma ação de desenvolvimento," O Globo, March 25, 2011.

Currency Crisis, Policy Switch, and Ideological Convergence

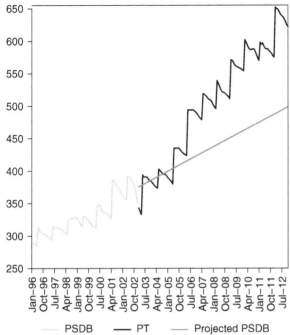

FIGURE 5.5. Evolution of Real Minimum Wage (constant R$).
Notes: Value of the nominal minimum wage, discounted the inflation of the previous month, as calculated by the National Index of Consumer Prices (INPC), from the Instituto Brasileiro de Geografia e Estatística (IBGE).
Source: Instituto de Pesquisa Econômica Aplicada (IPEA).

of the minimum wage in real terms (Figure 5.5), and a steady expansion of the Bolsa Família program (Figure 5.6).

Overall, Lula's second presidency was perceived to promote a shift to a mixed model of development, strengthening private–public partnerships and raising government intervention in the economy through a new industrial policy package. Analysts in the period frequently criticized Lula's ambivalent stance with respect to structural reforms, and the governments' diminishing resolve toward advancing them.

The Lula government has signaled a shift towards a mixed model of economic development in its second term. On one hand, it will continue to pursue an orthodox macroeconomic policy framework, encompassing fiscal discipline and inflation-targeting. It will also allow increased private-sector participation in areas traditionally controlled by the state, such as oil exploration and the management of ports and airports, which face growing bottlenecks. On the other hand, it will adopt a more interventionist stance in the economy through industrial policy measures and the creation of a public sovereign fund. Both initiatives

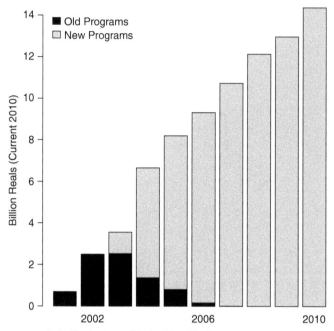

FIGURE 5.6. Evolution of Bolsa Família Program.
Notes: Total expenditures on the Bolsa Família Program.
Source: Social Development Ministry (MDES).

should be implemented in the first half of 2008 (Brazil Country Report, EIU, December 2007).

As illustrated in the preceding quote, the boom allowed the government to pursue a nonorthodox microeconomic agenda without provoking any market turbulence, provided that orthodoxy was maintained in the macroeconomic framework. In that sense, market constraints during the boom were arguably comparable to those incurred over governments in developed economies – strong, but narrow (Mosley 2003). Favorable fiscal prospects, by turning default risk negligible, boosted investors' complacency toward a more interventionist and redistributive agenda (Figures 5.5 and 5.6).[31]

Interestingly, this move to the Left in microeconomic policies occurred in parallel with capital markets' best years of Brazilian recent history, with primary issuances of around U.S.$190 billion between 2005 and 2008 and an increase in net foreign portfolio investment from U.S.$ 5.4

---

[31] It is worth noting that by mid-2013, as capital fled from emerging economies after expectations that the U.S. Fed would stop its quantitative easing, fiscal prospects worsened in Brazil and this agenda came increasingly under attack.

billion in 2006 to U.S.$ 58.6 billion in 2008 (Barbosa and Pereira de Souza 2010).

Yet, it is crucial to note that even though the PT used the wider room to maneuver to advance a microeconomic agenda closer to its historical preferences than it did until at least 2005, it did not return to the program it promoted until 2001. Even after the decrease in fiscal surpluses occurred during Lula's more "developmentalist" second term, the government still remained more fiscally conservative than its predecessor (2.3 percent between 2003 and 2008, compared to 1.9 percent between 1999 and 2002 under Cardoso).

Why Not a Return to PT's Historical Agenda?

Why did not Lula resume PT's leftist agenda during the boom?[32]

To understand this decision, it is important to take into consideration how different economies were affected during the commodity price boom started in 2004, and how that changed the reliance of public and private sectors on international financial flows.

The relevance of the commodity sector is more limited in Brazil than in any other Latin American emerging economy, with the exception of Mexico. Not only is the share of commodities over exports lower, owing to higher complexity and industrialization level, but so is the share of trade on GDP.

This implies that the Brazilian economy is less vulnerable to commodity price booms and crises than its neighbors. As an illustration, whereas in Brazil net barter terms of trade[33] increased 20 percent between 2004 and 2011, in Venezuela and Ecuador these values were 94 and 90 percent, respectively. Export revenues doubled between 2004 and 2008 in Brazil, compared to 2.4 and 2.3 times in these countries, and average GDP growth was 4.8, compared to 10.3 and 5.7.

In addition to commodities being less relevant to the Brazilian economy, the structure of the Brazilian commodity sector also contributes to explain the more limited impact price booms and crises have on the Brazilian government itself.

First, with the exception of state-owned oil company Petrobras, the commodity exporting sector in Brazil is explored by private companies

---

[32] Even though other leftist presidents took advantage of the boom to advance a "radical" leftist agenda that departed from markets' preferences both in the macro- and the microeconomic realms, Chávez was the only other case comparable to Lula's of one leader elected during "bad times" but who remained in office after the boom.

[33] Values, obtained from UNCTAD, were weighted by country's trade openness, calculated as a share of trade over GDP.

114 *The Politics of Market Discipline in Latin America*

such as Vale S.A., Bunge, BRF/Sadia. This means that the boom is channeled to the government mostly through taxes, both directly from the commodity sector and indirectly as the economy as a whole grows faster.

Second, the Brazilian commodity sector is less concentrated, and includes an important share of "soft" commodities – agricultural, poultry – which are less subject to the extraction of rent (Ananchotikul and Eichengreen 2007; Avendaño, Reisen, and Santiso 2008).

As a result, commodity price booms and crises have a more restricted impact on public revenues in Brazil; whereas the first presidencies of Chávez and Correa experienced an increase from 18 percent to 29.7 percent, and 16.6 percent to 25.8 percent of GDP respectively, Lula started his first term with central government revenues amounting to 21 percent of the GDP, reaching a maximum of 24.3 percent by the end of his second term.[34] In Mexico, the only Latin American emerging economy that is not primarily a commodity exporter, the difference between the share of public revenue immediately before the boom and its maximum during the boom was only 2 percentage points.

It follows that, as much as depressed commodity prices are not problematic to Brazil like they are for Ecuador and Venezuela, price booms do not provide as much leverage for the Brazilian government to prescind from international finance as they do in these two countries.

In addition, and very important, Brazil is one of the most financially integrated countries in the region, and certainly far more integrated than Ecuador and Venezuela even by the beginning of the boom.

In Brazil, not only the government but also private business and the banking sector are internationally integrated and therefore affected by the behavior of cross-border capital flows. Part of the Brazilian bonanza after 2005 happened as a result of this integration, as pro-cyclical flows were attracted by favorable economic prospects.

Whereas in Argentina, Ecuador, and Venezuela the main source of foreign currency was trade – capital flows were negative in most years since the mid-2000s – and in Chile capital inflows on average accounted for 30 percent of the inflows of currency to the country between 2006 and 2010, in Brazil they averaged 60 percent in the same period.

Actually, in Chile capital inflows only exceeded 40 percent of currency inflows in 2008, when they reached 60 percent of the foreign currency

---

[34] This, discounted the fact that in the end of 2003, the Brazilian Congress approved a tax reform ("mini-reforma tributária") that increased central government revenues in the following years, both nominally and as a percentage of the Brazilian GDP. See Barbosa and Pereira de Souza (2010) for a description of the main initiatives included in the reform.

that entered the country. In Brazil, they amounted to 50 percent or more since 2007, and reached 80 percent in 2010.

These numbers offer a measure of the exposure of the Brazilian economy to foreign finance. In the Brazilian conditions – relatively lower exposure to commodity price variation and higher exposure to foreign finance – it is harder for the government to afford a sudden loss of market credibility, even during a boom. Contrary to Venezuela and Ecuador, such loss has implications that go beyond governments' accounts, raising additional pressures from the domestic business community for "compliance."

Concluding, the commodity price boom started in 2004 did not afford the Brazilian government the same room to maneuver as it did in countries that, like Ecuador and Venezuela, are highly exposed to commodity price fluctuations and less reliant on international finance. Still, the boom contributed to improve public finances and make default risk negligible, which allowed Lula to implement supply-side policies more to the left, while respecting the limits imposed by macroeconomic orthodoxy.

THE 2010 PRESIDENTIAL ELECTION The presidential election of 2010 reaffirmed the convergence that observed in 2006 (Figure 5.7). Once

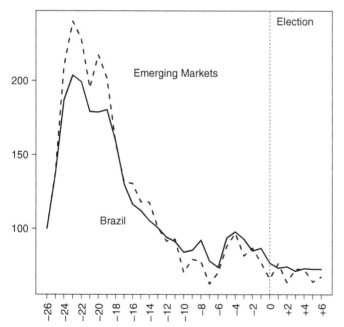

FIGURE 5.7. Brazilian Sovereign Spread: 2010 Presidential Election.
Notes: Spread of the JP Morgan Emerging Markets Bonds Index (EMBI+), for Brazil and Emerging Markets in the period that surrounded the Brazilian 2010 presidential election (denoted by the vertical dashed line).
Source: Global Financial Data.

116 *The Politics of Market Discipline in Latin America*

again there were no relevant distinctions between the programs of the PT candidate Dilma Rousseff and her main opponent, José Serra from the PSBD. Rousseff made sure to reassure investors that she would indeed stick to fiscal and monetary rectitude, by cutting taxes, reining in public spending, and controlling inflation, all "market-pleasing macroeconomic policies."[35]

Serra condemned high interest rates and promised to improve the quality of government expenditures and investment, but did not offer many alternatives to the program adopted under Lula. Similar to Geraldo Alckmin in 2006, Serra also announced he would not only maintain but also further the number of beneficiaries of the Bolsa Família.

Faster economic growth during Lula's second presidency, and the personal popularity of the PT leader, all contributed to make Rousseff an unbeatable candidate in 2010. The first Brazilian female president won in the second round, with a comfortable margin of 12 percentage points.

CONCLUSION

The election of Lula in 2002 marked a turning point for the Brazilian Left. After a financial panic of great proportions, Lula made a U-turn and announced an economic program that continued the agenda of the previous government, to which the PT had offered systematic opposition.

This chapter has shown the centrality of markets' confidence crisis to Lula's orthodox shift, as well as how the very restricted room to maneuver that marked the beginning of his first term was widened by the commodity price boom precipitated in 2004 and consolidated in the years that followed. The PT used this room to advance microeconomic policies to the left of those that characterized Lula's first presidency, including a revival of industrial policies, higher minimum wages, and a sharp expansion of the conditional cash transfers program. Yet these policies were implemented within the realm of an orthodox macroeconomic framework, established at the onset of the first mandate, and never quite challenged the economic status quo.

Lula's centrist stance persisted during the presidential campaign of 2006, and investors reacted with the expected indifference. The same trend remained in 2010, when the PT won a third term with Lula's political heir Dilma Roussef, evidencing the consolidation of the rightward move initiated in 2002.

---

[35] "Dilma Rousseff's economic team reassures suddenly nervous investors," *The Economist*, November 25, 2010.

Currency Crisis, Policy Switch, and Ideological Convergence   117

At last, I argued that the comparably limited impact of commodities on the Brazilian economy, in addition to its greater reliance on international financial flows, explains why Lula never returned to the PT's original agenda even after market constraints were released after 2004.

The next chapters reinforce these points, by examining countries that are highly exposed to currency booms and crises, and showing how this is associated with the persistence of a left-wing agenda comparable to the one promoted by the Brazilian Workers' Party before 2002.

6

Exogenous Shocks and Investors' Political Clout in Ecuador

The previous chapter unveiled how financial market panic, caused by the anticipation of Lula da Silva's electoral victory, influenced the appointment of his government's economic team and the agenda pursued in office in unexpected ways.

Most importantly, I have shown that even though market discipline was the strongest during the campaign and in the first year in office, when Brazil was subject to severe currency pressures, its effects remained visible even after international conditions improved and the government's external financing needs decreased. As a result, since 2002 the country has experienced a convergence of Left and Right around orthodox economic policymaking similar to that predicted by efficiency theories of globalization.

This chapter examines the presidencies of the leftists Lucio Gutiérrez and Rafael Correa, elected in 2002 and 2006 in Ecuador, and explains why market discipline did not produce a similar long-term convergence in the country. Four years after Gutiérrez switched to an orthodox program in response to a confidence crisis, Correa campaigned and governed on a leftist economic agenda, and responded to market panic by telling investors to "take a Valium."

I argue that these diverging behaviors cannot be understood without reference to the external scenario endured by each president, which determined governments' dependence on international sources of finance and in turn markets' leverage to influence policymaking.

Lucio Gutiérrez was inaugurated under severe currency pressures, precipitated by a sharp decrease in oil prices, the country's top export product, in addition to financial markets' risk averse behavior in the

Exogenous Shocks and Investors' Political Clout 119

aftermath of the Argentine default and of what was perceived as a Latin American "leftist wave."

In an attempt to avoid the financial collapse that could be potentially caused by a substantial loss of international reserves in a dollarized economy, Gutiérrez renounced his campaign promises, and advanced an investor-friendly program explicitly aimed at attracting foreign financial capital to the economy.

The limited power in the hands of the executive that characterized the Ecuadorean presidency, on top of long-increasing levels of political instability and party system fragmentation (Pachano 2005), contributed to Gutiérrez's switch by forcing him to gather political support from conservative parties.

Gutiérrez's orthodox economic agenda ended up warranting him an agreement with the International Monetary Fund (IMF), expected to raise the prospects of renegotiation of Ecuador's foreign debt, protect international reserves, and function as a "seal of approval" likely to induce much needed inflows of financial capital to the Ecuadorean economy. Yet political instability and fragmentation would later prove insurmountable barriers to the advancement of any coherent economic program, contributing to a crisis that culminated in his impeachment in 2005.

Different from Brazil, however, in which booming commodity prices after 2004 had a somewhat limited effect of the governments' leverage to deviate from markets' agenda, Ecuador's strong reliance on oil exports and limited financial integration prompted a dramatic change in this leverage between 2002 and 2006.

By the time Rafael Correa was elected, abundant inflows of foreign currency channeled through exports had reduced the country's external financing needs, lowered the public debt, and boosted international reserves (Table 6.1).

Figure 6.1 displays the evolution of currency pressures during Gutiérrez's and Correa's presidential elections.[1] It reveals that these pressures were close to zero in the beginning of 2002, rising sharply in the course of the year, and peaking a little after Gutiérrez's victory. In 2006, conversely, negative values captured a currency boom, which faded as the election approached, but never reached comparable levels.

---

[1] Currency pressures are calculated as detailed in Chapter 4, based on monthly relative changes in international reserves and exchange rates. They rise whenever reserves fall and/or the currency depreciates, and decrease when the currency appreciates and/or international reserves accumulate.

120   *The Politics of Market Discipline in Latin America*

TABLE 6.1. *Economic Indicators: 2002 and 2006 Presidential Elections*

	Gutiérrez (2002)	Correa (2006)
Foreign Debt/GDP	65.4	41.3
Public External Debt/GDP	56.8	32.6
Foreign Exchange Reserves (U.S.$ billion)	0.7	1.5
Short term/total external debt	14.2	12.9
Oil, spot price (U.S.$/barrel)	17.8	48.0
EMBI+spread Emerging Mkts	765	169
Exchange Market Pressure (preelectoral)	0.4	−3.0
Exchange Market Pressure (postelectoral)	0.9	−1.7

Source: Central Bank of Ecuador.

These favorable conditions allowed Correa to completely ignore markets' negative reactions to his victory and pursue the nationalist and redistributive agenda he had promised during campaign.

The benign scenario also facilitated Correa's successful strategy to confront the political fragmentation of the Ecuadorean political system. The president managed to dissolve the Congress, and to pass a new constitution that concentrated power in the executive branch and extended his term, policies that would have accelerated capital outflows and led to economic chaos had they been advanced by Gutiérrez four years earlier.

Ultimately, the room to maneuver Correa was afforded by the commodity boom prevented the consolidation of Gutiérrez' move rightward, and a convergence of the sort happened in Brazil from occurring in Ecuador.

Before examining market discipline during the presidencies of Lucio Gutiérrez and Rafael Correa, it is important to place these governments in the context of a recently dollarized economy, which had just experienced its worst financial crisis in 1999.

The Dollarization of the Ecuadorean Economy

Ecuador is endowed with abundant natural resources, but it is also vulnerable to crop disease and natural disasters such as earthquakes, volcanoes, and cycles of drought and excessive rain (Beckerman 2001). These characteristics, in addition to a dependency on primary commodities exports, have historically subjected the economy to internal and external shocks and to boom-and-bust cycles. Growing integration in international financial markets have magnified this volatility, as the

Exogenous Shocks and Investors' Political Clout

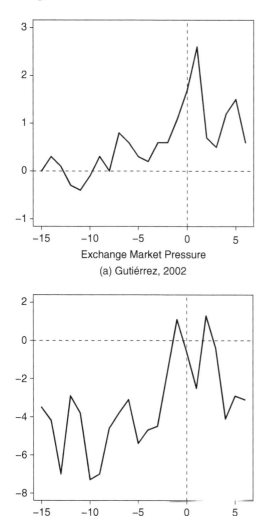

FIGURE 6.1. Currency Pressures in Ecuadorian Elections: 2002 and 2006.
Note: Evolution of currency pressures in the period around Lucio Gutiérrez's and Rafael Correa's inaugurations. Month of inauguration denoted by vertical dashed line. The horizontal dashed line marks $EMP = 0$.

country became further exposed to pro-cyclical cross-border financial flows.

The cycles of euphoria and panic experienced by other Latin American economies carry particularly severe consequences in Ecuador. This was the case during the abundance of petrodollars in the 1970s and that ended with the debt crisis of the 1980s. This was also true during the emerging markets' boom that collapsed with the Mexican crisis of 1995 and the Asian and Russian crises of the end of the decade.

Ecuador liberalized its financial system between the late 1980s and early 1990s, culminating with the Banking Law of 1994, which granted universal banking powers with low capital and lax licensing requirements, and caused a breakdown of monitoring in the context of new risks and competitive pressures.[2]

Like in other Latin American countries, the financial liberalization that followed the renegotiation of the Ecuadorean foreign debt under the Brady Plan, and the stabilization of the economy with the adoption of an exchange rate anchor,[3] led to a surge in capital inflows in the early 1990s. This, in the context of a deregulated financial system, produced over-indebtedness and an asset price bubble. This cycle ended in a sudden stop in late 1995, after the Mexican devaluation.

Starting that year, a series of events began to expose the fragility of the Ecuadorean financial system. Among them were the intervention in the Banco Continental, the liquidation or merger of about ten financing companies, and the injection of liquidity in another twenty by the Ecuadorean central bank.

Ecuador also entered in a brief but costly border war with Peru, and suffered the consequences of the El Niño rains. In October 1995 the vice president and architect of economic policymaking in the government of Sixto Durán-Ballén, Alberto Dahik, was forced to resign on account of a scandal (Beckerman 2005).

The crisis culminated in February 1997, with the impeachment of Durán-Ballén's successor Abdalá Bucaram, only ten months after his inauguration. Massive protests against structural adjustment policies left the government politically fragile, and the indigenous and social movements that helped raise Bucaram to power turned against him. The Ecuadorean Congress dismissed the president on the grounds of mental incapacity, and elected its leader Fabián Alarcón interim.

After a brief recovery between 1997 and 1998, when Alarcón avoided any major structural change in the financial system, Ecuador experienced another liquidity crisis following the collapses of Asian and Russian

---

[2] "Ecuador Financial Crisis Management," Augusto de La Torre, Roberto García-Saltos and Yira Mascaro. Presented at the University of Toronto in June 1, 2000.

[3] In August 1993 the authorities unified the foreign-exchange market and began a new policy of floating within a pre-announced crawling band. The nominal anchor was expected to help gradually to reduce the inflation rate (Beckerman 2005).

Exogenous Shocks and Investors' Political Clout

economies in parallel with a severe drop in commodity prices. In December 1998 the newly elected president Jamil Mahuad passed a fiscal emergency legislation, which included a 100 percent-plus adjustment in fuel prices, new taxes, and structural reform measures. Protests mounted.

After freezing bank deposits and increasing interest rates in an attempt to protect the value of the currency, the sucre was finally allowed to float in July 1999. The dollar jumped from 7,000 to 12,000 sucres and the currency entered in a free fall that led to rising insolvency and an implosion of confidence.

As a result, only four years after the Brady Plan left Ecuador with a debt that amounted to 36 percent of the GDP, this ratio had raised to 75 percent in 1998 and reached 90 percent in 1999 (Beckerman 2001). In September 1999, in response to demands from the civil society, and organizations such as the Confederation of Indigenous Nationalities of Ecuador (Confederación de Nacionalidades Indígenas del Ecuador [CONAIE]), Ecuador became the first country to default in its Brady bonds (Quispe-Agnoli and Whisller 2006). Consequently, the private sector was cut from international credit lines and the financial system collapsed. In that year, the GDP fell by 7.3 percent and inflation reached 61 percent (Hurtado Larrea 2006).

In January 2000, President Jamil Mahuad announced the full dollarization of the Ecuadorean economy, allegedly in an effort to avoid a complete breakdown of the banking system. The measure faced strong resistance among Ecuadorean economists and in the central bank, leading to the resignation of the majority of members of its executive board. Days later Mahuad was deposed and the legislature confirmed Gustavo Noboa, the vice president, as interim. Noboa maintained the dollarization, with the support of a stand-by agreement with the IMF that allowed the country to restart servicing its external debt and to access loans from other multilateral institutions.

The remainder of Noboa's presidency was dedicated to advancing structural reforms aimed at securing public finances. The government enacted policies aimed to restore the credibility and profitability of the still fragile financial system, and privatized major public companies.[4] Even though the economy started to show signs of recovery in 2001, with a real GDP growth of 5.1 percent, it slowed down again to 3.4 percent in the electoral year of 2002.

Yet the government's fragile support base in the legislature and an approaching presidential election posed major barriers to the implementation of the stringent conditions attached to the IMF agreement.

---

[4] "Ecuador Country Risk Service," Economist Intelligence Unit, March 2002.

124   *The Politics of Market Discipline in Latin America*

The Election of Lucio Gutiérrez

The 2002 presidential election in Ecuador was concurrent with the Brazilian poll. Analysts saw both cases as reinforcing a Latin American "move to the left," launched with the victory of Hugo Chávez in Venezuela in 1998.

By the time the campaign began, negotiations aimed at securing a new stand-by arrangement with the IMF to replace the previous deal had already collapsed. Given the conditions of the Ecuadorean economy, this implied that the next president would inherit a difficult fiscal situation. The price of oil, the country's main export product, was starting to recover after a substantial drop in 2001, which contributed to current account deficits in 2001 and in 2002.

Álvaro Noboa, a banana magnate who ran as an independent with the support of Ecuador's largest party, the Partido Roldosista Ecuatoriano, started ahead in the race. Noboa's major challenger, former president León Febres Cordero from the Social Christian Party (Partido Social Cristiano [PSC]), had decided not to run because of health problems. Rodrigo Borja, another former president, was then considered the most likely winner of the poll.

The name of Lucio Gutiérrez was largely ignored by the media and among analysts until he unexpectedly won the first round of the elections by a slight margin over Noboa.

Gutiérrez was a retired colonel, notorious for having led a coup backed by indigenous movements and the military to oust President Jamil Mahuad two years before. When his troops were sent to break up demonstrations in Quito by tens of thousands of Ecuadoreans of indigenous descent who were protesting against corruption and neoliberalism, instead of expelling the protesters Gutiérrez set up mobile army kitchens to distribute food and allowed them to take over the Congress building.[5]

Later, he would join indigenous leader Antonio Vargas and a judge, Carlos Solórzano, in announcing a government of "national salvation" to run the country. Interestingly, however, Gutiérrez did not agree to join the new government.

The coup failed, the old government was reinstated under the previous vice-president, and Gutiérrez was arrested. Released after six months in prison, he joined the 2002 presidential race as an outsider, with the support of a coalition named *January 21 Patriotic Movement* (*Partido Sociedad Patriótica 21 de Enero*) after the date of the attempted coup, and that included a small Marxist party, the Democratic

---

[5] "Lucio Gutiérrez: Ecuador's Populist Leader," BBC News, November 25, 2002.

Exogenous Shocks and Investors' Political Clout 125

Popular Movement (Movimiento Popular Democrático [MPD]), radical indigenous movements (represented in the CONAIE, the Ecuadorian Indigenous Nationalities Confederation), and leftist labor unions.

In the first round of the presidential election, Gutiérrez, a declared admirer of Fidel Castro and Hugo Chávez, wore green army fatigues in public appearances and was an outspoken critic of the dollarization of the Ecuadorean economy. His discourse had a conspicuous leftist tone; he condemned the "neoliberal globalization or any form of external intervention of international groups or foreign powers"[6] and claimed that "Ecuador's enemy was the enemy of all Latin Americans: neoliberalism."[7]

Among Gutiérrez's main campaign promises was the establishment of a "Debt Club" aimed at coordinating the restructuring of Latin American foreign debt. Gutiérrez also ruled out any prospects of Ecuador joining the Free Trade Area of the Americas (FTAA) in his government, which he considered "suicidal" to the country.[8]

In public speeches, the candidate reiterated his disapproval of market reforms advanced by previous administrations. He promised to increase social spending to reduce income inequality and boost the material conditions of the 60 percent of the Ecuadoreans who then lived below the poverty line, portraying his candidacy as the hope of the poor, the marginalized, and the excluded.

Gutiérrez's campaign rhetoric included expressions such as "fighting American neo-colonialism," and the candidate frequently referred to the importance of Latin America achieving a "second independence." Along these lines, he proclaimed the intention to revoke the American permission to operate a military base in Ecuadorean territory.

The fragile economic conditions of the end of 2001 deteriorated further in 2002. The country's current account balance moved from a negative U.S.$ 144 million between January and June 2001 to negative U.S.$ 805 in the same period in 2002, while international reserves decreased by U.S.$ 100 million in the first semester of that year. Oil prices reached a low of U.S.$16 per barrel in the second quarter of 2002, compared to U.S.$ 24 per barrel a year before.

Financial investors' confidence in the Ecuadorean economy also deteriorated in the months close to the election, as evidenced in the behavior of the spread of the country's sovereign bonds (Figure 6.2). Bond values decreased 30 percent in the six months before the election, along with a

---

[6] Party manifesto of the *January 21 Patriotic Movement*.
[7] Inter Press Service, January 16, 2004.
[8] *The New York Times*, November 22, 2002.

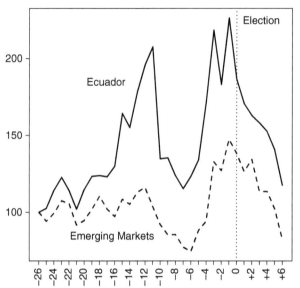

FIGURE 6.2. Ecuadorean Sovereign Spread: 2002 Presidential Election.
Notes: Spread of the JP Morgan Emerging Markets Bonds Index (EMBI+), usually taken as a proxy for the country risk, in the period that surrounded the Ecuadorean 2002 presidential election (denoted by the vertical dashed line).
Source: Global Financial Data.

more than 22 percent rise in bond yields, at this time only higher than post-default Argentina.

Higher sovereign bond spreads are usually associated with higher domestic interest rates and lower investment, and impose severe consequences not only to the governments but also to the private sector. For example, bank deposits fell steeply in the second half of 2002, and bank lending was restricted mainly to short-term capital.

The spread of the Ecuadorean bonds peaked after the results of the first round of the elections were released. According to a report published by the Economist Intelligence Unit (EIU) in November 2002, "both candidates have promised to devote resources to welfare and social investment, without increasing the prices of basic commodities and services or ending subsidies in the economy."[9] Moreover, none of the presidential candidates was expected to impose structural adjustment measures aimed at long-term stability, owing to their immediate impact in costs of living and employment.

---

[9] "Ecuador Country Report," Economist Intelligence Unit, November 2002.

Exogenous Shocks and Investors' Political Clout 127

Investors' negative response, in the context of highly unfavorable economic conditions aggravated by the fact that Ecuador had a dollarized economy and could not resort to currency devaluation, had a notable impact on Gutiérrez's behavior in the second round of the presidential election. Less than a week after his favoritism was confirmed, the candidate replaced his uniform with a business suit and visited Miami, Washington, and New York.

In the presence of potential creditors, Gutiérrez guaranteed that his government would maintain the dollarization of the Ecuadorean economy and meet foreign debt obligations, and that to meet these goals he considered the possibility of negotiating a new agreement with the Fund. Analysts quickly perceived the signals of change in Gutiérrez's agenda, and the EIU called attention that in a "remarkably rapid conversion to the centre ground, Gutiérrez has sought with some success to reassure ordinary voters, and foreign investors, that he is committed to sound public finances, and to the maintenance of dollarization. He has even pledged to hold talks with the IMF."[10]

The report also noted, however, that Gutiérrez's "political basis of support is very hostile to the role of the multilateral institutions and neoliberal economic policies in general. Those who supported Mr. Gutiérrez's fairly radical platform in the first round could stay away if he appears to be too much of a moderate."

According to a political ally, Gutiérrez's switch to orthodoxy was also influenced by campaign financiers who warned the candidate about the potential consequences of his leftist platform for investment in the country.[11] This influence can partly account for the invitation of Mauricio Pozo, an orthodox economist well regarded in the investment community, to advise Gutiérrez's economic team during the second round of the election.

Back in Ecuador, in the run-up to the second round of the presidential campaign Gutiérrez downplayed the conflicts that he had emphasized during the first round. To his much publicized intention to increase social expenditures, Gutiérrez added the commitment with maintaining fiscal discipline.

After promising to prioritize paying the "social debt" in the initial months of the campaign, in the second round Gutiérrez pledged to do so without defaulting on the public debt. The candidate justified the changed rhetoric by affirming that "if we are going to distribute wealth,

---

[10] "Ecuador Country Risk Service," Economist Intelligence Unit, November 2002, p. 2.
[11] Author's interview with a former finance minister of Gutiérrez, Quito, May 2008.

128   *The Politics of Market Discipline in Latin America*

we have to generate wealth,"[12] inadvertently illustrating the dilemma posed by electoral incentives for promoting income redistribution and the need to provide positive signals to investors, particularly pressing during currency crises. Yet the economic conditions Ecuador endured in 2002 left Gutiérrez with little room to accommodate both demands.

Any skepticism investors might still have about Gutiérrez's intentions proved unfounded shortly after his victory in December 2002, when the appointment of Mauricio Pozo for the Finance Ministry provided investors with a downright assurance that the government would follow an orthodox agenda. The president later announced the conclusion of a thirteen-month U.S.$ 200 million stand-by agreement with the IMF, which secured the country an additional U.S.$ 300 million from the World Bank, the Inter-American Development Bank, and the Andean Development Corporation (Hurtado Larrea 2006).

In the agreement, the government committed to maintaining dollarization and establishing inflation targets, raising oil prices, eliminating subsidies on cooking gas prices, granting the provision of public services to private concessions, assigning all oil revenues above and beyond what was estimated in the budget to servicing the country's foreign debt, and freezing public sector wages,[13] among other policies demanded by the Fund, which went far beyond macroeconomic targets and rendered redistributive promises made during the campaign unattainable.[14] The president also proclaimed that Ecuador would be the "US' best ally in the region," and reasserted the U.S. permanence in the military base of Manta.

Not surprisingly, Gutiérrez's first year in office was marked by a crisis in his supporting coalition. In Chapter 4 we saw that policy switches are more likely to occur in institutionalized party systems, and conjectured that one of the reasons for that arises from the fact that voters punish switchers more strictly than nonswitchers for bad economic results (Stokes 2001). In a poorly institutionalized system, and with a very fragile basis of political support among the Ecuadorean electorate, Gutiérrez's switch to orthodoxy sparked protests among political allies, with indigenous movements immediately demanding the removal of the finance minister, the revoking of the agreement with the IMF and of all the policies on which the agreement was conditional. Protests and marches culminated in the rupture of the government's original support

---

[12] Dudley Althaus, "Latin America's leftist prominence," *Houston Chronicle*, November 24, 2002.
[13] The wage freeze, initially set for 2003, ended up lasting three years.
[14] See Correa (2003) for an analysis of the first months of Gutiérrez's term.

Exogenous Shocks and Investors' Political Clout 129

base in August, and Gutiérrez ended the year with an approval rating of 15 percent, compared to almost the 60 percent during his inauguration.[15]

We also observed in Chapter 4 that strong constitutional powers granted to the executive are an important condition for successful policy switches. Even though Gutiérrez clearly initiated a conservative agenda, he lacked constitutional powers to overcome legislative opposition, and was never able to gather enough support to advance a coherent program. With the collapse of his electoral coalition, he managed to assemble a majority in Congress that included seven parties and some independents, which between them controlled fifty-five votes. The major partners in the coalition were the Partido Roldosista Ecuatoriano (PRE), with fifteen seats, and the Partido Renovador Institucional Acción Nacional (PRIAN) with nine, both right of center.

Gutiérrez actually attempted to expand his political powers; among other initiatives, the replacements of justices at the Supreme Court were the most controversial, for they were considered unconstitutional and accused of serving political purposes. The crisis in the Supreme Court, in addition to the rapprochement with former impeached president Abdalá Bucaram – in exchange for support from the PRE – sparked new marches and popular protests that precipitated Gutiérrez's ousting in April 2005.

The Election of Rafael Correa

The election of 2006 was held in a scenario quite distinct from that of 2002. Oil prices had doubled in the period between the two polls, raising tax revenues and lowering the public debt. Alfredo Palacios, former vice president in charge since the impeachment of Lucio Gutiérrez, had already started using oil revenue to fund an expansion of social spending. His strategy was to stimulate higher rates of growth and, in doing so, cut indebtedness and lower Ecuador's risk premium, which was in turn expected to boost private investment.[16]

On the financial side, however, even though the debt restructuring concluded in 2000 had alleviated immediate pressures on public finances, amortizations were still high. This, in addition to current account deficits between 2001 and 2004, projected increasing financial requirements in the following years.

Despite repeated attempts, Ecuador never fully recovered access to international financial markets after the 1999 collapse. As a result, the

---

[15] "Ecuadorean Country Risk Service," *Economist Intelligence Unit*, December 2003.
[16] "Ecuadorean Risk Service," *Economist Intelligence Unit*, June 2006.

130 *The Politics of Market Discipline in Latin America*

government remained dependent on multilateral creditors and commercial banks for international funding, leaving the country vulnerable to its relations with the IMF.

The front runners in the 2006 election were León Roldós, a former vice president, and the banana magnate Álvaro Noboa, who had also run in 1998 and 2002. The candidate of the conservative Partido Social Cristiano (PSC), Cynthia Viteri, and Rafael Correa also stood chances of advancing to the second round.

Formerly an economics professor, and holding an American Ph.D., Correa had served as a finance minister in Alfredo Palacios' administration. In that period, he reverted part of the funds Gutiérrez had set aside to pay foreign debt, confronted the World Bank, and was an unequivocal critic of the IMF and the country's debt management, all of which granted him the reputation of a "radical left-winger."[17]

These initiatives gathered the support of workers and indigenous movements, which launched a series of protest marches when Correa resigned after only three months with a popularity higher than the president's.[18] This support was also manifested in Correa's last press conference as a minister, which included representatives of labor organizations such as the umbrella Frente Unitario de los Trabajadores (FUT) and the Confederación Ecuatoriana de Organizaciones Sindicales Libres (CEOSL); the Confederation of Indigenous Nationalities of Ecuador (CONAIE); and the anti-FTA group "Ecuador Decide."[19]

A year later, in 2006, Rafael Correa would run for president portraying himself as an anti-neoliberal and anti-establishment candidate, with a rhetoric in many ways comparable to that of Gutiérrez in 2002. He condemned the dollarization of the Ecuadorean economy, referring to it as "the biggest mistake ever committed in the economic management of the country,"[20] and vigorously denied any possibility of joining a free trade agreement with the United States. The candidate made no effort to disguise his close relationship with Hugo Chávez and, following the example of the Venezuelan president, announced intentions to call a constitutional assembly as well as to "do away" with the Congress.

Contrary to Gutiérrez, though, Correa did not moderate his discourse after the first round of the election, which he lost to Álvaro Noboa by 4

---

[17] "Ecuadorean Risk Service," *Economist Intelligence Unit*, September 2006, p. 7.
[18] World Markets Analysis, August 5, 2005.
[19] Latin American Weekly Report, August 9, 2005.
[20] World Markets Analysis, April 22, 2005.

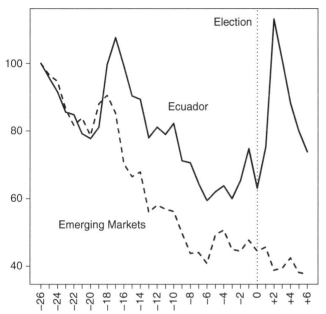

FIGURE 6.3. Ecuadorean Sovereign Spread: 2006 Presidential Election.
Notes: Spread of the JP Morgan Emerging Markets Bonds Index (EMBI+), usually taken as a proxy for the country risk, in the period that surrounded the Ecuadorean 2006 presidential election (denoted by the vertical dashed line).
Source: Global Financial Data.

percentage points. Rather than reassuring investors, the candidate disclosed the prospects of an Argentine-style debt restructuring were he elected president.

Markets' behavior during the 2006 election was also comparable to that observed during the 2002 race; not even the fast improving economic conditions of the country sufficed to prevent sovereign bond spreads from rising as the race approached. Spreads peaked soon after Correa's victory, as he announced that Ecuadoreans were "leaving the night of neoliberalism behind" and called for twenty-first century socialism in reference to Chávez's government in Venezuela (Figure 6.3).

Yet in the context of a currency boom fostered by an unprecedented rise of oil revenues – about 40 percent of Ecuador's official revenue – [21] markets' "signals" had no influence on Correa's programmatic choices, as they did in the case of Gutiérrez.

---

[21] Asad Ismi, "Correa's Re-election in Ecuador: Sweeping Triumph of Socialist Economic Program," *Global Research*, May 20, 2013.

132 *The Politics of Market Discipline in Latin America*

Early in office, Correa declared to have no interest whatsoever in the evolution of the country's risk measures.[22] In his words: "If the country risk goes up because of speculators worrying over our ability to pay the debt, I don't care. The country risk I care about is children suffering. If they're nervous, let them take a Valium. What else can I do?"[23]

In his discourse, the president made no attempt to build investors' confidence or to attract foreign finance to the economy, and was explicit about the intention to "act on behalf of our citizens, not on behalf of finance capital" (Correa 2013, p. 91). Coherent with this rhetoric, Correa's economic program largely deviated from the investor-oriented agenda that had prevailed during Gutiérrez's years. Rather, it boosted labor conditions while strengthening the control over the financial sector.

The government enacted and reinforced labor laws that inhibited sub-contracting, increased the minimum wage in real terms, and promoted state-bolstered mortgage, vacation, and social security programs. In parallel, it established a Domestic Liquidity Coefficient according to which 45 percent of all banks' liquid assets were held domestically, later raised to 60 percent.

New rules set additional requirements for categories of assets that must be included in banks' minimum liquid reserves, and placed a tax on capital outflows of 0.5 percent in 2008, raised to 5 percent in 2011 (Weisbrot, Johnston, and Lefebvre 2013).

Correa also revoked the independence of the Ecuadorean Central Bank, and defaulted on a third of the country's foreign debt, declared "odious" – incurred by a former regime that did not have Ecuador's best interests in mind.

The president renegotiated telecommunications, mining, and oil contracts, the latter explicitly designed to raise the state's share of oil windfalls.[24] He also increased the size and the regulatory authority of the government, the progressivity of the tax system, and efforts aimed at tax collection.[25]

Between 2006 and 2013 government revenues almost tripled, with oil accounting for about half of the rise.[26] The other half came from increased funds from buoyant non-oil tax collections, extra budgetary

---

[22] See Acosta, Gorfinkiel, Gudynas, and Lapitz (2005) for a detailed description of what the Correa government would later denominate "The Other Country Risk."

[23] Monthe Hayes, "Ecuadorean Leader Eyes Wealth Distribution," The Associated Press, December 2, 2006.

[24] Ecuador Weekly Report, Analytica Securities, May 2008.

[25] Mark Weisbrot, "Why Ecuador Loves Rafael Correa," *The Guardian*, February 15, 2013.

[26] "The Man with the Mighty Microphone," *The Economist*, February 9, 2013.

Exogenous Shocks and Investors' Political Clout

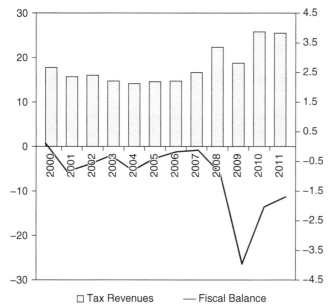

FIGURE 6.4. Ecuador – Central Government Budget (% GDP).
Note: Total Revenue and Grants and Total expenditure and lending minus repayment for the Ecuadorean central government.
Source: CEPALstats.

revenues arising from a change to the Hydrocarbons Law that forced private oil companies to hand over to the state 50 percent of the revenues above a contractually set oil price, and extra funds from the takeover of Occidental's assets.[27]

As a percentage of GDP, these revenues went from 14.7 to 25.5 percent from 2006 to 2011, and were matched by a dramatic increase in public spending, which almost doubled as a percentage of GDP in the same period – from 14.9 to 27.3 (Figure 6.4).

Increased social expenditures were channelled to expanding access to medicare, government-subsidized housing credit, to an ambitious cash transfer program, and to doubling education expenses in real terms. Remarkably favorable conditions allowed this expansion of the size of the State to occur in parallel with a reduction of interest payments to less than 1 percent of GDP (from 3.5 percent in 2006), and of the public debt-to-GDP ratio from 35 in 2006 to 25 percent in 2013.

As a result of these initiatives, social indicators greatly improved; unemployment fell to 4.1 percent in the end of 2012, a record low for at

---

[27] Nouriel Roubini, "Ecuador debt watch: What Would Correa Do?," *RGE Analysts Blog*, November 28, 2006.

least twenty-five years.[28] Poverty rates fell from 64 to 27 percent between 2000 and 2013.[29] Not surprisingly, when Correa was reelected in 2013 his government was approved by 85 percent of Ecuadoreans. [30]

Conclusion

The divergent paths followed by presidents Lucio Gutiérrez and Rafael Correa in Ecuador illustrate how the effectiveness of market discipline varies over time in a country highly vulnerable to cycles of currency booms and crises.

Governing under severe dollar scarcity, Gutiérrez was pushed to abandon his campaign promises in favor of an orthodox economic program designed to attract IMF funds expected to pave the Ecuadorean return to international financial markets after the economic collapse of 1999.

Four years later, his successor Rafael Correa was elected during a currency boom driven by an unprecedented rise in oil revenues. Remarkably favorable international conditions allowed him to deviate from investors' agenda, and to pursue the nationalistic and redistributive economic program he announced during the presidential campaign.

This chapter also highlighted how, different from Brazil, Gutiérrez's embrace of economic orthodoxy did not initiate a long-term moderation of the Left in Ecuador.

These different outcomes are explained by the fact that, contrary to Brazil where reliance on international finance remains relatively stable between "good" and "bad" times, in Ecuador this reliance is extremely high during crises but remarkably low during currency booms, affording a wide room to maneuver to presidents elected during the latter.

As a result, in Brazil once market constraints were learned, and given that they do not change substantially, there was no point for the Left to promise an agenda it will never be able to fulfill – financial integration, thus, should promote long-term moderation.

In Ecuador, conversely, market constraints change substantially between "good" and "bad" times. Whereas they were very high when Gutiérrez was elected, making an IMF agreement and the return to international financial markets a priority in the president's agenda, they were low under Correa to a point that the government never even bothered to raise funds internationally.

---

[28] Mark Weisbrot, "Why Ecuador Loves Rafael Correa," *The Guardian*, February 15, 2013.

[29] "The Man with the Mighty Microphone," *The Economist*, February 9, 2013.

[30] Mark Weisbrot, "Why Ecuador Loves Rafael Correa," *The Guardian*, February 15, 2013.

Exogenous Shocks and Investors' Political Clout 135

In the longer term, the fact that leftist presidents can fully promote their agenda during currency booms, even though they frequently switch to orthodoxy during crises, prevents the Left from converging rightward as in Brazil. This happens because, as leftist policies remain credible, candidates on the Left have the incentive to promise redistributive and nationalist policies whenever they are expected to boost electoral prospects, even if they are not sure they will be able to fulfill their promises.

Still, it is always possible to argue that Correa's and Gutiérrez's governments were different owing to characteristics of presidents that are hardly comparable, the former being more of a "true leftist" than the latter. To address these claims, the next chapter examines the presidency of Hugo Chávez in Venezuela, and shows how the effectiveness of market discipline can vary *even under the same president* in a country highly exposed to cycles of currency booms and crises.

7

One President, Different Scenarios: Crisis, Boom, and Market Discipline in Venezuela

Venezuela had been experiencing two decades of economic deterioration, when Hugo Chávez was elected in 1998. Since the early 1980s, GDP growth had slowed dramatically, poverty had increased, and income had become more unequally distributed. The percentage of the poor in the population doubled between 1981 and 1999.[1]

Partly as a result of the long economic downturn, these years were also a period of political turmoil, when successive governments proved incapable of dealing with increasing poverty and corruption. The result was a "detachment" between the political bureaucracy and society, not only affecting the image of specific leaders or governments, but also increasing Venezuelans' disillusionment with the political system itself (Buxton 2003; Hellinger 2003; Levine 2001; López Maya 2005; Penfold-Becerra 2001).

The two governments that preceded Chávez's were marked by an unequivocal break with campaign promises (Stokes 2001). Carlos Andrés Pérez, from the Acción Democrática (AD), was elected in 1989 on the vow to revive the golden years of his first presidency (1974–1979), when booming oil revenues were channeled into income redistribution and incentives to domestic industry.

Venezuelans expected a similar agenda in 1989 and were surprised by the announcement of an orthodox program that included harsh austerity measures and prompted widespread popular reaction (Stokes 2001). After two coup attempts, Pérez was finally forced out of office by the Venezuelan Supreme Court on embezzlement charges.

After two years of interim administrations, Venezuelans elected Rafael Caldera, a former member of the Social Christian Party of Venezuela (COPEI), who ran as an independent in 1993. During the campaign,

---

[1] ECLAC, Base de Datos Estadísticos.

136

One President, Different Scenarios   137

Caldera criticized Pérez's neoliberal agenda and promised to never resort to the International Monetary Fund (IMF) for financial help.

Two years after a persisting currency crisis, Caldera announced a stand-by agreement with the Fund, followed by harsh austerity measures that included a sudden rise in oil prices, a sharp devaluation of the bolívar, an increase in sales taxes, the liberalization of exchange and interest rates, and the opening of the Venezuelan oil sector to foreign investment.[2]

These experiences help explain the value attributed, especially but not only by the poorer strata of the population, to an outsider whose discourse centered on criticism of Venezuelan democratic institutions and social injustice (Lander 2007). Recurring political and economic crises since the late 1980s polarized the political arena along an elite–mass cleavage, and Chávez's appeal was particularly pronounced in this context (Buxton 2003; Hellinger 2003; Roberts 2003).

Once in office, however, the president surprised analysts who expected a radical leftist government by maintaining the incumbent finance minister, promising fiscal discipline, and restraining increases in the minimum wage. Chávez pleased the investment community in his first visit to the United States, announcing plans to increase private participation in the oil sector.[3]

Yet after oil prices started to soar in 2004, producing a currency boom unprecedented in Venezuela's history, Chávez reverted to his original agenda. This included nationalizations, and a dramatic increase of State control of the economy, continually furthered since then.

The presidency of Chávez in Venezuela reinforces the argument posed in the previous chapter; it reveals how the effectiveness of market discipline varies in countries highly vulnerable to cycles of currency booms and crises, even under a single administration. Venezuela is an extreme case in Latin America; oil provides between 75 and 90 percent of the country's exports and accounts for more than half of the government budget.[4]

---

[2] See Petkoff (1997) for a narrative of the motivations for Caldera's policy switch.

[3] In that sense, the narrative I offer in this chapter is in line with Corrales and Penfold (2011), who claim that most authors incorrectly label Chávez as a radical anti-market reformer from the beginning. Instead, they argue that "Chávez's economic policy *became* radical – heavily anti-market and redistributive – only when the removal of institutional constraints *and* the rise in oil revenues allowed him to seize the opportunity and tighten political competition" [p. 48].

[4] "Venezuela Country Risk Service," Economist Intelligence Unit, first quarter 1999, and July 2011.

138   *The Politics of Market Discipline in Latin America*

Before discussing the first election of Hugo Chávez, however, the next section describes the trajectory of the Venezuelan economy and political system in the years prior to 1998.

BACKGROUND: NEOLIBERALISM IN VENEZUELA

After a decade of fast economic growth driven by an unprecedented rise in oil prices, the debt crisis hit Venezuela in February 1983. In what became known as "Black Friday," President Luis Herrera Campins from Christian Social Party (Partido Social Cristiano [COPEI]) allowed the bolívar to devalue with respect to the dollar, in response to a fall in international oil prices and massive capital flight (Lander and Fierro 1996).

This marked the beginning of a long period of disarray in the Venezuelan economy; by the end of the Campins administration, the country had experienced severe trade and current account deficits, international reserves were dangerously low, and the public external debt had reached unprecedented levels – tripling since 1978. In 1983, an election year, the country's GDP was expected to fall by 3 percent and unemployment to climb from 7 percent to 13 percent. Not surprisingly, Herrera Campins had a 12 percent public approval rating.

In this context, Jaime Lusinchi from the opposition party Acción Democratica was elected in 1983 on an expansionist platform, promising a social pact with labor, a rescheduling of the country's foreign debt, and intentions to resist the IMF's orthodox agenda. Bolstered by Venezuela's relatively high international reserves as a result of a recovery of oil exports, Lusinchi successfully avoided austerity policies during his tenure. The government also managed to reschedule 75 percent of the country's foreign debt, without ties or conditions of any kind, after taking a tough stance in negotiations with creditors. Because Venezuela – unlike Mexico, Brazil, and Argentina, in the period – did not need fresh bank money, the country was in a better position to negotiate with bankers.

Closer to the end of Lusinchi's term, however, oil prices dropped dramatically, and the president tried to implement a contingency clause included in the agreement with creditors to improve the terms of the debt payments. As they refused to accept a renegotiation, however, the process stalled and was left for the next administration to reinitiate. Lusinchi ended his term with the highest approval ratings obtained by a Venezuelan president until then (Luongo 2007), which facilitated the election of his successor, the former president Carlos Andrés Pérez.

One President, Different Scenarios 139

Pérez won his second presidential term in 1989 promising to revive the good years of his previous tenure (1974–1979), when he advanced an expansionary and nationalist plan know as *La Gran Venezuela* (The Great Venezuela).

As early as in his inauguration speech, however, the president revealed that by the end of 1988 international reserves had reached levels lower than in 1982, and that harsh austerity measures were necessary if the country were to pay its foreign obligations. After that, Pérez's second presidential term would make a U-turn with respect to his first administration.

The president immediately announced an economic plan named *Gran Viraje* (Great Turnaround). Based on IMF recommendations, the plan aimed at both macroeconomic stabilization and structural reforms. Policies included restrictions on public expenditure and wages, free exchange and interest rates, reduction of subsidies, increases in basic prices – 100 percent for gasoline, 133 percent for natural gas, and 30 percent for public transportation (Stokes 2001, p. 53) – and trade liberalization, among other measures.

The government later signed a letter of intent with the IMF, which tied renewed access to Fund resources to a structural adjustment program. The agreement was expected to facilitate the renegotiation of the country's foreign debt with private creditors.

Popular reaction to Pérez's plan was unexpectedly strong and would be later referred to as the "Caracazo" (Hernandez and Giusti 2006). The process started with protests against the sudden rise in the price of public transportation, following the government's decision to raise oil prices. As the wave of protests intensified and disseminated throughout the country, with little immediate resistance by the government, traffic was interrupted on major routes, local businesses were pillaged, and violence spread in Venezuelan streets. The response finally came with the intervention of the army, and the Caracazo ended with more than 100 deaths, 800 people injured, and 1,000 arrests, causing irremediable damage to the Pérez presidency (Luongo 2007, p. 276).

The measures agreed with the IMF were followed by recession and an almost fifty percent increase in unemployment, but they were successful in restoring investors' confidence – the government managed to borrow additional funds, to re-attract foreign investment and to halt capital flight. The plan was also successful in guaranteeing resources for the payment of foreign debt. Between 1989 and 1992, Venezuela paid U.S.\$9.6 billion and U.S.\$5.9 billion in interest and principal, respectively, for a total debt of U.S.\$15.5 billion.

140   *The Politics of Market Discipline in Latin America*

In 1992, however, macroeconomic indicators had deteriorated once again and the debt had grown further. Between 1988 and 1991, the share of the poorest decile of the population fell from 2.3 percent to 1.8 percent of GDP, whereas the share of the richest decile rose from 30.3 percent to 43 percent (Lander and Fierro 1996), increasing the already high level of income inequality.

Broad dissatisfaction with the consequences of the adjustment and corruption allegations led to Pérez's impeachment, and Rafael Caldera was elected in 1993 promising honesty and autonomy from international institutions. The candidate ran as an independent, after leaving the party that he had founded and headed, itself an evidence of the extent of the deterioration of Venezuela's highly institutionalized two-party system.

Caldera's economic agenda, designed by economists that were highly critical of the previous structural adjustment program, contemplated more nationally oriented policies focused on employment, industrial development, wages, and income redistribution. The candidate promised to create jobs by reducing taxes, increasing public spending, keeping state control of the crucial oil sector, and protecting domestic industries. As reported in the international media during campaign:

Both Caldera and Velásquez [candidate of the leftist Causa R] are vowing to reverse the free-market reforms begun by Pérez four years ago, which they say have placed an extraordinary burden on the poor. While Venezuela's economy has grown substantially over the past three years, Pérez's massive cuts of state subsidies have led to increases in food and transportation prices. "We cannot automatically carry over economic policies that have worked in developed countries to underdeveloped ones," Caldera said. "The rigorous application of free-market policies can be beneficial in some segments [of the economy] but can have disastrous effects in others."(*The Miami Herald*, November 14, 1993.)

The media also reported the deep concern among powerful business owners and the military provoked by the popularity of Caldera and Velasquez. They feared that the rich would be taxed, central planning and nationalization would be restored and power would pass from the traditional elites to new unknowns. Elites were apprehensive that a Caldera victory represented a backlash against orthodoxy, after the free-market tide that had swept Latin America in the previous years.

In light of the theory advanced in this book and its implications for long-term ideological convergence, it is plausible that the credibility of Caldera's promises after Pérez reneged on a very similar agenda a few

One President, Different Scenarios 141

years before, was granted by previous presidents' like Lusinchi, who managed to sustain the leftist program announced during his presidential campaign.

In these circumstances, typical of a country that is highly vulnerable to cycles of currency booms and crises during which governments' room to maneuver varies tremendously, voters and investors learn that presidents elected on a left-wing discourse live up to their redistributive promises, if not always, at least sometimes. This belief creates incentives for leftist candidates to differentiate themselves from the right even when they are not sure of their capacity to advance the policies announced, whenever they believe a leftist discourse will boost chances of victory.

Unexpectedly, however, the first year of the Caldera presidency was marked by the collapse of the Banco Latino, the second largest Venezuelan bank. To avoid a major financial crisis, the government decided to bail out the bank. Yet the initiative not only failed to prevent the crisis from spreading but also led to a process of financial assistance that was largely beyond the capacity of the Venezuelan state, calculated to cost 13 percent of the GDP.[5]

The consequences were a rise of fiscal deficit, inflation, capital flight, and, ultimately, a currency crisis reflected in sharp losses of international reserves. The government responded by imposing exchange controls and regulating the prices of essential services (Luongo 2007), but the Venezuelan GDP contracted by 3.3 percent in 1994.

The crisis did not recede, and actually worsened as oil prices decreased. In 1996, Caldera finally promoted a turnaround in his economic policies, embracing neoliberalism and announcing a series of structural reforms under the name of *Agenda Venezuela*. The reforms, led by Planning Minister Teodoro Petkoff, included the opening of the oil sector to private investment, a reduction of the size of the state through privatizations and bureaucratic reform, fiscal adjustment through higher taxes and lower government expenditures, and privatization of sectors such as telecommunications and steel.

The government also signed a stand-by agreement with the IMF, aimed to provide Venezuela with a seal of approval that would boost its access to international finance.[6] Yet considering that Caldera was elected in part due to his criticism of the economic reform program Pérez had promoted under the IMF, the agreement carried high domestic political costs.

---

[5] "Venezuela Country Risk," Economist Intelligence Unit, first quarter 1998.
[6] Interview with a former minister of the Caldera government, Caracas, March 2008.

142   *The Politics of Market Discipline in Latin America*

The temporary recovery engendered by the *Agenda Venezuela* came to a crushing halt with a new precipitous drop of international oil prices in late 1997, which prompted a severe budget crisis. The negative perceptions about renewed economic deterioration induced more and more Venezuelans to become risk acceptant and advocate drastic changes. Weyland (2002, p. 244) reports that:

> In May 1998, 82.8 percent of the population advocated profound reforms or changes in Venezuela's system of government. As a result, they rejected the established political class and embraced newcomers and outsiders as candidates for the presidential contest of December 1998.

Conditions were, thus, propitious for a candidate like Hugo Chávez Frías.

THE 1998 PRESIDENTIAL ELECTION

According to his biographers, Chávez's identification with the Latin American Left was established early in his life. His mentors, Ruiz Guevara and Luis Miquilena, were both self-declared Marxists and militant communists. Besides Simón Bolívar, his role model, Chávez revered general Juan Velasco Alvarado, the nationalist leader of the 1968 Peruvian revolution (Marcano and Tyska 2005).

Chávez became notorious in Venezuela after leading a failed attempt to oust President Pérez in 1992, in protest against his IMF-inspired austerity program. Yet there is evidence that, ten years before the coup attempt, he was already involved in the organization of the Exército Revolucionário Bolivariano (Revolutionary Bolivarian Army), which aimed at establishing a nationalist autocracy in Venezuela inspired by Velasco Alvarado's experience in Peru.

After two years in prison following the failed coup, Chávez was released by President Rafael Caldera in 1994. Four years later, he would run for the presidency as an outsider, on an anticorruption radical leftist platform.

During a campaign that split Venezuela across class lines, Chávez promised to halt illegitimate foreign debt payments, to reverse prior liberalizing reforms, and to redistribute income. According to Venezuelan pollsters, the candidate was supported by most of the 80 percent of the country's 23 million people living in poverty, whereas his opponent, the Yale-educated businessman Henrique Salas Römer, drew most of his support from a wealthy minority: "While Mr. Chávez preaches to the have-nots seeking political revenge and radical change, Mr. Salas appeals

One President, Different Scenarios 143

to people concerned with his opponent's military background and leftist agenda."[7]

Chávez proved to be a charismatic and effective campaigner, who successfully capitalized on Venezuela's deteriorating economic situation. His nationalist, state capitalist economic platform tapped into popular hostility to Caldera's economic policies. Chávez exploited voters' dissatisfaction with the status quo and set the terms of the electoral debate by proposing a referendum on the dissolution of Congress and the election of a Constituent Assembly. Government and leading parties condemned the proposal, at the same time that the electorate was reassured about Chávez's commitment to reform.[8]

In addition, the candidate announced plans to overhaul the national oil company, Petróleos de Venezuela (PDVSA), and to put an end to Venezuela's dependence on oil revenue. Toward this end, he promised a shakeup of PDVSA's management and a revision of the state oil company's ambitious investment program oriented to doubling crude production by 2006. Production targets would be scaled back, and 15 percent of PDVSA's budget would be redirected toward social programs.[9]

In flagrant opposition to Chávez's rhetoric, Salas Römer announced his intention to advance a harsh program of stabilization and economic liberalization. His orthodox, market-based program would include public-sector cutbacks and development based on investment in oil.

Chávez's rhetoric unnerved the Venezuelan elite and was received with alarm. International investors, risk averse in consequence of the recent Asian crisis, panicked with the prospect of his victory. As a result, the Venezuelan country risk peaked and capital outflows accelerated in the course of the presidential campaign (Figure 7.1).

According to Datanálisis, a local polling company, 29 percent of local companies trimmed investment plans in the first half of 1999, while 35 percent canceled projects, wary of Chávez's campaign.[10] The market capitalization of the Bolsa de Valores de Caracas (the major Venezuelan stock market) fell to U.S.$7.6 billion in December 1998 from U.S.$14.6 billion at the end of 1997, as confidence evaporated and investors liquidated their positions.[11]

---

[7] "Coup Leader Favorite To Win Venezuelan Vote," *The Globe* and *The Mail* (Canada), December 5, 1998.

[8] "Venezuela Country Report," Economist Intelligence Unit, third quarter 1998.

[9] Ibid.

[10] "Venezuela Country Report," Economist Intelligence Unit, fourth quarter 1999.

[11] "Venezuela Risk Report," Economist Intelligence Unit, January 1999.

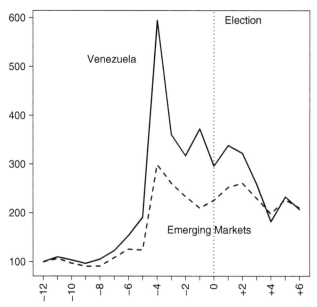

FIGURE 7.1. Venezuelan Sovereign Spread: 1998 Election.
Note: Spread of the Standard & Poor's Emerging Market Bond Index (EMBI+) in the period that surrounded the Venezuelan 1998 election.
Source: Global Financial Data.

Financial analysts noted that "while popular with the poor, some of Mr Chávez's radical postures left him open to accusations of having contributed to the downturn in the economy by accelerating capital flight and the withdrawal of investors from Venezuela, particularly during August and September."[12]

Chávez responded to investors' fears by moderating his discourse as the election approached. Backtracking on previous statements, he emphasized the importance of foreign investment and promised to honor Venezuela's debt commitments. Financial market reports issued during the campaign suggested that Chávez would likely take a pragmatic approach once in office, and emphasized that "promises in the early days of his campaign to freeze payment of the foreign debt and to close the economy to foreign investment have been replaced recently with a more market-friendly stance."[13]

[12] "Venezuela Country Report," Economist Intelligence Unit, fourth quarter 1998.
[13] "Venezuela Country Report," Economist Intelligence Unit, fourth quarter 1998.

One President, Different Scenarios 145

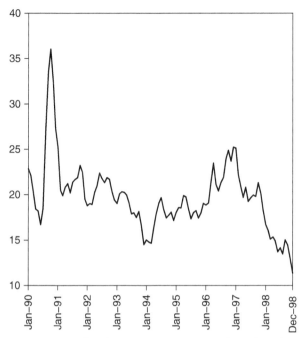

FIGURE 7.2. Oil Reference Price (WTI, U.S.$ per barrel) – Pre-Chávez.
Source: OPEC.

Hugo Chávez was elected in December 1998 with 56 percent of the vote, while his coalition Polo Patriótico won a third of the congressional seats.

CHÁVEZ'S FIRST PRESIDENTIAL TERM

First Year: Honeymoon with the Markets

Chávez was elected in the midst of an international economic scenario that was even less favorable than that experienced by Lucio Gutiérrez in Ecuador or Lula in Brazil. The international price of the Venezuelan oil barrel averaged U.S.$8 compared to U.S.$100 in 2011 (Figure 7.2).

After signaling a move toward a more pragmatic program by the end of the presidential campaign, Chávez consolidated his turnaround with the decision to keep Caldera's well-regarded finance minister Maritza Izaguirre, rather than appointing left-leaning economists who helped him draft his electoral economic program (Corrales and Penfold 2011). Under Izaguirre, the government would advance a surprisingly orthodox macroeconomic agenda in 1999.

146 *The Politics of Market Discipline in Latin America*

An Economist Intelligence Unit report released in the first quarter of that year confirmed expectations raised during the campaign that:

Reverting to the moderate, pragmatic approach which he had adopted in meetings with business and the IMF prior to the election, Mr. Chávez reiterated his commitment to fiscal discipline and urged his supporters to be patient.[...] Despite the populist tone of his campaign, orthodox fiscal austerity measures designed to curb the escalating deficit are dominating his policy agenda ("Venezuela Risk Report," Economist Intelligence Unit, January 1999).

According to the report, since the election Chávez had tried to convince financial investors and business that he would be fiscally prudent and implement pro-business market reforms: "Now president-elect, he is appearing statesman-like and prudent, wooing business, investors and multilaterals alike." The document highlighted that as part of Chávez's new pragmatic approach to the economy, the president had sought special fast track powers to implement specific fiscal measures immediately.

Among these measures, aimed at cutting the deficit by two-thirds, was a financial transaction tax of 0.5 percent, the substitution of the wholesale tax of 16.5 percent for a more widely applied value-added tax rate of 15.5 percent, the transformation of social security and tax laws, and the streamlining of government (including a reduction in the number of ministries from twenty-three to fourteen). The measures were expected to allow the government to contract U.S.$1.4 billion worth of new debt. Investors showed approval:

[T]he Enabling Law shows that Mr Chávez is not averse to adopting orthodox solutions to Venezuela's economic problems.[...] Realism appears to have replaced rhetoric, and the retention of Maritza Izaguirre as finance minister seems to have convinced business that the government intends to pursue a prudent fiscal agenda, and press ahead with market reforms ("Venezuela Country Report," Economist Intelligence Unit, first quarter 1999).

Despite having displayed intentions to renegotiate the Venezuelan foreign debt with the Paris Club during his campaign, once in office Chávez assured investors that he would not take any unilateral measures, and that contracts would be respected.

The president also committed to maintaining the prevailing structure of the oil sector and the contracts with multinationals that had been signed under Caldera, and so he did. He went so far as to approve a decree concerning investment protection and promotion, and to open telecommunications to foreign investment based on a market-friendly regulatory framework (Corrales and Penfold 2011).

One President, Different Scenarios

FIGURE 7.3. Oil Reference Price (WTI, U.S.$ per barrel) - Chávez Presidency. *Source:* OPEC.

In addition, still part of the cost-cutting exercise, Chávez announced intentions to review the strategic value of a number of foreign refineries with a view to selling some holdings and to examine the possibility of opening up the natural gas sector to private-sector participation.[14]

After panicking during the presidential campaign, markets responded positively to Chávez's moderation. This recovered confidence was reflected in the fall of Venezuelan sovereign bond spreads in the context of still low oil prices; the fall started in the end of the presidential campaign and persisted throughout 1999 (Figure 7.1).

Regaining markets' confidence was particularly important considering that the government was expected to resort to multilateral agencies and international capital markets for around half of its estimated U.S.$5.5 billion international financing requirement. The administration negotiated a U.S.$500 million loan from the Inter-American Development Bank (IDB), which followed a U.S.$1.6 billion loan made in 1998, and the World Bank would provide another U.S.$900 million. In addition, the government held discussions with the IMF managing director, Michel Camdessus, and Chávez publicly remarked that he was committed to

[14] "Venezuela Country Report," Economist Intelligence Unit, third quarter 1999.

148   *The Politics of Market Discipline in Latin America*

maintaining the adjustment program agreed with the Fund (Corrales and Penfold 2011).

The remaining funding of government's international obligations was expected to come from new issues in international capital markets, as well as from recent debt swaps and buybacks. The Chávez administration planned to launch its first international bond by mid-1999, with another issue later in the year when debt-service payments fell due.

The Economist Intelligence Unit reports that "access to international capital is likely to be forthcoming, despite the deep economic crisis, in recognition of Venezuela's strong liquidity position."[15] Chávez's visit to the United States in June 1999, the first since his inauguration, was broadly regarded as a major success by U.S. investors.

These first impressions began to fade as Chávez was perceived to put an excessive focus on political reforms, at the expense of economic ones. Except for some fiscal austerity measures, Chávez never clearly outlined an economic program, and investors feared the interventionist attitude signaled in the new constitution, which forbade the privatization of major assets; extended agricultural subsidies; and placed excessive demands on fiscal accounts in mandating social security provisions:

> In line with the spirit of the new document, the government plans to repeal market-oriented labour and social security reforms, provide subsidized credit to agriculture and small and medium-sized enterprises (SMEs), exercise greater discretion over import quotas and tariffs to protect domestic producers, and take a much more active role in price setting, monetary policy and the management of the state oil company ("Venezuela Risk Service," Economist Intelligence Unit, first quarter 2000).

Since the beginning of 1999, when Brazil devalued the real and oil prices hit a twenty-five-year low, investor sentiment toward Latin America had improved and capital flows had been restored. However, as the United States tightened interest rates in August of that year, international investors sought liquid and "quality" investments in the region. In the process, they largely shunned Venezuela on the basis of its increased political uncertainty and rising government interventionism.

In response, the Chávez administration resorted to domestic financial markets to fund the public debt, announcing that it planned to raise U.S.$1.3 billion in 2000. Considering the few alternatives that were available to Venezuelan banks as a result of the predominance of the oil economy, the government had no problem raising the money.

The new Bolivarian constitution, enacted in December 1999, improved the previous one in terms of social policies and human rights.

---

[15] "Venezuela Country Report," Economist Intelligence Unit, second quarter 1999.

One President, Different Scenarios 149

It also established mechanisms of direct democracy, strengthening local power and civil society organizations along with the strengthening of the executive relative to other government branches. Still in 2000, Chávez called new presidential elections, and by winning extended his term for six more years. In the same process, allied parties won absolute majorities in the legislature and seventeen out of twenty-four state governments in state elections. All these events reinforced the consolidation of political power in the hands of the president.

Second Phase: Confrontation and Instability

By the end of 2000, Chávez was still perceived by the international financial community as a pragmatist:

Since his re-election in July 2000 in fresh polls called to re-legitimize public posts following the introduction of a new constitution, Mr Chávez has shown himself to be relatively pragmatic. Notwithstanding the frequent use of rabble-rousing rhetoric, his government's few economic policy initiatives to date, such as a new telecommunications law, have generally been well received by private investors ("Venezuelan Country Report," Economist Intelligence Unit, fourth quarter 2000).

In this period, the government still reiterated its openness to foreign investors, even though markets viewed Venezuela with increasing suspicion in light of the recent political developments. International investors demanded structural reforms to the public finances, as well as signs of government's willingness to hold down labor costs, which Chávez seemed reluctant to accept.

Initial efforts to cut the budget deficit faded as oil revenues rebounded. In 2000, the Venezuelan government allocated 50 percent of the budget to public-sector salaries, 40 percent more than in the previous year, and also boosted spending in priority areas such as health care and education.

In the realm of structural reforms, the government seemed to be taking the opposite direction from what was expected after Chávez's policy switch in 1999; following the approval of the new constitution, the president used powers delegated by the Congress to pass laws that raised the Venezuelan State's share in the oil sector and initiated the expropriation of lands destined for an agrarian reform.

These measures marked the beginning of a period of rising confrontation between the government and the private sector, in a scenario of restricted fiscal capacity due to still low oil prices. The government's timid economic results, after the high expectations raised by campaign promises, severely hurt Chávez's popularity; in 2002, he reached the lowest level of support since his inauguration. Only 36 percent of

150   *The Politics of Market Discipline in Latin America*

Venezuelans approved of the government, compared to 67 percent a year before.[16]

The crisis culminated with a coup attempt in April, led by Venezuelan elites with strong support of the media. Chávez was deposed and Pedro Carmona – leader of the most important business association of Venezuela (Fedecámaras) – assumed the presidency. For numerous reasons, among them Chávez's strong support in the military, the pressure of popular protests in favor of the elected government, and the political inability of Carmona, the president was returned to power in less than forty-eight hours.

From that moment on, however, the fissure between government and business became inevitable (López Maya 2005). Confrontation continued with a general strike organized between December 2002 and February 2003, which involved not only private companies but also the state oil company PDVSA, and that severely damaged the country's economy – Venezuela's GDP (in dollars) dropped 31 percent in nominal terms in 2003.

Chávez reacted to the events of 2002–2003 by radicalizing his already polarizing discourse. In the economic realm, the president recovered and strengthened his hold over PDVSA's operation[17] and established price controls on basic products. He also imposed capital controls, initially in an attempt to prevent an already significant capital flight from the Venezuelan economy, but that progressively turned into an instrument of political control over private investors.

Third Phase: Boom and Consolidation

The consolidation of Chávez's economic power followed the consolidation of his political power initiated with the new constitution. Rising oil prices were key to this process (Figure 7.3).

Higher export revenues boosted inflows of foreign currency, dramatically reducing the government's external financing requirements. This freed the Chávez administration from multilateral conditionality and from the need to address markets' demands for economic reforms. Moreover, prospects of strong economic growth increased the attractiveness of Venezuelan financial assets, further boosting the government's capacity

---

[16] "Análisis del Entorno Sociopolítico Venezolano," Alfredo Keller y Asociados, May 2002.
[17] See Corrales and Penfold (2011) for a detailed account of Chávez's capture of political control in PDVSA.

One President, Different Scenarios 151

to advance its preferred policies with little regard to investors' preferences and concerns.

As a result, starting in 2003, Chávez established a successful strategy of channeling oil revenues to poorest citizens, through projects controlled directly by the executive branch. Among the most important of these projects were the *misiones* (missions), social initiatives based on the Cuban experience (Agullo 2006; Rodriguez 2006). Exchange controls and firm oil prices enabled a major expansion of public spending.

It was also in this period that what would be later called *boliburguesía* – a new political elite that took command of the main political and economic institutions in the country and that reported directly to Chávez – emerged.

In the context of a significant drop in direct investment caused by investors' fears of the Chávez government, the oil price boom was the main driver of the country's fast economic growth (Figure 7.4).

Higher spending also boosted the president's popularity, especially among the poor. Polls suggested that the initial impact of the *misiones* was a key factor in the recovery of Chávez's support between 2003 and 2004 from the crisis faced in the first years of the government.[18] In 2004, 60 percent of voters in a popular referendum approved of his government.

The establishment of the *misiones* occurred at the same time as the dismantling of Chávez's political opposition, consolidating the process initiated with the collapse of the *Puntofijismo*.[19] The opposition itself largely contributed to the hegemony of Chávez's Movimiento Quinta República (MVR); on allegations of "lack of transparency," parties refused to join the 2005 elections.

This decision allowed Chávez's allies to win twenty out of twenty-two state government elections, in addition to almost all congressional seats. The electoral process was declared free and fair by local and international observers, legitimizing a level of concentration of power in the hands of the executive unprecedented in Venezuela's democratic history. On top of that, Chávez reformed the Supreme Court in 2004 increasing the control of the executive over the judicial branch.

Owing to high economic growth, the public-sector debt fell from 47 percent of the GDP in 2003 to 24 percent in 2006. At the same time,

---

[18] Interview with Alfredo Keller, from pollster firm Alfredo Keller and Associates in Caracas, Venezuela, March 2008.

[19] The term comes from the Punto Fijo Pact, a series of agreements made by the Acción Democratica and the COPEI that set the terms of political competition in Venezuela, characterized by the alternation of the two parties in the leadership of national unity governments.

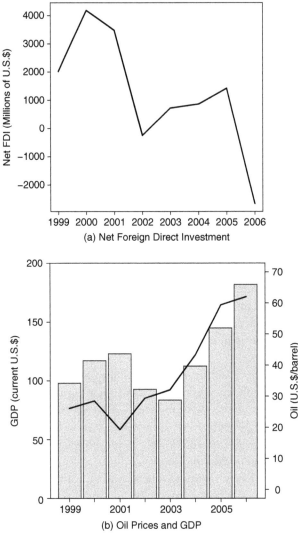

FIGURE 7.4. Foreign Direct Investment, Oil Prices, and Economic Growth. *Source:* Venezuelan Central Bank.

debt management operations reduced interest rates and lengthened the average maturity of the public debt, reducing the debt-service burden. In this favorable scenario, with few questions about the government's capacity to meet debt service commitments, Chávez was again capable of tapping international markets for funds.

Even though costs were higher than would be expected in a country in such a good financial situation, it is worth noting that the spread of the

One President, Different Scenarios 153

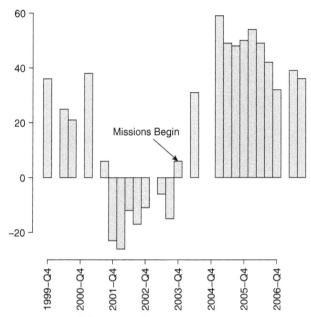

FIGURE 7.5. Chávez's Popularity.
Note: Difference between approval and disapproval of the Chávez' administration.
Source: Alfredo Keller y Asociados, 2007.

Venezuelan bonds followed a downward trajectory from 2003 on, similar to other "better behaved" Latin American economies (Figure 7.6). Still, foreign investors' fears, coupled with the captivity of local markets, led to a change in the composition of the Venezuelan public debt (Figure 7.7).

Higher social expenditures and the establishment of the *misiones* were also fundamental in explaining Chávez's reelection in 2006 (Figure 7.5), interpreted by the president as a mandate to furthering his "twenty-first-century socialism."

CHÁVEZ'S REELECTION: SOCIALISM IN THE TWENTY-FIRST CENTURY

Similar to what happened in 1998, the events following the third election of Hugo Chávez took investors by surprise. This time, however, the surprise took the opposite direction – markets reacted to the election with indifference but panicked after the president's inauguration, as the radicalization of Chávez's leftist platform became evident (see Figure 7.8). Still, very favorable conditions limited the impact of these reactions (Figure 7.9).

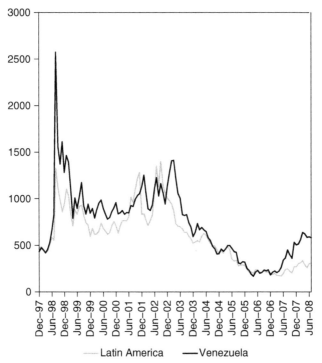

FIGURE 7.6. Venezuelan Sovereign Risk, Compared to Latin America.
Note: Venezuelan and average Latin America sovereign bond spreads (EMBI+).
Source: S&P, Global financial data.

Investors quickly realized that an expected post-election fiscal retrenchment would not happen. Still, even though access to fresh external debt could be limited by the government's increasingly radical policy stance, the captive liquidity created by exchange controls forced the existence of a domestic market for public debt.

The period starting in 2007 marked a new phase of Chávez's relations with investors. Strengthened by historically high oil prices and by the autonomy provided by control of the Congress,[20] the Central Bank, and PDVSA and helped by a favorable judiciary, Chávez revealed his intention to reassess the role of the state in the Venezuelan economy and to nationalize companies deemed strategic to the country's development.

This process initiated in the oil sector, where concessions in the region known as Faja del Orinoco were replaced by societies in which

---

[20] Chávez managed to obtain congressional approval to another set of enabling laws. These granted the president the right to govern by decree in the first eighteen months of the new presidential term.

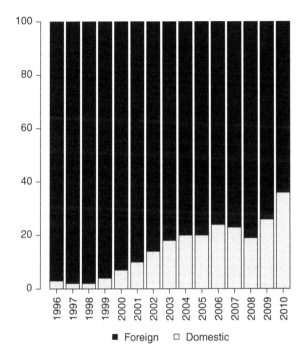

FIGURE 7.7. Venezuelan Debt Composition.
Note: Venezuelan debt composition.
Source: Economist Intelligence Unit.

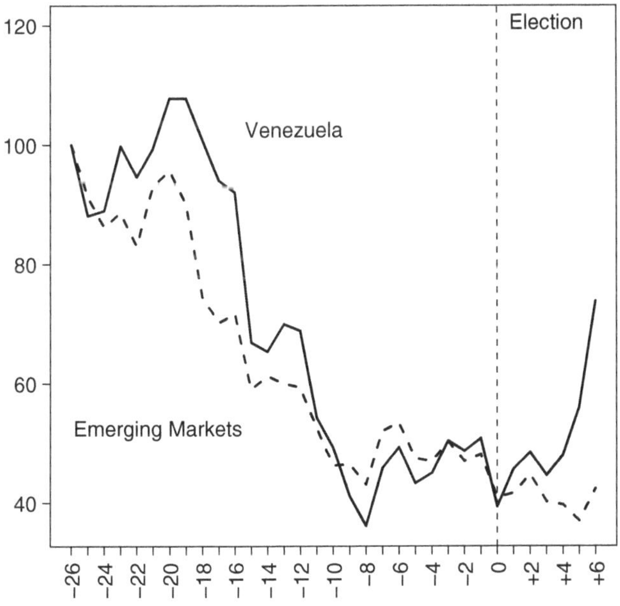

FIGURE 7.8. Venezuelan Sovereign Spread: 2006 Election.
Note: Spread of the Standard & Poor's Emerging Market Bond Index (EMBI+) in the period that surrounded the Venezuelan 2006 election.
Source: Global Financial Data.

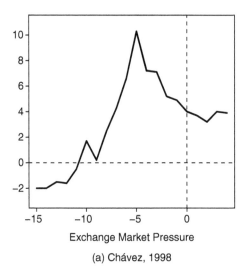

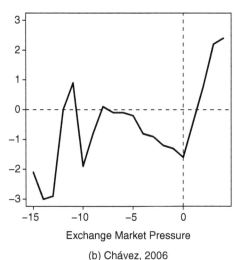

FIGURE 7.9. Currency Pressures in Venezuelan Elections: 1998 and 2006.
Note: Evolution of currency pressures, as calculated in Chapter 4, in the period around Chávez's inaugurations in 1998 and 2006. Month of inauguration denoted by the vertical dashed line. The horizontal dashed line marks $EMP = 0$.

PDVSA became the majority shareholder. Chávez also nationalized CANTV, the monopolist firm operating in the telecommunications sector bought by Verizon in 1992, and the Electricity of Caracas, a private company acquired by the American AES Corporation in 2000. Later, the government privatized SIDOR, the country's largest steel company. In all these cases, shareholders were willing to accept the

One President, Different Scenarios   157

financial compensation proposed by the government, with the exception of ConocoPhillips and ExxonMobil, which decided to contest the decision in international arbitration courts.

Arguably, the first round of nationalizations were consistent with Chávez's announced intention to regain control of "strategic sectors" and reflected the government's capacity to confront investors in an economy in which high oil prices and exchange controls largely reduced the government's reliance on private finance. Using the same rationale of previous governments that justified privatizations on the basis of a lack of public resources for investment, the oil boom allowed Chávez to renationalize. A typical example of this logic is the case of SIDOR, bought by the Italian-Argentine consortium Techint during the wave of privatizations promoted under Caldera's *Agenda Venezuela*, and always considered strategic by the new administration.

Later on, this confrontation intensified, as Chávez decided to nationalize businesses never before classified as strategic but that became key to guaranteeing the victory of the president's allies in the regional elections of 2008. To boost the government's capacity to build housing for the poor, the president announced the nationalization of cement companies. Aiming to combat food scarcity, Chávez nationalized Cealco, the country's major food warehouse, as well as Lacteos Los Andes, producer of 30 percent of Venezuela's milk.

Analysts concerned with the excessive power of the *chavismo* in Venezuela since 2006 have speculated about the conditions under which market discipline could once again occur in Venezuela. One of these occasions occurred after Chávez's defeat in the December 2007 referendum on constitutional reform, then again later during the financial crises of 2008. In none of these cases, however, did Chávez display any signal of a new turnaround.

In contrast to the period that followed his first election, the president concentrated political power to the point at which his response to political or economic setback could result in an even more confrontational approach toward investors, in an attempt to further extend the state's control over the Venezuelan economy. The second wave of nationalizations observed after the referendum evidences that trend.

CONCLUSION

Returning to the central theme of this chapter, an unprecedented oil windfall allowed Chávez to promote state-led economic growth and promote an aggressive redistribution of income to the poorest Venezuelans. The country grew an average of 30 percent in nominal terms, while the Gini coefficient[21] dropped from 0.50 to 0.44 between 1999 and 2009.

Market discipline, which was effective in constraining Chávez's policies in the first years of his presidency, became irrelevant to policymaking after the export boom consolidated in 2003. The boom freed the government from the necessity of submitting to multilateral conditionality or addressing investors' demands to attract capital inflows, as Chávez clearly did in the aftermath of his inauguration in 1998.

This process is comparable to the one observed in Ecuador (Chapter 6). Nevertheless, although part of the variation between Gutiérrez's and Correa's behaviors might be attributable to their different personalities and backgrounds, Chávez's case in Venezuela allowed us to "control" for the incumbent's identity and political preferences, making it possible to observe the effect of changing exogenous conditions (once again export prices) on markets' capacity to influence policy choices.

After portraying himself as a left-wing alternative in the 1998 presidential race, once inaugurated, Chávez adopted more moderate behavior toward private investors, as well as an orthodox macroeconomic program. Even though the new constitution consolidated the president's political power and displayed signals that Chávez might revert to his original political agenda, it was only after oil prices soared that the president acquired the capacity to actually advance it.

Although indebtedness was reduced relative to the economy because of the oil bonanza, it is important to note that Chávez was still able to tap into international markets, even deviating tremendously from investors' policy preferences. Exchange controls and other regulation maintained domestic financial markets captured, further reducing the government's dependence on foreign portfolio investors. As a result, after 2003 Chávez's initially moderate stance was replaced by the so-called twenty-first-century Venezuelan socialism.

Contrary to Brazil, where a more complex economy cushions the effects of currency booms (and crises) and limits the differences between good and bad times, in Venezuela (as in Ecuador), these differences are substantial. Consequently, the government's dependence on international finance and, therefore, the necessity to build investors' confidence varies markedly in both countries. Uncertainty about the constraints imposed by market discipline explains a pattern of leftist policy switches in bad times and radical redistribution in good times, preventing ideological convergence from occurring in the long run.

---

[21] The Gini coefficient is a measure of the inequality of a distribution, a value of 0 expressing perfect equality where everyone has equal shares of income and a value of 1 expresses maximal inequality where only one person has all the income.

8

"Vivir con Lo Nuestro": Default and Market Discipline in Argentina

The chapters on Ecuador and Venezuela have highlighted how market discipline varies with cycles of currency booms and crises that, in both countries, were triggered by factors exogenous to governments' decisions.

The experiences of Lucio Gutiérrez and Hugo Chávez illustrate the argument that leftist presidents elected under severe dollar scarcity frequently chose to renounce campaign promises and advance orthodox economic policies in an attempt to boost market confidence and attract capital inflows to the economy.

In contrast, both Rafael Correa and the same Chávez after 2003 benefitted from a wide room to deviate from market preferences, in a scenario of oil price boom and high international liquidity. Rather than advancing (or maintaining, in the case of Chávez) an investor-friendly agenda, both seized the opportunity to pursue an interventionist and redistributive economic program.

The experience of Argentina since 2002 is also one in which a government gained substantial autonomy from financial market discipline compared to its predecessors. Different from Ecuador and Venezuela, however, this autonomy did not result primarily from an exogenous shock; it was rather a consequence of a previous governmental decision to default on the country's public debt. By unilaterally reducing Argentina's external financial obligations, the default relieved following governments from the need to resort to financial markets or to the International Monetary Fund (IMF) to fund them.

Contrary to the cases of Chávez and Correa, in which an increased supply of foreign exchange widened governments' autonomy from international finance, under Néstor Kirchner this autonomy resulted from a drastic reduction of Argentina's foreign obligations. After 2004, the commodity price boom that encompassed most Latin American

159

emerging economies, coupled with the refusal of some bondholders to accept the terms offered by the debt restructuring, limited both the Kirchner and later the Fernández governments' necessity and capacity to return to international financial markets for the following decade.

The combination of the default and the commodity boom allowed President Kirchner to advance policies substantially distinct from those demanded by investors and multilateral institutions, in both the macro- and microeconomic arenas. The strategy prevailing in Argentina since then has been one of "living with their own resources" – *vivir con lo nuestro*. Put simply, this implies restricting international obligations to the amount that can be funded with resources generated through exports. To accomplish this goal, the administration maintained an underval- ued peso, actively stimulated exports and limited imports, and imposed capital controls.

The autonomy from financial markets allowed Kirchner to main- tain subsidies to basic goods, increase the number of public jobs, and renationalize the social security system. It is unlikely that any of these policies had been advanced in a scenario like the one Argentina expe- rienced during the 1990s, when economic policymaking was oriented toward building confidence in the international financial community. The principle of *vivir con lo nuestro* itself starkly contrasts with the phi- losophy of growing with foreign savings that prevailed in the previous decade.

To understand the political and economic scenario in Argentina since 2002, it is important to consider the period that starts with the election of Carlos Menem in 1989. The crisis that led to the default was the most tragic consequence of years of a regime of currency convertibility that tied the government's hands in monetary policy and demanded a fiscal orthodoxy stricter than Argentina was ever capable of maintaining. The convertibility imposed a dependence on foreign capital inflows to fund structural imbalances in external accounts that put market confidence at the center of the Argentine political stage. The default was the critical juncture after which this scenario started to change.

CONVERTIBILITY AND CONFIDENCE

The first democratic alternation of presidents in almost sixty years occurred in Argentina in the midst of a hyperinflationary crisis in May 1989.

The "Primavera Plan," announced nine months earlier, had been Pres- ident Raúl Alfonsín's last attempt to curb hyperinflation and assure his party – the Unión Cívica Radical (UCR) – some prospects of winning the

"*Vivir con Lo Nuestro*" 161

race. The plan relied on an exchange rate anchor, but was launched when international reserves were at a bottom level. The anchor was initially maintained by short-term capital inflows, but this proved unsustainable.

Rumors that the World Bank would suspend funds to Argentina triggered a speculative attack that sent the plan to an early end after the government spent U.S.$ 900 million to defend the value of its currency. Capital flight persisted, provoking a 193 percent devaluation in April 1989 followed by another 111 percent devaluation in May.

On top of the economic crisis, a confidence crisis emerged with respect to the front runner in the presidential race, the candidate from the *justicialismo*[1] Carlos Menem. Stock markets collapsed, and capital flight accelerated in the months preceding the election. Markets' suspicion was such that all the due dates for the repayment of fixed-date deposits were concentrated in the last day of Alfonsín's term (Gerchunoff and Llach 2003).

This reaction was not unfounded. The Partido Justicialista had been traditionally associated with leftist policies in Argentina, and its constituency was composed mainly of poorer voters and unionized workers. The tone of Menem's campaign was not unexpected for a Peronist candidate; he criticized the orthodox economic policies advanced in the second half of Alfonsín's term and promised, instead, to launch a "productive revolution" driven by a "demand shock" (*salariazo*). His program promoted state ownership of heavy industries, utilities, and oil; a social pact to deal with inflation; and the suspension and renegotiation of the country's debt service (Stokes 2001).

In May 1989, Menem was elected in the first round, under hyperinflation rates that had reached 78 percent a month. The presidential office was transferred six months earlier than the official date because Alfonsín lacked credibility to confront the crisis.

Menem's cabinet surprised voters and analysts alike and completely reversed markets' expectations with respect to the new government. The president appointed a conservative unionist as his labor minister, and the vice president of the Argentine multinational Bunge y Born to the Economy Ministry. Menem also announced an economic agenda far more orthodox than the one advanced by Alfonsín, which he had fiercely attacked during the presidential campaign. Previously scared investors were reassured, and the Argentine stock market immediately resumed an upward trajectory.

---

[1] Candidate from the Partido Justicialista (PJ), sometimes referred to as "Partido Peronista."

The first initiatives of the new administration – the laws of economic emergency and state reform – were both designed to foster price stability and curb hyperinflation. The government also suspended industrial policies and exports promotion regimes, among other measures allegedly aimed to destroy the prevailing logic of "assisted capitalism." In addition, it launched an aggressive privatization program in 1990, which encompassed telecommunication concessions, transports, and heavy industrial sectors such as steel and petrochemicals.[2]

Yet efforts were not sufficient to stabilize prices, and by October 1990 the monthly inflation rate was 7.7 percent. This initial failure triggered a political crisis that culminated with the replacement of the economic cabinet.

During the first two years of Menem's presidential term, antiinflationary policy followed the monetarist receipt, under a floating exchange rate regime. After accumulating a considerable amount of foreign reserves with the privatization program, Menem and the new minister of the economy Domingo Cavallo understood that the conditions were forcing a new and radical gamble against inflation – the Convertibility Law.

The law was more than a traditional exchange-rate-based stabilization plan.[3] It established that the Central Bank had the obligation to keep foreign reserves sufficient to buy the country's entire monetary base at the rate of one peso/one dollar. This peg, expected to reestablish the credibility Menem had lost in his first anti-inflationary attempt, also implied that the government renounced its ability to use monetary policy as a macroeconomic instrument, which would later prove to be an extremely costly decision.

The plan was unquestionably successful in fighting hyperinflation. A combination of trade competition and a fixed exchange rate, in a period of high international liquidity, reduced the annual rate from more than 3,000 percent in 1989 to 25 percent in 1992.

With the end of the inflationary tax, credit became more predictable in Argentina, triggering a consumption boom that accelerated economic growth. From 1990 to 1994, the GDP grew at an 8.8 percent annual rate, a record in the century, while both consumption and investment increased 50 percent.

---

[2] Menem's initial economic plan was dubbed Plan BB, in reference to the Bunge y Born executives appointed to the Economy Ministry and responsible to launch it.
[3] Exchange-rate-based stabilization (ERBS) plans are those with which an exchange rate peg provides a nominal anchor to the domestic currency.

"*Vivir con Lo Nuestro*"

Strong economic growth provided for increased tax collection, which allowed the Argentine government to balance its budget. The increase in the GDP more than compensated for the negative consequences of the stabilization in the first years of the Convertibility Law; the downsizing effects of privatizations and imports competition were barely felt until 1994.

Yet the reduction of import barriers – between 1989 and 1993, the average import tariff dropped from 26 percent to 10 percent – led to a fivefold increase in the amount of imports, whereas exports grew at a 6 percent rate in the same period (Figure 8.1). This process transformed a trade surplus of U.S.$ 8.3 billion in 1990 into a U.S.$ 5.7 billion deficit in 1994, putting pressure on the country's external balance.

The persisting external imbalances were justified by the fact that a large share of the new imports was composed of capital goods. The expectation was that this strategy would increase the competitiveness of domestic production, which should, in the longer term, boost exports (Gerchunoff and Llach 2003, p. 434). The government also advanced policies to stimulate exports, but that ended up reverting the 1993 budget surplus into deficits in 1994. This reversal occurred at the same time as the external imbalance peaked (Table 8.1).

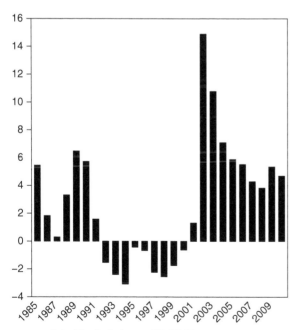

FIGURE 8.1. Trade Balance (% GDP).
Source: Instituto Nacional de Estadística y Censos de la Republica (INDEC).

164 *The Politics of Market Discipline in Latin America*

TABLE 8.1. *Fiscal Results under Convertibility (% GDP)*

1991	1992	1993	1994	1995	1996	1997	1998	1999	2000	2001
−0.9	−0.1	0.3	0.0	−0.5	−1.9	−1.5	−1.4	−1.7	−2.4	−3.2

Notes: Central government budget: deficit/surplus (% GDP).
Source: Argentine Central Bank.

Productivity actually increased – the average production of the urban sector rose 7.3 percent per year between 1990 and 1994. Its side effect, however, was unemployment. In the first two years of the plan, economic growth compensated for the downsizing effect of imports competition and privatization; in the following two years, the economy grew at an annual rate of 6.5 percent, and new jobs increased only 0.5 percent. The reasons why the growth of the Argentine economy in the 1990s was not labor intensive are disputed, but the main result of this process was a sharp rise of urban unemployment between 1992 and 1994.

With fiscal deficits, external imbalances, and rising unemployment, the only source of optimism were the conditions of the external scenario: the devaluation of the dollar, the convergence of local and American inflation, the depreciation of the peso relative to neighbor currencies, and finally the creation of the Mercosur.[4]

It is important to remember that in the model adopted under Menem, persisting current account deficits were financed by the inflows of foreign portfolio capital (Figure 8.2). In the first half of the decade, about 70 percent of the increase in the external financial obligations of Argentina were held by the private sector (Burgo 2011).

After 1994, however, the privatization of the social security system forced the Argentine government into a spiral of indebtedness; the state continued paying its obligations to retired workers, but no new contributions were coming in (Levitsky and Murillo 2003). From the mid-1990s on, thus, the public sector became increasingly indebted, and consequently more vulnerable to market sentiment.

This vulnerability became evident with the reversal of the favorable international scenario in 1995; it peaked when an increase in American interest rates, coupled with the devaluation of the peso, raised fears of a Mexican default. Investors' panic provoked substantial capital flight from emerging economies, as they anticipated other defaults to follow.

---

[4] The Mercosur is an economic and political agreement among Argentina, Brazil, Paraguay, and Uruguay, founded in 1991, and with the purpose of promoting the free movement of goods, people, and currency, indicated good prospects for the economy after 1994 (Gerchunoff and Llach 2003, p. 442).

"*Vivir con Lo Nuestro*"

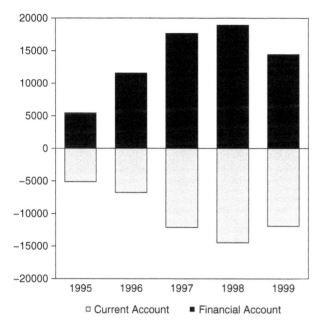

FIGURE 8.2. Balance of Payments (U.S.$ billion).
Note: Current account and financial account balance (U.S.$ billion).
Source: ECLACstat.

Argentina was subject to even stronger pressure because of the rigidity of its exchange rate system, suffering severe consequences of the confidence crisis. Stock markets dropped, the sovereign risk rose, and the country lost 25 percent of its international reserves between the end of 1994 and the first quarter of 1995.

The government responded to the loss of market confidence by reinforcing its commitment to convertibility. It increased interest rates and in March 1995 signed an agreement with the IMF that was conditional on the maintenance of the fixed exchange rate regime. Argentina also started a program of fiscal austerity and economic adjustments that led to a 4.5 percent fall in the country's GDP. Menem was reelected in the same month that the unemployment rate reached 19 percent.

Austerity coupled with IMF funds helped maintain market confidence in convertibility after 1995, but from then on the economy adjusted to lower standards compared to the pre-crisis period.

The recovery that occurred between 1995 and 1998 strengthened the belief that maintaining convertibility had been the right choice. Despite the drop in 1995, GDP in 1998 remained 15 percent higher than in 1994. Unemployment decreased from 19 percent to 12 percent. Growth became more labor intensive, and was sustained not by consumption, but by

166   *The Politics of Market Discipline in Latin America*

investment. It was also spurred by the astonishing growth in exports (64 percent between 1994 and 1998) driven by the Mercosur, which further contributed to alleviate the pressures on the current account. These gains were partly offset by an 80 percent increase on interest payments in the same period (Gerchunoff and Llach 2003, p. 446).

Based on the transcript of a press conference in October 1998, the IMF's Independent Evaluation Office reported:

> In October 1998, the performance of Argentina received the attention of the world when President Carlos Menem shared the podium of the Annual Meetings with the IMF Managing Director, who characterized the experience of Argentina in recent years as "exemplary." The Managing Director further remarked: "Argentina has a story to tell the world: a story which is about the importance of fiscal discipline, of structural change, and of monetary policy rigorously maintained." (IMF 2004, p. 12.)

Ironically, the relative tranquility observed since 1995 was already set to end in Argentina as a result of the Russian crisis of 1998. From late 1998 on, the economy was hit by successive exogenous shocks, including a reversal of capital flows to emerging markets after the Russian default, a fall in commodity prices, the general strengthening of the dollar against the euro, and a weakening of demand in major trading partners. The coup de grâce came in early 1999, with a 70 percent devaluation of the Brazilian real against the dollar. This destroyed the competitiveness of Argentina's exports and aggravated its dependence on external funding, setting the country into a downward spiral that culminated in the end of convertibility and default.

COLLAPSE AND DEFAULT

Despite evidence that convertibility would not be sustainable for much longer, it is interesting to note that no candidate in the presidential election of 1999 dared to challenge the model.

The widespread support of convertibility among the Argentines left no space for questioning; considering the level of dollarization of the economy, a devaluation of the peso would have striking consequences not only to firms but also to a large share of the population that had debt and contracts in dollars.

It comes as no surprise, thus, that the newly elected president Fernando De La Rúa from the Unión Cívica Radical (UCR) was inaugurated in 2000 promising "one peso/one dollar." Protecting convertibility in such an unfavorable scenario demanded, however, renewed efforts to regain the confidence of financial markets. According to the new minister of the economy, José Luis Machinea, the strategy was straightforward:

"Vivir con Lo Nuestro" 167

government's harsh fiscal austerity should reduce the country's risk, lower interest rates, and reattract foreign capital to reactivate the economy.[5] As market sentiment emerged as the key driver of policymaking, the trade-off between investors' and other societal demands reached its highest in the De La Rúa administration.

To reduce the U.S.\$ 7.5 billion fiscal deficit, the government first imposed a tax increase that heavily penalized the middle class. The reversal of the feeble economic recovery of 1999 would later be attributed to this single measure. It followed a 12 to 15 percent cut on public sector wages that exceeded U.S.\$ 1,000 to U.S.\$ 6,500 a month, respectively (Gerchunoff and Llach 2003).

Both policies raised strong opposition not only in UCR's traditional constituency – the Argentine middle class – but also in the business community, because they reduced consumption and strangled any prospects of economic recovery. Reactions forced Machinea to back down and to announce a tax reduction on investment that later proved ineffective to recover business confidence.

The loss of UCR's traditional political base and the conflict with industrialists, in conjunction with a stigma in the financial community owing to his passage by the Economy Ministry during hyperinflation, all contributed to undermine Machinea's strength as minister of the economy.[6]

Problems intensified in 2000 as insolvency concerns were exacerbated by the appreciation of the dollar and a further drying up of capital flows to emerging economies. Market confidence did not recover, and the country lost access to funding later in the year.

In March, President De La Rúa announced an agreement with the IMF that would provide Argentina with exceptional financial support amounting to U.S.\$ 7.2 billion. The funds were later increased by U.S.\$ 13.7 billion, and with additional financing arranged from private sources amounted to U.S.\$ 39 billion. According to the IMF, the country faced a liquidity crisis, and "any exchange rate or debt sustainability problem was manageable with strong action on the fiscal and structural fronts" (IMF 2004, p. 5). The most pressing problems of Argentina were attributed to adverse but temporary shocks and were expected to recede with an improvement of external conditions in 2001.

Markets' positive response to what was later called *blindaje* was reflected in a drop in the country risk and a 28 percent rise in the Argentine stock markets. The main condition for the IMF disbursement, however, was a social security reform that lowered the value of payments

[5] "Machinea não conseguiu estimular crescimento," *Valor Econômico*, May 3, 2001.
[6] "Ultraliberal assume hoje Ministério da Economia," *Valor Econômico*, May 3, 2001.

and increased women's retirement age by five years. The government also committed to reforming the health system and to negotiating a five-year freeze in local governments' expenditures.

Another deterioration of external indicators and the explosion of the fiscal deficit destroyed the effects of the *blindaje*. Without the support of UCR's core constituency and having lost all remaining confidence in financial markets, Machinea resigned in February 2001.[7]

Machinea was replaced by Ricardo López Murphy, former minister of defense. The appointment of the well-known orthodox economist reinforced De La Rúa's commitment to the strategy of confidence building through fiscal austerity.[8]

Markets expected the new minister to accelerate budget cuts. In the past, Lopez Murphy had defended a 10 percent reduction in nominal wages, encompassing public and private jobs, as a means to boost the country's competitiveness.[9]

The cabinet change was also believed to widen the coalition in favor of the fiscal adjustment program and, therefore, to secure United States' support for further IMF help. Investors' optimism was reflected in an 8 percent rise in stock markets and a 5 percent drop in the country risk.

The Argentine industrial sector did not manifest the same enthusiasm over the appointment of Lopez Murphy as did the financial markets. With a recession that lasted for 32 months, the business sector did not recognize the ultraliberal new minister as having the tools necessary to actively promote economic growth.

In the words of the president of the Argentine Industrial Union (UIA, Unión Industrial Argentina), "the resignation of Machinea is part of the failure of recessive measures recommended by the financial sector, multilateral institutions and neoliberal economists."[10]

The Union anticipated that Murphy's measures would be harsher than Machinea's and claimed that their only goal was to produce the budget surpluses creditors explicitly demanded. It did not help that the new minister had previously defended the end of all fiscal exemptions and mechanisms of industrial promotion to save U.S.$ 2.9 billion in public expenditures.

---

[7] "Os 14 meses sob Machinea," *Valor Econômico*, May 3, 2001.

[8] In that period, investors explicitly quantified potential decreases of the country risk if De La Rúa would appoint more orthodox economists such as Ricardo López Murphy and Domingos Cavallo. (Interview with a former Minister of Economy in the De la Rúa administration, Buenos Aires, June 2011).

[9] "Mercado reage com euforia à mudança," *Valor Econômico*, June 3, 2001.

[10] "Empresário não compartilha ânimo," *Valor Econômico*, October 3, 2001.

"*Vivir con Lo Nuestro*" 169

Murphy's plan confirmed expectations. It included cuts in public expenditures in all three levels of government, as well as in federal transfers to the provinces, the privatization of Banco de La Nación, the end of special retirement, and an ambitious state reform designed to downsize the public sector and halve the number of public employees. The minister also announced cuts in health and education expenditures.

Of a total of U.S.$ 2 billion budget cut in 2001, only U.S.$ 105 million would require legislative approval; the executive would pass the remainder in the form of emergency decrees.[11] These measures were portrayed as the only way to maintain the convertibility regime.

Markets' initial enthusiasm rapidly turned into apprehension with the political constraints imposed on the minister; investors speculated whether Lopez Murphy would gather enough political support to implement his orthodox program. Legislative elections, to be held that year, put additional pressures on government expenditures.[12]

Skepticism was not unfounded; following Murphy's announcement of the new program, the ministers of Interior, Education, and Social Development, as well as the secretary-general of the presidency, resigned. The Confederation of Workers in Education called a national strike, and students organized protests and the occupation of major Argentine universities.

Less than a week after his appointment, political tensions along with an IMF public declaration that Argentina needed radical change fostered rumors that Lopez Murphy was about to be dismissed. Murphy resigned a few days later and was replaced by Domingo Cavallo, the mentor of the convertibility plan. Meanwhile, De La Rúa requested additional decree powers from the legislature, justified on the need to advance the economic agenda.

Cavallo's appointment renewed prospects of wider political support for austerity measures because of his ties with the *justicialistas*. The minister allied market confidence – lacking in the case of Machinea – to political ability not to be found in the technocrat Lopez Murphy. Cavallo was quick to reinstate Argentina's commitment to creditors and intentions to expand its sources of funding.

The new economic plan consisted of a tax on financial transactions and changes in other taxes and tariffs (IMF 2004, p. 61), among them the end of a tax exemption on capital gains and interest, new taxes on banking transactions, tax reductions on imports of capital goods, and increased tariffs on consumer goods.

---

[11] "Analistas: o risco agora é de caos político," *Jornal do Brasil*, May 17, 2001.
[12] "Fôlego depende de apoio político,"*Valor Econômico*, March 6, 2001.

170 *The Politics of Market Discipline in Latin America*

The minister also launched sectoral competitiveness plans and announced the intention to promote a 20 percent reduction in production costs through measures that included cuts in public employees' benefits and the reduction or even elimination of employers' contribution to social security.[13]

In June, Cavallo sent to Congress a bill designed to modify the convertibility law and change the currency anchor to an equally weighted basket of the euro and the dollar. The measure boosted expectations that the peg would be abandoned, upsetting investors and the IMF.[14]

In an effort to calm markets and to rebuild confidence, Cavallo announced a new package of budget cuts – the "zero-deficit plan,"aimed at eliminating the federal government deficit from August 2001 onward.[15] Actually, at that point there were no other options if Argentina wanted to keep its IMF agreement, as the target for government expenditures had already been met.[16]

To achieve the zero-deficit goal, the government announced additional budget cuts of U.S.$ 1.5 billion in six months, cuts in public sector wages and pensions to employees/retirees who had an income above U.S.$ 300 per month, and the end of all tax exemptions on financial transactions. It also established that private sector salaries should be paid through banks, thereby adding the taxes on banking transactions.

At last, Cavallo communicated that wages, pensions, and payments to suppliers would be subject to additional cuts if other initiatives were not sufficient to guarantee a zero deficit. Such extreme measures raised concerns of a widespread loss of political support, likely to accelerate the collapse of the De La Rúa administration. On the day after the announcement of the package, the seventh under De La Rúa, withdrawals in the Argentine banking system reached U.S.$ 700 million, in addition to the U.S.$ 5 billion of the previous weeks (Gerchunoff and Llach 2003).

Protests were widespread. The State Employees Union (Associación de Trabajadores del Estado [ATE]) demonstrated in front of the Economy Ministry and demanded Cavallo's resignation. The Union of State Suppliers suspended the delivery of goods and services to the government until the magnitude of the adjustment was clear. About 85 percent of the union members were the so-called PyMEs (*pequeñas y medianas empresas*, small and medium companies), which were put under serious risks

---

[13] "Plano Cavallo tenta cortar 20% de custos de produção," *Valor Econômico*, March 22, 2001.
[14] "Pacote argentino é mal recebido," *O Globo*, June 19, 2001.
[15] "A Argentina tenta de novo,"*O Globo*, 07/09/2001; and "Argentina tem novo pacote," *Valor Econômico*, July 10, 2001.
[16] "As preocupações de Cavallo,"*O Globo*, September 7, 2001.

"Vivir con Lo Nuestro" 171

by the government measures.[17] The main workers federation, the Central General de los Trabajadores (CGT), called a general strike and organized occupations of public offices.

At that point, markets had already incorporated a default in their valuation of Argentine financial assets, and creditor governments and both international and domestic media considered the default inevitable. As cited in Duhalde (2007), "The convertibility is over to Moody's. There are not enough dollars in the formal system to sustain the parity established by the law."[18]

The situation started to collapse in the October legislative elections, when the Alliance lost about 50 percent of its share of the valid legislative vote, and the percentage of voters who cast blank or invalid ballots in protest reached an unprecedented 22 percent of the overall vote (Levitsky and Murillo 2003). In November, the government responded to increasing capital flight with the establishment of the *corralito* (playpen), which froze bank accounts and forbade withdrawals from dollar-denominated accounts.[19]

In December, after an explosion of protests and brutal repression that caused at least two dozen deaths, both Cavallo and De La Rúa resigned. In the absence of a vice president, the president of the Senate Ramón Puerta, from the PJ, temporarily assumed the office.

Still in December, a divided legislature elected Adolfo Rodríguez Saá as president.[20] Among other measures, Rodríguez Saá declared the default on the Argentine public debt. The default amounted to U.S.$ 103 billion in the hands of private savers, U.S.$ 21 billion of which were interest rates. The remaining debt, estimated at around U.S.$ 90 billion, was in the hands of privileged creditors: the International Monetary Fund, the World Bank, the Inter-American Development Bank, and the Paris Club,[21] among others. In Rodríguez Saá's words, payment would, from then on, be reverted to job creation (Duhalde 2007, p. 23).

---

[17] "Alvos do ajuste, funcionários protestam,"*O Globo*, July 14, 2001

[18] "Para Moody's finalizó la convertibilidad,"*La Nación*, June 12, 2001.

[19] With the aggravation of the crisis, the *corralito* turned into the *corralón* ("big corral"), where most deposits were forcibly exchanged for peso-denominated bonds. Dollar-denominated accounts were automatically exchanged for pesos and peso bonds at a predetermined rate.

[20] There were 169 votes in favor and 138 against his election.

[21] The Paris Club is a voluntary, informal group of 19 creditor nations that have agreed to act with a common approach to negotiate debt relief for developing countries unable to meet their external obligations. Members of the Paris Club agree to restructure and/or reduce official debt owed to them on a case-by-case basis, provided certain conditions are met. J. F. Hornbeck. "Argentina's Defaulted Sovereign Debt: Dealing with the 'Holdouts'." Congressional Research Service. February 6, 2013 (Hornbeck, 2010).

172   *The Politics of Market Discipline in Latin America*

In spite of the president's reaffirmed commitment to keeping convertibility, pressures from the industrial and financial sectors mounted, as many bankers and business owners demanded the straightforward dollarization of the economy.[22] After a very short honeymoon, violent demonstrations resumed and citizens would bang pots, pans, and other utensils outside their windows (the *cacerolazos*).

A failed meeting, at which the absence of a significant number of governors revealed the lack of political support for the president, was the trigger to Saá's resignation. The president of the Chamber of Deputies, the Peronist Eduardo Camaño, assumed office on a temporary basis.

Finally, in January 2002, the Congress elected Eduardo Duhalde, also from the PJ. Duhalde ruled over a collapsed economy; the Argentine GDP contracted by 16 percent in the first quarter of 2002, and the unemployment rate reached nearly 25 percent. More than 5 million people fell into poverty between October 2001 and June 2002, when more than half of the population lived in poverty (Levitsky and Murillo 2003). Inequality levels also rose steadily throughout the 1990s, more than in any other Latin American country, despite the strong rates of growth observed in most of the period (Singer and Rosas 2007).

The president's economic plan encompassed the end of convertibility, the maintenance of zero deficit, the pesification of debts, and the promotion of "new productive alliances" (Duhalde 2007). The government adopted a provisional fixed exchange rate of 1.4 pesos to the dollar, equivalent to a 29 percent devaluation. The total devaluation of the peso would reach 75 percent in only four months.

It is worth noting that when the government forced banks to convert their dollar-denominated accounts and debts to pesos, it mandated that deposits be converted at an exchange rate of 1 U.S.\$ = 1.4 pesos, while credits were converted at a 1 U.S.\$ = 1 peso rate. This so-called "asymmetric pesification" was designed to prevent widespread defaults that could threaten the financial system, at the expense of substantially reducing the value of banks' net worth. The asymmetric pesification was, then, partially compensated (estimates point to a 70 percent to 80 percent compensation of losses) by the government's decision to issue about U.S.\$27 billion in compensation bonds to banks in 2002, in September 2003.

---

[22] Some of the most powerful banks operating in Argentina, under the leadership of HSBC's executive Emilio Cárdenas, presented a proposal to Duhalde that included the full dollarization of the Argentine economy – the Plan Cárdenas. "Los Cruzados Del Dólar,"*Página 12*, January 20, 2002. Cited in Duhalde (2007, p. 205).

"Vivir con Lo Nuestro"   173

In its short tenure, the Duhalde administration ended convertibility, managed to stabilize the exchange rate, and avoided a major collapse. Nominated by the legislative assembly to serve until December 2003, Duhalde brought forward the date of the presidential elections in response to a crisis of governability.[23] In May 2003, Néstor Kirchner, Peronist and the former governor of Santa Cruz, was inaugurated as the fifty-fourth president of Argentina.

ROOM TO MANEUVER IN THE KIRCHNER AND FERNÁNDEZ YEARS

Even though sovereign risk increased dramatically after the Argentine collapse (Figure 8.3), Néstor Kirchner's inauguration occurred under considerably improved conditions compared to the aftermath of the 2001 default (Figure 8.4). In 2002, the Argentine economy had already started to show consistent signals of recovery, and hyperinflation had been averted. The budget was balanced, interest rates had fallen, and investment had resumed. Most important to the argument advanced here, the country's external financial requirements had dropped substantially, for two main reasons.

First, the devaluation of the peso stimulated the recovery of exports vis-à-vis imports. Exports increased from 11.5 percent of GDP in 2001 to 27.7 percent in 2002, whereas imports went from 10.2 percent to 12.8 percent of GDP. After a U.S.$ 3.9 billion deficit in 2001, which reverted to a U.S.$ 9.1 billion surplus in 2002, Argentina would produce consistent current account surpluses under Kirchner.

Moreover, the policy of de-indebtedness (*desendeudamiento*), which prevented new borrowing from multilateral agencies and maintained the cessation of payments to private creditors, further reduced the country's need of external funds. The foreign debt service, which was U.S.$ 24.0 billion in 2001, fell to U.S.$ 5.8 billion in 2002.

It was in this scenario of decreased demand for external funding – and therefore increased autonomy from creditors' influence – and with the legitimacy of a president who had not been the one to declare default,[24] that Kirchner started the renegotiation of the Argentine foreign debt.

Debt Renegotiation

The Kirchner administration had already started efforts to restructure the public debt in the beginning of 2003. Yet after the failure of initial

---

[23] "Argentina Country Report," Economist Intelligence Unit, December 2001.
[24] Kirchner stressed in his inaugural speech that "debt default was not his project." "The empty-handed social democrat," *The Economist*, May 29, 2003.

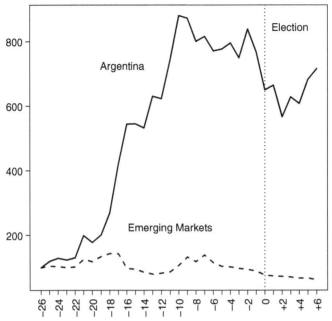

FIGURE 8.3. Argentine Sovereign Spread: 2003 Presidential Election.
Note: Spread of the Standard & Poor's Argentine Emerging Market Bond index (EMBI+) in the period that surrounded the Argentine 2003 election, 0 represents the month of the presidential election.
Source: Global Financial Data.

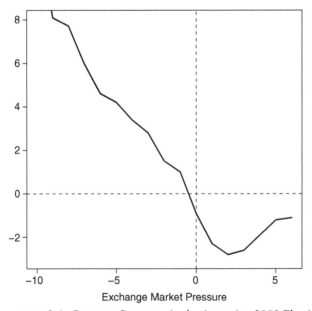

FIGURE 8.4. Currency Pressures in the Argentine 2003 Election.
Note: Evolution of currency pressures in the period around Néstor Kirchner's inauguration in 2003. Month of inauguration denoted by the vertical dashed line. The horizontal dashed line marks $EMP = 0$.

"*Vivir con Lo Nuestro*" 175

negotiations the government reached an impasse with creditors and decided to act on its own.

The first unilateral offer was presented in a meeting with bondholders in Dubai, in September of that year, almost two years after the default had been declared. The government proposed to reduce the amount owed from U.S.$ 82 billion[25] to U.S.$ 21 billion, a 75 percent haircut.[26] Taking into consideration the present value of the debt determined by the price of the bonds in secondary markets at that time, the haircut would reach 90 percent (Broder 2005).

Néstor Kirchner would make his second and last offer in 2005. This time it included a lower haircut, along with a substantial reduction in interest payments and an extension of the debt profile. The proposal had a 76 percent acceptance rate, equivalent to U.S.$ 62 billion (the "old debt"), with U.S.$ 20 billion remaining in hands of the so-called holdouts.[27] The old debt was distributed in 152 bonds in different currencies and exchanged for U.S.$ 35 billion of new debt.[28]

The renegotiation allowed Argentina to reduce its total debt from around U.S.$ 190 billion to U.S.$ 125 billion (113 to 72 percent of GDP). The average maturity of the debt increased from eight to fourteen years, while yearly interest payments dropped from U.S.$ 10 billion in 2001 to U.S.$ 3 billion in 2005. The share of dollar-denominated debt dropped from 66 to 37 percent.

Even though the country had reached a point at which the default was inevitable, and financial markets recognized that, investors were frustrated:

In the eyes of institutional creditors, the 2005 Argentine restructuring set a precedent that could not be condoned, even though a majority of bondholders accepted the terms. Although Argentina continues to argue that the restructuring was a negotiated solution, it was not a mutually agreed one. Bondholders had to accept or reject the offer with the alternative being no restitution at all (Hornbeck 2010, p. 5).

After rejecting the Argentine offer, some holdouts have sought legal remedies in the United States and other countries, as well as at the World

---

[25] The government renegotiated the principal of its private debt; debt held by multilateral agencies or the Paris Club was never included in the negotiations.

[26] In debt restructuring agreements, the *haircut* is the reduction in the amount of debt to be repaid to creditors (*Financial Times* Lexicon).

[27] Holdout creditors are those who did not accept the terms of the offer and have since then pursued litigation to force repayment.

[28] A detailed account of the terms of the renegotiation can be found in Broder (2005, p. 45).

176 *The Politics of Market Discipline in Latin America*

Bank's International Center for the Settlement of Investment Disputes (ICSID), where Argentina became the champion of lawsuits.

According to the U.S. Congressional Research Service (CSR) report quoted above, 158 suits have been filed in the United States alone. By the time this book was concluded, an additional 34 proceedings were underway at the ICSID, brought by investors under the numerous bilateral investment treaties (BITs) Argentina had signed in the 1990s. By 2010, awards had been rendered in eight ICSID cases totaling U.S.$ 913 million, but none had been executed.

U.S. creditors complained that Argentina had not fulfilled its obligations under either the bond contracts or its bilateral investment treaty with the United States. It is important to note that even if the government decided to return to global capital markets, these lawsuits would have hampered its bid to do so.

Should Argentina launch a new issue in international capital markets, it faced the threat that some of its assets could be seized. The so-called "vulture funds" – funds that purchased the defaulted Argentine debt with the goal of returning a profit on restructuring – vowed to try to block any new debt operations by Argentina. Although some of these litigations have been granted to holdouts in court, U.S. sovereign immunity laws that protected assets owned by a country abroad prevented creditors from effectively receiving this money.

Argentina, for its part, did not deny that it owed investors money for the defaulted bonds. But the government affirmed that it was "legally unable and also unwilling to pay holdouts at a more favorable rate than the creditors who accepted its swaps."[29] In light of these events, the fact that after Kirchner's offer in June 2005 and until the end of his term in 2007, the Argentine country risk was at the same level as that of Brazil points to markets' short memory in the context of the economic boom experienced in the period.

"Vivir Con Lo Nuestro"

According to Argentine political leaders and bureaucrats, the main lesson learned from the crisis was that if the country were to maintain its autonomy in economic policymaking, it would need to keep macroeconomic balance and limit its dependence on foreign finance.

Regaining and maintaining autonomy from financiers was a recurring topic in the interviews I held in Argentina, both with high bureaucrats

---

[29] "Argentina still haunted by the holdouts from the 2001 default," *MercoPress*, February 4, 2011.

"*Vivir con Lo Nuestro*" 177

involved in the debt negotiations and with members of the Fernández's administration.

The skepticism toward policies promoted by investors and multilateral institutions is evident in the words of Roberto Lavagna, the finance minister responsible for the debt renegotiation:

Argentina can not live subject to the economic politics demanded from the outside. Part of the success of these almost three years is associated with the limits we imposed. Some have even proposed, in May 2002, that we should provoke a hyperinflation that liquidated the passive of the banks. We have attempted to recover a wider room to maneuver to the country.[30]

Also,

While the party lasts the profits go to the bankers; when the "bicycle" breaks, the losses extend to the whole society (Lavagna 2011, p. 64).

Along the same lines, Kirchner declared in the presence of the most important representatives of business and financial sectors, in a meeting with the UIA:

It is time that the financial system looks beyond its own interests and thinks about the whole society; we do not ask for altruism but intelligence.... Our plan does not satisfy these strange capitalists that dislike business risks and clear rules, and only want the protection of their own interests.[31]

The Kirchner administration marked a break with the pro-market, orthodox policies of the 1990s, which the majority of Argentine voters blamed for the 2001 crisis. The government adopted a more interventionist role which sometimes strained relations with the business community but paid off in opinion polls.[32]

This strategy also set Argentina apart from the United States in the foreign realm, and all efforts under Kirchner were directed to Latin American integration and to strengthening the Mercosur. As a symbolic gesture, Brazil was the first country visited by the president.[33]

In general terms, Kirchner preserved the strategy of de-indebtedness and strict fiscal discipline inherited from Duhalde, running both fiscal and external surpluses. This strategy has been frequently referred to as living within one's own means, or *vivir con lo nuestro*.[34]

---

[30] "Roberto Lavagna: El desafío es no volver a perder una década," *La Nación*, December 11, 2004.

[31] "Kirchner fustigó al FMI y a los bancos," *La Nación*, September 03, 2003.

[32] "Argentina Country Report," Economist Intelligence Unit, December 2006.

[33] "Argentina Country Profile," Economist Intelligence Unit, 2003.

[34] This expression is attributed to Aldo Ferrer, former minister of the economy and professor of Roberto Lavagna. In its "soft" version, it refers to a need to mobilize domestic rather than external resources for development.

178   *The Politics of Market Discipline in Latin America*

Benefiting from the room to maneuver acquired after the default, Kirchner was able to advance policies that frequently collided with creditors' demands, something hardly feasible in the 1990s. These policies aimed at strengthening the productive sector (in contrast with the priority assigned to the financial sector during the Menem and De La Rúa years) and domestic income and at boosting economic growth based on consumers' demand and exports.

Macroeconomic Policies

In the macroeconomic realm, contrary to the overvalued currency of the Menem years, Kirchner maintained a cheap peso. The government targeted a competitive exchange rate and intervened in the currency market to avoid appreciation. This, in addition to import restrictions[35] and an industrial promotion law (*Ley de Promoción Industrial*) were part of a strategy of import substitution and export-led growth, aimed at running external surpluses and reducing the dependency on capital inflows.

The government also kept interest rates from rising and occasionally attempted to coerce banks into reducing lending rates, indicating the priority placed on growth promotion over inflation control.[36] As a result, the Argentine economy grew on average 8.8 percent a year from 2003 to 2007, while inflation reached 8.5 percent in 2007. The government's response to inflation was also non-orthodox; it refused to adopt inflation targets recommended by the IMF and instead resorted to administrative measures such as price agreements, caps on utility tariffs, and restrictions on food exports.

Finally, Kirchner maintained Duhalde's strategy of strict fiscal discipline. A booming economy allowed the government to increase consumption and investment while still keeping budget surpluses (Table 8.2).

Microeconomic Agenda

Kirchner's microeconomic agenda was also characterized by increased state intervention. The government nationalized private companies, subsidized and controlled tariffs of public services, and actively promoted exports while restricting imports. Public expenditures were channeled into subsidies, social programs, and public works aimed at job creation.

---

[35] An estimated 65 percent of import items need to request a discretionary license from the Ministry of Industry, which analyzes their impact on local industry before making a decision.

[36] "Argentina Country Report," Economist Intelligence Unit, December 2007.

"Vivir con Lo Nuestro"

TABLE 8.2. *Macroeconomic Indicators (% GDP) – Kirchner Years*

	2003	2004	2005	2006	2007
GDP Growth	8.8	9.0	9.2	8.5	8.3
Primary Balance	2.3	3.9	3.7	3.5	3.1
Fiscal Balance	0.5	2.6	1.8	1.8	1.2
Government Consumption	1.5	2.7	6.1	5.2	6.5
Lending Rates (%)	19.1	6.8	6.2	8.6	10.1
Consumer Prices	3.7	6.1	12.3	9.8	8.5
Unemployment (%)	17.3	13.6	11.6	10.2	8.9
Trade Balance	13.0	8.6	7.2	6.5	5.0
Reserves excl. Gold (U.S.$ million)	14,1	19,7	28,1	32,0	47,5
Gross Fixed Investment	38.2	34.4	22.7	18.2	11.5

Source: "Argentina Country Report," Economist Intelligence Unit, 2008.

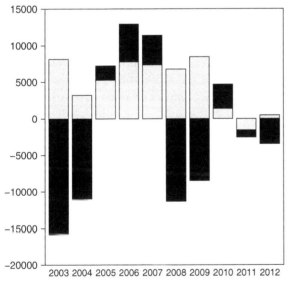

FIGURE 8.5. Balance of Payments in the Kirchner Years (US$ billion).
Note: Current account and financial account balance.
Source: ECLACstat.

NATIONALIZATIONS The Kirchner administration nationalized a number of important Argentine companies. The first was the Correo Argentino, which was renationalized in response to a debt owed by the concessionary to the state. The original plan was to restructure and later privatize the company, but good results under public management in

180   *The Politics of Market Discipline in Latin America*

2003 ruled this option out. Kirchner also nationalized water services, first by canceling the contract maintained by the state with Aguas Argentinas S.A. (AASA), and then by creating the Agua y Saneamientos Argentinos (AySA), which provides water services to 12 million citizens in Buenos Aires and 17 other municipalities. Finally, the government nationalized railroads (Ferrocarriles Belgrano Cargas y San Martín), shipyards (Domecq García), and an aeronautical pole (Polo Aeronáutico de Córdoba), among other businesses.

TRADE POLICY A report of the World Trade Organization (WTO) released in 2007 stated that:

The Kirchner administration has reiterated its commitment to an open economy, taking the view that regional and multilateral liberalization will foster social well-being. However, Argentina also considers that trade liberalization cannot be detached from the need of governments to retain sufficient room to conduct active policies in pursuit of their economic and social objectives ("Argentina trade policy review," World Trade Organization, February 2007).

Since the 2001 crisis, Argentina made wide use of antidumping measures.[37] The country also prohibited imports of several product categories and required an automatic preimportation license for all products, as well as nonautomatic import licenses or prior authorization for sanitary, environmental, and other reasons.

The Kirchner administration increased the rates and scope of export duties, mainly in the case of commodities; duties accounted for 10 percent of total tax revenues between 2002 and 2005. The government also applied suspensions and other restrictions on exports, as in the case of copper and aluminum tailings.

At the same time that Kirchner had restricted and taxed commodity exports, allegedly with the goal of keeping prices below world levels and limiting exchange rate volatility, he also promoted exports of manufactured products through the use of fiscal incentives and tax refunds, special customs areas, and the free-zone regime. The government also created special credit lines to stimulate small and medium-size businesses and incentives for companies to buy components locally.

SUBSIDIES TO PUBLIC SERVICES Public services tariffs were mostly frozen throughout the Kirchner presidency, and the few tariffs for which this was not the case were readjusted in levels lower than inflation. The government subsidized these services in order to keep them affordable and

---

[37] Between 1999 and 2006, the government initiated 111 antidumping cases and adopted 62 provisional and 88 final measures.

"Vivir con Lo Nuestro" 181

at the same time to reduce companies' losses after the crisis of 2001. The same policy of price adjustments lower than inflation and subsidies has been applied to short-, medium-, and long-distance transportation, including the subway and trains managed by private companies.

PUBLIC WORKS AND JOBS The budget of the Ministry of Planning and Public Works was raised from 2.1 million pesos in 2003 to 49.2 million in 2010. Investments were channeled into public-works programs to spur jobs and growth. Between 2003 and 2009, the Kirchner government doubled the length of Argentine railways, from 569 to 1,252 miles, while electric generation went from 17,900 to 23,800 megawatts. Gas transportation increased from 118.6 to 139.3 million cubic meters a day. In the same period, the government built 480,000 houses and repaired another 240,000, benefiting a total of 3.6 million citizens. In addition, the Kirchner administration launched the *Programa Jóvenes con Más y Mejor Trabajo*, *Programa de Trabajo Autogestionado*, and *Programa de Empleo Comunitario*, all programs that used public funds to generate jobs and promote training of individuals and small companies.

WAGE AND SOCIAL SECURITY The first initiative of Kirchner's Labor Ministry was to reestablish the National Council of Minimum Wage (*Consejo Nacional del Salario Mínimo Vital y Móvil*) after fourteen years of inactivity. The minimum wage had been fixed at 200 pesos per month throughout the 1990s and was equivalent to U.S.$ 50 per month in the beginning of 2003; it was raised to 980 pesos by the end of the Kirchner years – approximately U.S.$ 300.

The government also stimulated collective negotiations of wage agreements between workers and firms. Whereas in 2003, there were 203 collective wage agreements, in 2007 this number had doubled.

These measures led to praises by the general secretary of the World Labor Organization (WLO), the Chilean Juan Somavía:

> The experience of your country in the social dialogue is a clear manifestation of the importance of these processes in overcoming the crisis and rebuilding the nation. Argentina has shown that social dialogue and tripartism constitute an essential element of democratic governability and of the sustainability of public policies ("Elogios en la OIT a Cristina Kirchner," *La Nación*, June 8, 2007).

Somavía and the WLO complimented Argentina as an "example of a country that grew recovering employment and refusing to apply neoliberal recipes or to resort to new debt with the IMF." Finally, in 2007,

182   *The Politics of Market Discipline in Latin America*

Kirchner responded to a long-term demand of Argentine labor unions and allowed workers to choose whether to join the private pension system or a public system with a common pool. This measure was a heavy blow in the operation of the AFJPs, as prior to that they did not need to attract new members, who were automatically shared between the various providers (*administradoras*).[38]

SOCIAL POLICIES In the social front, the president attempted to recover a role that the government had lost in the 1990s – that of assisting the poor (Broder 2005, p. 149). The administration expanded programs such as the *Jefes de Hogar* and the *Manos a la Obra* and advanced plans for social inclusion of families and retired workers in the *Hambre Más Urgente*.

Other programs such as the *Programa Federal de Emergencia Habitacional* and the *Programa Federal de Reactivación de las Obras* addressed housing needs and at the same time generated jobs in public works. Kirchner also advanced programs in health (*Remediar* and *Programa Nacional de Salud Materno-Infanto-Juvenil*) and in education (*Programa Nacional de Becas Estudiantiles* and *Plan Nacional de Alfabetización*).

RELATIONS WITH CREDITORS The default and later the boom in commodity exports provided the Kirchner government with room to deviate from the investors' agenda. This room was furthered, also, by the president's decision to use Central Bank reserves to cancel Argentina's U.S.$ 9.8 billion debt with the IMF in 2005. International reserves, which reached U.S.$ 9 billion in 2001, amounted to U.S.$ 27 billion in the period. It was argued that the country would save U.S.$ 1 billion in interest rates as a result of this action.

Questionable from an economic perspective, given the relatively low interest rates charged by the IMF, the payment had clear political connotations. Kirchner accused the Fund of using the public debt to push Argentina to adopt policies that damaged economic growth, provoked pain and injustice, and presented the payment as the path to full independence from the IMF's influence.

Concurrent with the cancellation of its debt with the IMF, Argentina announced the decision to sell sovereign bonds, in a total of U.S.$ 2.5 billion, to the Venezuelan government. The declared purpose of this action was to replenish Argentine international reserves after over a third of them were used to pay the IMF. Whereas the bonds were sold at market rates, they allowed the government to delay its return to

---

[38] Interview with a congressmen specializing in the Argentine pension system, May 2011.

"Vivir con Lo Nuestro" 183

international financial markets or to IMF conditionality. Politically, the decision strengthened regional ties and the position of Venezuela vis-à-vis the United States as a source of funding to Latin American countries.[39]

With the economy growing strongly and unemployment easing toward single-digit levels for the first time in almost two decades, Kirchner maintained his popularity at around 66 percent between 2003 and 2006,[40] and managed to have his wife Cristina Fernández de Kirchner elected as his successor in 2007.

Room to Maneuver and the Reintegration into International Markets Under Cristina Fernández

Contradicting market expectations of a more "investor-friendly" presidency, Cristina Fernández, inaugurated in 2007, maintained and even furthered the economic agenda of the former administration.

Fernández maintained public expenditures on social programs and job-generating public work and nationalized the major Argentine air transportation company, Aerolíneas Argentinas. The government further raised the minimum wage from 980 to 1,740 pesos, reaching a higher than 800 percent increase since 2002. Relative to other Latin American economies, the minimum wage in Argentina was 33 percent higher than in Chile, 52 percent higher than in Brazil, and 93 percent higher when compared to that in Uruguay.[41] Collective wage agreements reached a record number of 1,286 in 2009.

Fernández also furthered the trade policy advanced under Kirchner. In 2009, the government went as far as to implement a so-called one trade policy, forcing companies that bring imports to the country to match their value with exports. According to Claudio Loser, the former IMF head for the Western Hemisphere, the country "has introduced about one hundred restrictive measures since 2009 – more than any other individual country" in the world.[42] In the macroeconomic realm, more expansive fiscal and monetary policies put pressure on inflation and wages, eroding currency and wage competitiveness.

Measures to control inflation remained non-orthodox, with efforts to control supply rather than rein in demand, and under consistent critique of the financial community.

---

[39] "Venezuela to Buy Argentine Bonds, Backs IMF Payoff," Venezuelanalysis.com, December 2, 2005.

[40] "Indicadores de opinión pública y escenarios políticos de la Argentina pos-electoral," *Poliarquia Consultores*, August 28, 2009.

[41] "El salario mínimo creció un 820 por ciento desde 2002," *Economía y Negocios*, August 9, 2010.

[42] "Argentina: Beggaring our neighbors," *Financial Times Beyond Brics*, July 14, 2011.

184   *The Politics of Market Discipline in Latin America*

The government's intervention in the National Institute of Statistics (Instituto Nacional de Estadística y Censos de la Republica Argentina [INDEC]), the organization responsible for releasing data on inflation, has also been in clear confrontation with investors, especially those who bought Argentine bonds that remunerated based on inflation rates. Markets claim that the Fernández government systematically downplayed real inflationary rates.

As previously pointed out, the convergence of Argentine and Brazilian risks in 2005 and 2006 is not compatible with backward-looking behavior on the part of investors and contradicts the expectation that markets would punish a bad debtor. The detachment of the Brazilian and Argentine EMBI+ during the Fernández presidency only strengthens the case for investors' forward-looking behavior. Interviews with portfolio investors in Argentina and an analysis of investment bank reports reveal that perceptions of increased Argentine risk are associated with the government's decreased transparency in dealing with inflation, to the more expansive macroeconomy, and to regulatory insecurity, among other policies advanced by the Fernández presidency, and not to the 2001 default.

Yet the Fernández administration resumed communication with global financial markets. In September 2009, the president announced the reopening of the debt negotiation, now imposing a 66 percent haircut on the remaining debt in the hands of holdouts. This reopening was in response to an initiative of foreign banks such as Barclays Capital and Deutsche Bank y Citigroup, in an operation named "reverse inquiry."[43]

In December, the government passed a law that allowed a new series of bonds to be bought by private creditors who did not accept the 2005 terms. The renegotiation reached a 66 percent acceptance, and with that Argentina managed to renegotiate its debts with 92 percent of its creditors, a high rate of success. According to the rating company Fitch, the renegotiation "represents a step forward to normalizing Argentina's relations with creditors."[44] Nevertheless, holdout creditors – then mainly "vulture" funds that purchased the defaulted Argentine debt with the goal of returning a profit on restructuring – still refused the terms offered in the exchange.

At the same time that it moved closer to financial markets, the government of Cristina Fernández adopted an even tougher stance than

---

[43] Reverse inquiry happens when creditors, and not the debtor, take the initiative to request the reopening of debt negotiations.

[44] "Mejora la calificación de la deuda argentina, tras el cierre del canje," *La Nación*, July 12, 2010.

"Vivir con Lo Nuestro"

Kirchner's with respect to the IMF. After the cancellation of the Argentine debt with the Fund, the administration ceased to abide by the fourth article of the IMF charter and rejected any surveillance by the Fund.

The government also remains in default of U.S.$ 6.7 billion with the Paris Club – payments have not been made since 2001. The Club typically requires debtors to have an agreement with the IMF to reschedule debt payments owed to it. However, the Fernández government resists the IMF's policy recommendations and any program with the IMF that would require structural reforms, lowering the prospects of any agreement with the Club in the near future.[45]

Argentina's isolation from international financial markets prevented major spillover effects from the international crisis of 2008, which the government took as evidence of the success of this strategy. Nonetheless, the country was not completely shielded from the effects of the crisis on commodity exports, and lower fiscal and external surpluses raised financing needs.

Fernández responded with measures that, while preserving and even enhancing the country's autonomy from finance, were also severely criticized by the international community. Among these measures were paying foreign debt with Central Bank reserves, borrowing additional funds from Venezuela, and renationalizing the social security system.

Lately, the government has disclosed intentions to return to global capital markets. Interviews with government bureaucrats and investors and presentations at meetings of the Emerging Markets Trading Association all confirm not only Argentina's willingness to rejoin the international financial community, but also the eagerness of investors to lend to the country.

Argentina's attractiveness, paradoxically, arises from the fact that the country has very low financial obligations, as most of its debt is funded by the state itself (social security system, public banks). Furthermore, a scenario of a long economic boom and abundance of foreign exchange guarantees the government's capacity to repay debt. The leadership has also signaled its willingness to do it, and its credibility is arguably boosted by Kirchners' previous condemnation of the default.

CONCLUSION

This chapter traced the relations between government and financial markets in Argentina since the 1990s to explain the substantial variation in markets' capacity to discipline four Argentine administrations.

---

[45] "Argentina Country Finance," Economist Intelligence Unit, 2010.

It started with Carlos Menem, inaugurated in the midst of an inflationary crisis that was aggravated by a confidence crisis. Markets expected the Peronist candidate to adopt an expansionary program and were surprised by his orthodox switch. Menem advanced a pro-investor agenda that included all major demands from financial markets and multilateral institutions: deregulation, privatization of companies and the pension system, priority to inflation over employment, and attempts to discipline central and local governments' fiscal policies.

Menem's program spurred euphoria in the international investment community, and turned Argentina into the poster child of emerging markets' successful neoliberalism, with its convertibility plan and the end of hyperinflation. While capital inflows persisted, current account deficits caused by an overvalued currency and trade liberalization were comfortably financed. An appreciating dollar and external crises in Mexico, Asia, Russia, and Brazil uncovered the fragility of the model, dependent on a level of fiscal discipline that was never achieved and on an exchange rate anchor that spread its rigidity to the whole economy.

Fernando De La Rúa was elected in the midst of a confidence crisis and promised to maintain convertibility, at times when even the mention to a floating exchange rate could produce panic in financial markets. Generalized dissatisfaction with ever-harsher adjustments demanded to regain markets' confidence, and therefore sustain the convertibility, led political confrontation to a level that terminated De La Rúa's government.

If during the first years under Menem the currency stabilization and a favorable international scenario created a win–win situation for citizens and investors, under De La Rúa the trade-offs involved in responding to one or the other's demands became evident. The government prioritized investors' confidence, and the crisis that followed threatened citizens' commitment to democracy itself. The slogan *que se vayan todos* ("that all of them leave") reflects the severity of the situation.

The collapse of the De La Rúa mandate was followed by a succession of provisional presidents, among them Adolfo Rodríguez Saá, who declared the default on the Argentine public debt. The Peronist Eduardo Duhalde was the last of them, and the one who finally abandoned convertibility. After a period of widespread uncertainty and fears of the return of hyperinflation, Duhalde managed to stabilize the economy once again and to turn the government to his successor Néstor Kirchner in significantly improved conditions.

Kirchner also inherited the mandate to renegotiate the defaulted debt. The deal he proposed, despite a significant haircut, was accepted by a large share of bondholders. Nevertheless, the drastic reduction of external obligations, the trauma of the crisis, and legal impediments on the part of holdouts prevented Argentina from returning to international capital markets for the following decade. A boom in commodity prices starting in 2004 boosted export revenues, further decreasing Argentina's need to access external funding.

Kirchner used this room to maneuver to break with the pro-market policies of the 1990s and to advance a redistributive, pro-poor agenda. He kept an overvalued peso that promoted exports and restrained imports, prioritized employment and growth over inflation, and maintained strict fiscal discipline that ensured autonomy from external finance. The government subsidized the prices of basic goods and services, nationalized private companies, advanced an active industrial and export promotion policy, while raising barriers to imports and imposing capital controls. It raised the budget of public works and infrastructure substantially, with the explicit goal of promoting employment.

Cristina Fernández benefited from the commodity boom and the insulation from international financial markets to further the agenda initiated during her husband's tenure.

It is still to be seen, though, whether it will be possible to maintain such autonomy in face of a deterioration of the international scenario in which commodity prices fall and/or the United States restarts to raise interest rates.

9

Who Governs? Market Discipline in the Developed World

The previous chapters disputed the conventional wisdom that markets have a strong capacity to constrain left-leaning governments in emerging economies.

The experiences of Brazil, Ecuador, Venezuela, and Argentina reveal how market discipline varies substantially over time and among countries, with most of this variation depending on factors that are exogenous to governments' and investors' choices – fluctuations in commodity prices and international interest rates.

Whereas bondholders' influence on economic policymaking is certainly substantial in periods of dollar scarcity, it is rather limited when commodity prices are high and international interest rates are low, and Latin American emerging markets experience abundant inflows of foreign currency.

In Ecuador, Rafael Correa defaulted on what he considered "illegitimate" public debt and renegotiated utility contracts in extremely favorable terms when remarkably high oil prices released the government from the necessity of building market confidence. This happened only a few years after his predecessor Lucio Guitérrez, elected on a similar agenda but under strong currency pressures, embraced a surprisingly orthodox program to receive an International Monetary Fund (IMF) loan expected to reopen Ecuador's access to international financial markets.

During a commodity boom, the government of the Justicialista Néstor Kirchner in Argentina intervened to lower interest and exchange rates, increased social spending, and nationalized key sectors of the economy, policies that conflicted with markets' preferences, while still maintaining

Who Governs? 189

risk levels comparable to the "well-behaved" Brazil. A decade earlier, a government of the same Partido Justicialista had advanced one of the most encompassing neoliberal programs in Latin America, boosting market confidence and managing to attract substantial inflows of capital in a period when they were desperately needed throughout the region.

I argued that variation in the effectiveness of market discipline between good and bad times is related to changes in the demand and supply of foreign funding available to governments in each scenario.

When commodity prices are low, Latin American low-savings-commodity-dependent economies slow down, hard currency becomes scarce and public revenues fall, forcing governments into searching for additional funds in international financial markets to meet their external financial obligations. When low commodity prices coincide with high interest rates, which prompt investors to flee emerging economies, the result is high demand but low supply of foreign funds available to governments, subjecting them to strong market discipline in an effort to attract much needed capital inflows.

In booming times, these conditions reverse; the abundance of foreign currency channelled through trade, and higher public revenues due to faster economic growth reduce governments' need to tap into international financial markets. When this concurs with a period of low interest rates, in which investors are more prone to divert capital to emerging economies, the result is low demand and high supply of foreign funds. This favorable scenario puts leftist governments in a much better position to ignore market pressures and advance their preferred agenda.

Moreover, consistent with Mosley (2003), the previous chapters have shown that whereas in "bad times," when default risk is considerable, investors extend their attention beyond the macroeconomic scenario, in "good times" leftist governments that respect the limits imposed by macroeconomic orthodoxy are able to attract strong inflows of foreign capital even while adopting a more interventionist and/or redistributive microeconomic agenda than investors would prefer.

I concluded that in good times, when default risk is negligible, bondholders' complacency in the microeconomic level and focus on macroeconomic indicators resembles the behavior claimed to be the norm in the Organisation for Economic Co-operation and Development (OECD).

After focusing on the workings of market discipline in *emerging economies* during *good times*, this chapter delves into the opposite case – the means through which discipline is imposed on leftist governments in *developed economies* during *bad times*.

190   *The Politics of Market Discipline in Latin America*

I examine the experiences of the socialist governments of Spain, Portugal, and Greece after the great recession started in 2008; in all three countries the Left was either elected or reelected in the aftermath of the crisis[1] and, even though economies had followed very different trajectories during the boom, all governments suffered and ended up acquiescing to similar market pressures toward adopting austerity measures after the crisis erupted.

Before starting, it is important to note that eurozone countries display some important differences relative to the Latin American cases discussed. First, the participation in a monetary union eliminates the effect of financial flows on the exchange rate. This circumstance is comparable to that of a dollarized Ecuador and to Argentina under a currency board, explored in Chapters 6 and 8 respectively, but quite different from Brazil, Venezuela, and Argentina after 2002.

The monetary union limited the scope for counter-cyclical monetary and fiscal policies in Spain, Portugal, and Greece. Unless governments chose to abandon the euro, their options in response to severe capital flight were restricted to a default, with all the economic and political costs involved, and/or imposing a recession aimed at restoring the balance of payments. Another alternative would be to somehow manage to re-attract private – or raise official – financial inflows, which in both cases necessarily involved advancing policies designed to reestablish market confidence.

In addition to a monetary union, the institutional context is also quite distinct from most Latin American cases, as bargaining ensued not only with private but also with public creditors over the terms of eurozone support. In Latin America, the influence of public creditors, when relevant, occurred through the IMF, which was also a key player in the eurozone crises. Yet there are no institutions comparable to the European Commission or the European Central Bank.

On one side, the existence of such institutions can be argued to reinforce market discipline. Yet from another perspective, such an international institutional framework, and the resulting stakes other eurozone members have in avoiding contagion, potentially create conditions for distressed countries to regain fiscal and external balance without the need to devalue – an alternative not available to Argentina in 2001, for example.[2]

---

[1] The Spanish PSOE (Partido Socialista Obrero Español), and the PS (Partido Socialista) in Portugal were in office before the crisis, whereas in Greece the socialists were elected soon after it started.

[2] See Mario Blejer and Guillermo Ortiz's article "What Argentina tells us about Greece," *The Economist*, February 16, 2012.

Who Governs? 191

Considering these differences, however, the eurozone cases evidence that in a scenario of severe capital flight – here also caused by a common exogenous shock, that is, the American subprime crisis – financial market discipline works in the developed world quite similarly to the way it has been shown to do in the emerging markets under similar conditions.

First, when confronted with non-negligible default risk, investors' attention in Europe expanded beyond macroeconomic indicators to encompass a far broader range of governments' supply-side policies. Second, the need to build market confidence in times of capital scarcity prompted leftist governments in all three countries to renounce their agenda in favor of an orthodox economic program.

Boom and Crisis in the Eurozone

The creation of the eurozone in 1999 led to a very quick convergence of risk perceptions among financial investors with respect to member countries. Figure 9.1a shows the yields of sovereign bonds paid by Spain, Portugal, and Greece, compared to Germany, the lowest yield in the region. Between 2002 and 2008 the difference between these yields became practically inexistent, evidence that in this period bondholders attributed similar risks to bonds issued by the Greek and the German governments.

In consequence of the remarkable adjustment of risk perceptions, these economies were swept by a wave of capital inflows that accelerated economic growth (Figure 9.1b) but also led them into widening current account (Table 9.2) and, in some cases, fiscal deficits (Table 9.1).[3] After a decade of bonanza, the American subprime crisis led these inflows to a sudden stop, with severe consequences to governments and the private sector in all cases, irrespective of the trajectory each economy had followed in the previous years.

Even though signals of contagion had already been felt when the Bank of England had to offer emergency funding to Northern Rock in 2007, in the first bank run in the United Kingdom since 1866, the fall in British stock markets of January 2008 – the largest since September 11, 2001 – was considered to mark the spread of the American crisis to European markets. By that time, the crash was interpreted as a response to U.S. President George W. Bush's emergency U.S.$145 billion package, considered by analysts to be "too little, too late."[4]

---

[3] Spain, Portugal, and Ireland were part of the states that originally formed the eurozone in 1999; Greece entered the zone in 2001.

[4] "London shares in biggest fall since 9/11," *The Guardian*, January 21, 2008.

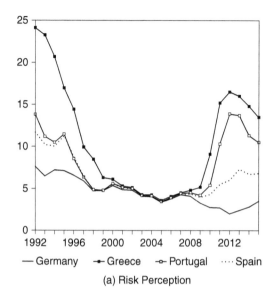

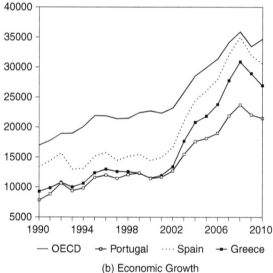

FIGURE 9.1. The Eurozone Boom.
Note: Long-term sovereign bond yields (basis points) and gross domestic product per capita (current U.S.$).
Source: Economist Intelligence Unit.

A few months later, in September 2008, Fannie Mae and Freddie Mac, two American government-sponsored enterprises (GSE) responsible for providing a secondary market in home mortgages and owing U.S.$5 trillion of mortgage-backed securities, were taken over by the U.S.

Who Governs?

TABLE 9.1. *Fiscal Results (% GDP)*

	2000	2001	2002	2003	2004	2005	2006	2007	2008	2009
Spain	−0.5	0.2	0.3	0.7	−0.3	1.3	2.0	2.4	−2.0	−8.6
Portugal	−2.6	−3.9	−2.5	−2.7	−3.3	−5.5	−3.9	−2.6	−2.6	−8.7
Greece	−3.7	−4.6	−4.8	−5.7	−7.3	−5.3	−5.9	−6.6	−9.5	−15.3

Notes: Central government budget: deficit/surplus (% GDP).
Source: OECD Statistics.

government. In the same month, Lehman Brothers – the fourth largest investment bank in the United States – filed for bankruptcy protection after incurring billions of dollars in losses due to the mortgage crisis, and the U.S. government spent U.S.$85 billion to bail out the multinational insurance corporation American International Group (AIG).

In response to these events, U.S. Treasury Secretary Henry Paulson proposed a rescue plan,[5] which authorized the government to buy troubled assets at discounts from financial institutions.

In October, Hungary, Ukraine, and Iceland suffered sudden banking and currency crises as foreign funds dried up. Hungary was the first to receive IMF help, followed by Ukraine a month later. In November, the Fund approved a loan to Iceland, at the same time that the euro area officially entered into recession.

The contagion took different forms in each country; in Greece, a highly indebted government experienced a collapse of available funding as international capital markets became dramatically risk averse, the same happening to some measure in Portugal even though public deficits had never reached Greek levels. In Spain, where the government had been fiscally conservative until the crisis, contagion started as investors' panic raised costs of financing to a point in which markets started to question whether the government would be able to serve its debt. In common, only the fact that in all cases crises were triggered by the sudden stop of capital inflows in economies that got used to abundance, and in which currency devaluation was not an option.

GREECE After joining the eurozone in 2002, improved risk perception prompted a sudden availability of international funding to the Greek economy, lowering interest rates and spurring a spending splurge that made the country increasingly reliant on foreign finance. During this period, an average growth of 4 percent a year shortened the gap between Greece and other OECD economies (Figure 9.1b).

---

[5] The "Troubled Assets Relief Program."

194   *The Politics of Market Discipline in Latin America*

TABLE 9.2. *Current Account (% GDP)*

	1990-7	2000	2001	2002	2003	2004	2005	2006	2007	2008
Spain	−1.7	−4.0	−4.0	−3.2	−3.5	−5.3	−7.4	−9.0	−10.0	−9.7
Portugal	1.6	−10.4	−10.3	−8.2	−6.5	−8.4	−10.4	−10.7	−10.1	−12.6
Greece	−2.1	−7.8	−7.2	−6.5	−6.6	−5.9	−7.5	−11.2	−14.3	−14.8

Notes: Current Account surplus/ deficit (%of GDP).
Source: OECD Statistics.

Abundant inflows of capital allowed the Greek government to refinance its huge debt – equivalent to more than 100 percent of the GDP – on increasingly favorable terms, lowering the debt service as a share of the country's GDP. Nevertheless, different from countries like Spain and Ireland, capital inflows also funded a dramatic rise in budget deficits (Table 9.1).

Moreover, inflation higher than in other eurozone countries mined the competitiveness of the Greek economy, and caused a fast deterioration of the country's current account. The deficit reached 14.3 percent of GDP in 2007 (Table 9.2).

Still, early in 2009 markets' worst-case scenario for Greece predicted a shallow recession.[6] It was in this context of mild pessimism that the socialist Pasok won a landslide victory in the October general election, promising a €2.5 billion stimulus package in response to the crisis that would be partly financed by tax increases for high-income earners, as well as a crackdown on tax evasion.[7]

The election was perceived as a rebuke of the recent European strengthening of right-of-center parties, with the Communist Party winning 7.1 percent of the vote, and the leftist Syriza 4.6 percent. The conservative New Democracy Party, which had already lost popularity over a series of financial scandals, was defeated after announcing intentions to advance a two-year wage freeze, tax increases, and further liberalization measures in response to the crisis.

After inauguration, however, the new prime minister Georges Papandreou disclosed fiscal conditions that worsened the prospects for the Greek economy dramatically. To the shock of other European governments and the financial community, the deficit for 2008 was revised upwards and provisional estimates for 2009 were calculated in 14

---

[6] "A very European crisis," *The Economist*, February 4, 2010.
[7] "Greek Socialists win landslide victory," *Financial Times*, October 4, 2009.

Who Governs? 195

TABLE 9.3. *Government Debt (% GDP)*

	2002	2003	2004	2005	2006	2007	2008	2009
Spain	43.9	40.7	39.3	36.4	33.0	30.0	33.7	46.1
Portugal	58.7	60.2	63.0	68.2	69.8	69.2	71.2	81.1
Greece	109.2	105.8	108.3	110.3	107.5	105.8	109.6	125.7

Notes: Central Government Debt (%of GDP).
Source: OECD Statistics.

percent, while public debt was expected to reach 115 percent of GDP at end-2009 (Table 9.3).[8]

Even though Greece had been consistently incurring substantial fiscal and current account deficits and yet paying interest rates comparable to Germany for a decade, the news provoked panic among holders of the country's sovereign bonds, and justified Fitch and S&P downgrades of Greek sovereign bonds below the A rating for the first time in ten years, marking the beginning of the confidence crisis.[9]

PORTUGAL Different from Greece, the global crisis hit Portugal after a decade of sluggish economic growth when, rather than catching up with its European partners, the Portuguese GDP per capita fell from 78.3 percent of the European Union average to 75.3 percent (Figure 9.1b).

As in the other two cases, lower interest rates after joining the euro spurred a consumption boom in Portugal, with citizens borrowing heavily to buy houses, cars, and airline tickets. Easy credit and rising wages, which reduced the country's competitiveness relative to China and Eastern Europe, contributed to a current account deficit that averaged 9.6 percent of GDP between 2001 and 2008 (Table 9.2). In a country once considered an exemplary saver, the net foreign debt reached 96 percent of GDP in 2008.

Homeowners and businesses borrowed most of this capital; banks' gross debt hit 120 percent of GDP. Low savings and a large share of foreign debt left the country highly vulnerable to a sudden change in market sentiment. Feeble economic growth and cheap money contributed to deteriorating public accounts (Table 9.1).

Amidst unfavorable economic prospects, the Socialist Party (PS) was reelected in September 2009 with a legislative minority, in an poll in

---

[8] "Greece: Staff report on request for stand-by arrangement," IMF Country Report No. 10/110, May 2010.

[9] Under normal circumstances, which had been provisionally relaxed after the 2008 crisis, a BBB rating meant that the government would lose access to the European Central Bank's liquidity operations.

196   *The Politics of Market Discipline in Latin America*

which 40 percent of the Portuguese electorate did not vote. Expectations of a 3 percent contraction of the GDP, and a 9 percent unemployment rate substantiated the negative outlook placed by Fitch by the end of 2009, and the warning of the first downgrade of the Portuguese sovereign debt, which did not take long to occur.

SPAIN The years preceding the crisis were extremely favorable to the Spanish economy. Between 1995 and 2008, real output increased by 58 percent in the country, allowing a fast catch-up with other OECD economies (Figure 9.1b). Inflation remained low, and unemployment fell from 24 percent to 8 percent despite women and immigrants' increased participation in the labor force.

Strong capital inflows were key to these results; Spain had been the largest single beneficiary of EU regional funds and private inflows increased dramatically after the country's admission to the eurozone. A sharp fall in interest rates and in the costs of mortgages – from 18 percent to below 5 percent rates – prompted a housing boom, during which more homes were built in the country than in France, Germany, and the Benelux combined.[10]

Economists attributed most of Spain's differential growth rates with the EU to the credit-fueled property boom, and the country was at some point described as a "monoculture of bricks and mortar alone."[11]

As a result of the boom, a fast growing construction sector boosted jobs and attracted immigrants. Between 1999 and 2007, more than a third of all new jobs in the eurozone were generated in Spain (Harrington 2011), and the population grew by 13 percent.

Growth and consumption spurred a substantial rise in imports, which, in addition to external borrowing to acquire housing units and land, raised the current account deficit from around 3 percent in 2002 to 10 percent of the GDP in 2007 (Table 9.2). Foreign borrowing reached €870 billion, or 80 percent of the GDP by the end of 2008 (Harrington 2011).

As in other cases, the immediate effect of the international financial turmoil was a credit squeeze at home. Once the European Central Bank raised interest rates in response to the crisis, credit available to the government and the private sector was restricted, causing a sudden burst of the housing bubble.

The crisis in the real estate market imposed major consequences to the Spanish economy. Because the construction sector accounted for 13

---

[10] "The morning after," *The Economist*, August 11, 2011.
[11] "Boomtime Spain waits for the bubble to burst,"*Financial Times*.

Who Governs? 197

percent of total employment in Spain, as housing prices began to fall and demand halted, unemployment jumped to 10 percent, and payment of unemployment benefits increased correspondingly. In addition, a fall in indirect taxes (income and corporate profits taxes) and in the value-added tax led to a 4.4 percent decrease in government revenues over GDP between 2007 and 2008.[12]

Falling housing prices and an increasing number of foreclosures put financial institutions that lent to the housing sector under extreme pressure. Even though the Spanish financial system was initially stronger than many of its counterparts, half of the banking system was composed of regional savings banks – the cajas – that loaned mostly to clients considered undesirable by larger banks.[13] The construction industry also owed billions of euros to Spanish banks.

Reflecting the downturn, Spain grew by just 0.1 percent between the first and the second quarters of 2008, its slowest pace since 1993. By the fall of 2008, inflation had turned into deflation and unemployment reached 11.3 percent, a third higher than a year earlier.

Still, when the crisis hit, the Spanish government was in relatively good conditions compared to its Western European counterparts. In 2007, the budget surplus had reached 2.4 percent of the GDP (Table 9.1). Public debt was only 30 percent of GDP, down from 44 percent in 2002, and low compared to 104 percent in Italy and even 44 percent in Britain.

It was under these conditions that the socialist José Luis Zapatero was reelected as prime minister in March 2008, promising to rely on the government's solid fiscal position to launch a stimulus program designed to revive the economy and create jobs.

The Confidence Game: Markets' and Governments' Responses to the Crisis

Higher interest rate spreads, economic slowdown, and initial stimulus policies raised public indebtedness and speculations about European governments' actual capacity to honor their obligations. By mid-2008 the price of credit default swaps – an insurance against bond defaults and

---

[12] Similar to Ireland, tax collections generated by the value-added tax and a capital gains tax associated with the real estate boom were the main components of government's revenues during booming years (Fernández-Villaverde and Ohanian 2010, p. 12).

[13] The cajas were less regulated than other banks, less subject to supervision, and more deeply invested in the Spanish real estate market than the government was aware when the crisis hit. By 2008, cajas owned 56 percent of the country's mortgages, and loan payments from property developers accounted for a fifth of their assets (Harrington 2011, p. 7).

indicators of risk in debt markets – had jumped for many European economies, among them Greece, Spain, and Portugal.

As market sentiment spiraled, investors' concern with budget tightening, and demands for specific policies that would make it credible became more explicit. To roll debt and fund widening deficits, governments were forced into a structural redesign of the role of the state in the economy, which involved cuts in welfare policies, consolidation of the public sector, and privatization.

Leaders' capacity to advance structural programs depended on the cohesiveness of the incumbent party or the ruling coalition, its status in the legislature, and the level of support offered by the opposition. In Greece and Spain, strong public reaction raised even further the political costs of an austerity agenda. What started as strikes organized by major labor unions later extended to private-sector workers and non-organized citizens. Yet neither political opposition nor protests or strikes were sufficient to counteract pressures toward austerity.

In a first moment, risk agencies and institutional investors, through financial and risk reports, drove the policy agenda by signaling what measures should be advanced if governments were to restore confidence. Newspapers such as the *Financial Times* and *The Economist* were also key players in Europe's confidence game, as they offered political leaders and finance ministers an outlet for communicating with markets, one in which they could reveal new plans, reinforce their resolve, or express frustration with downgrades or with an unsuccessful bond issuance.

Once governments actually initiated bailout programs, however, economic policies became increasingly determined by the so-called troika – the European Commission (EC), the International Monetary Fund (IMF), and the European Central Bank (ECB) – and attached to loan agreements.

Even though it could be argued that these policies were mainly influenced by the preferences of leading European economies, most likely Germany, throughout the period of negotiation they were still conspicuously justified as necessary conditions to reestablishing market confidence.

In the letter of agreement with Greece, for example, the IMF specified restoring confidence and fiscal sustainability as the program's first priority.[14] The Fund explained that previous measures taken by the Greek government had "failed to calm the market," and that "markets were further unsettled by what was perceived to be insufficiently clear financing assurances from euro partner countries." As a result, "concerns about

---

[14] The others were to restore competitiveness and safeguard financial sector stability.

Who Governs? 199

fiscal sustainability deepened and market sentiment weakened further, triggering a confidence crisis."

Still in the letter, the IMF declared that, to bolster confidence, regain market access, and put the debt-to-GDP ratio on a declining path, it envisaged the necessity of "an exceptionally strong frontloaded fiscal effort, with fully identified measures through 2013."

The same applies to the letter of intent of the Portuguese government, which also justified the initiatives agreed as necessary to restore market confidence, a term used in nine pages out of a twenty-seven-page document.

Ultimately, evidence that austerity policies were primarily oriented toward the need to build confidence in the investment community is the fact that Spain, even in the absence of an IMF bailout,[15] pursued an agenda similar to that imposed on Portugal and Greece.

Greece

In December 2009, Standard & Poor's (S&P) and Fitch downgraded Greece's sovereign bonds from A– to BBB+, the first lower-than-A grade in ten years.

George Papaconstantinou, the country's new finance minister, responded with the promise of doing "whatever was required" to reduce the record budget deficit and achieve medium-term fiscal targets. Toward this end, the government announced an ambitious three-year stability and growth program (S&GP), including among other measures the reduction of civil service employment through a hiring freeze in 2010, and a 5:1 rule from 2011 onward (one new hire for every five retirements); a 10 percent cut in salary entitlements coupled with no nominal wage increases for monthly salaries exceeding €2,000 in the public sector for 2010, and a significant consolidation in public sector institutions. The program was portrayed as "Greece's passport" to borrowing almost €54 billion on international markets to fund its public debt.[16]

Investors regarded the plan as too vague; cuts to the public-sector wage bill were considered small when set against Greece's huge deficit, and timid when compared to actions that were being taken in Ireland in the same period. Greece had one of the most generous, and therefore expensive, state pension systems among OECD countries, and analysts no longer considered this sustainable.

---

[15] It was only in mid-2012 that Spain finally accepted rescue funds to its stressed banking sector.

[16] "Summary of Greek stability & growth programme," Reuters, January 14, 2010.

200   *The Politics of Market Discipline in Latin America*

Reflecting the skepticism toward the country's economic prospects, the costs of insuring Greek debt rose to fresh heights, bonds markets dipped to a twelve-month low and yields reached their highest levels since 2004. As reported by the Economist Intelligence Unit, markets were "dissatisfied with a rhetoric of long-term, structural change, rather than specific, drastic measures."[17]

Pasok's reluctance was interpreted as a preference for consensus with trade unions and other social groups, and as evidence of the fears of provoking a crisis with "populists" from within the party, who pushed for increases in government spending.

Trade unions, however, reacted to the announcements by staging a symbolic takeover of the Finance Ministry and threatening to organize a twenty-four-hour strike. As highlighted in the *The Economist*, the Greek leadership was faced with the choice of either accepting markets' demands and deeply cutting the country's welfare state, or refusing to do so and suffering the damages imposed by intense capital flight:

A bolder package of budget cuts might secure bond-market finance at tolerable interest rates. The Greek government says it has to strike a balance between budget cuts and keeping its "social partners" happy. But if it is too kind to public-sector workers, pensioners and so forth, it will struggle to find buyers for its bonds. If the bond markets are closed to Greece, the country will face bail-out or default. Neither option is likely to contribute much to social peace. ("Greece's sovereign-debt crunch: A very European crisis," *The Economist*, February 4, 2010.)

As panic escalated, in April eurozone members announced a rescue package of up to €30 billion over the following year, to be supplemented by €15 billion in IMF funds. After three previous rounds of austerity measures, which failed to convince financial markets that Greece could bring its public finances under control, fears that markets may drive up yields again following Fitch's downgrade of Greece's sovereign rating forced Prime Minister Papandreou to finally activate the package. In the words of the premier of Luxembourg and president of the Eurogroup, this was the step of clarification the markets were waiting for.[18]

In May 2010, Greece finally received not the initially expected €30 billion, but a €110 billion rescue loan – equivalent to 47 percent of the country's nominal GDP in 2010. The package was conditional on expenditure measures that included the elimination of the Easter, Summer, and Christmas pensions and wages, cuts in allowances and high pensions, employment reductions, cuts in discretionary and low priority

---

[17] "Greek Country Report," Economist Intelligence Unit, January 2010, p. 3.
[18] "Eurozone in €30bn loans deal for Greece," *Financial Times*, April 12, 2010.

Who Governs?

investment spending, untargeted social transfers, consolidation of local governments, and lower subsidies to public enterprises.

On the revenue side, the government committed with increasing the standard value-added tax (VAT) rate from 21 to 23 percent and the reduced rate from 10 to 11 percent, moving lower taxed products such as utilities, restaurants, and hotels to the standard VAT rate, and increasing excises on fuel, cigarettes, and tobacco to bring them in line with EU averages, among other measures.

In response, Greek trade unions promised strikes to protest against any measures that threatened salaries, pensions, and employment rights, warning they would "take the road of social resistance and increased mobilization."[19]

Though harsh, the measures agreed on in the rescue package did not prevent Standard & Poor's from downgrading Greece's credit rating a few days later, then to junk status. The downgrade happened *in tandem* with widespread protest among Greek citizens, in response to the austerity package announced. In spite of the increasing violence of the protests, the prime minister reiterated his commitment to implementing the package.

Alex Tsipras, the leader of the small but vocal left-wing party Syriza, called for a snap election[20] on the grounds that the Socialists did not have a mandate to carry out austerity measures, having been elected on the promise of increasing welfare spending as the country moved deeper into recession.

In February 2011, a month after Fitch finally joined Standard & Poor's and Moody's in another downgrade of Greek sovereign bonds, and amid skyrocketing financing costs, the Greek parliament passed tax legislation to remove several legal and administrative obstacles to effective revenue administration. In addition, the Ministry of Finance published its first comprehensive anti-tax-evasion action plan.

The government later announced the details of an ambitious privatization program, which included selling stakes in public telecommunications, banking, transportation, and water companies to constitute a sovereign-wealth fund that would be used to buy back heavily discounted government bonds. Initial plans to raise €7 billion by asset sales were expanded to €50 billion, after the troika concluded that other reforms were not bearing fruit.

---

[19] "Greece grasps for €30bn rescue package," *Financial Times*, April 23, 2010.

[20] Snap elections – called earlier than required, either by law or convention – are a feature of some parliamentary systems, often used to capitalize on a unique electoral opportunity or to decide a pressing issue.

202 *The Politics of Market Discipline in Latin America*

By June 2011, Greece's GDP had shrunk by 5.5 percent on a yearly basis, while investment had decreased to 19.2 percent and household consumption to 7.8 percent, discouraging recovery hopes and feeding fears of a default. Two-year bond yields had jumped to 30 percent.

Loans to pay debt maturing in July were conditional on the Greek parliament backing new austerity measures, with the prime minister fighting to persuade his own party, let alone the opposition, of the need to pass them. Political backlash led to the replacement of Finance Minister George Papaconstatinou – unpopular with the Socialist Party and seen as the harsh face of austerity – with the former minister of defense Evangelos Vernizelos.

In July, after the Greek parliament passed a €28 billion austerity bill, the European finance ministers approved a €8.7 billion aid payment likely to prevent Greece from defaulting. Still in the same month, EU leaders finally agreed on a new €109 billion bailout, now including a €37 billion participation of private bondholders, with the goal of "supporting Athens until it is able to return to the financial markets."[21]

Yet once again, instead of calming markets, the initiative raised expectations of a default; Greek one-year bonds traded at 172 percent, compared to 20 percent in June. For the sake of comparison, a close-to-default Belize had eighteen-year bonds trading at 15 percent, while Venezuela had nine-year bonds trading at 14 percent.[22]

More than 100,000 striking workers did not prevent the Greek parliament from approving the new austerity bill on its first reading, expected to increase the chances that the country would receive another €8 billion tranche from the European bailout loan.

Popular protests mounted after Greece agreed to another €7 billion of spending cuts and tax increases in the 2012 budget. Protestors threw petrol bombs, as well as marble paving slabs at police officers. The latest round of austerity measures was denounced as an unprecedented blow on job security, with 30,000 public-sector workers expected to lose their jobs by December 2011. Workers employed in the private sector, where more than 250,000 jobs were cut since 2009, also protested against the government's decision to suspend sectoral wage agreements.

Private banks, shops, cafés, and supermarkets were closed, along with government offices, schools, museums, ancient sites, and passenger shipping services. Air-traffic controllers staged a 12-hour strike that

---

[21] "EU leaders agree on a €109 billion Greek bail-out,"*Financial Times*, July 21, 2011.
[22] "Greek Bond yields rise to unprecedented levels," *Financial Times*, September 13, 2011.

Who Governs? 203

caused 150 flight cancellations and delays.[23] Prime Minister Papandreou pledged to stand firm against protests.

Amid escalating political crisis, European leaders finally reached a new €130 billion rescue package aimed at reducing Greek public debt to 120 percent of the GDP by the end of the decade (note that early during the crisis this level was 113 percent, and already considered far beyond sustainability). Greece agreed to put €15 billion of the revenues raised by privatization of state companies back into the European Stabilization Facility (EFSF),[24] on top of previous commitments.

Political tension increased as protests continued, sparked by additional hostility raised as a pan-European task force – a team of EU civil servants – arrived in the country with the goal of sharing its administrative expertise in activities such as privatization, tax collection, small business lending, accelerating the disbursement of EU funding, and ultimately assisting in the "modernization" of the country's public administration.

Surprising EU leaders, party allies, and voters alike, Prime Minister Papandreou announced plans to call a referendum to approve the second €109 billion EU bailout deal less than a week after it was agreed to with international creditors at an EU summit.

The move reinforced concerns that political pressures and popular reactions to austerity measures were getting beyond control of the government and caused alarm in the international community. European leaders threatened to cut off an already overdue tranche of €8 billion in international aid to Greece as they put pressure on Athens over the referendum. Such pressures forced the Greek opposition to take a favorable stance with respect the new package, which provided Papandreou with a justification to back down from the referendum.

With no remaining support, the prime minister resigned. In November 2011 Lucas Papademos, a former central banker, agreed to serve as caretaker prime minister until new elections were called. Among his main priorities were the ratification of the €130 billion rescue package and implementation of the policies attached to it.[25]

Portugal

In response to the negative outlook placed by Fitch in September 2009, the newly reelected socialist prime minister José Sócrates immediately

---

[23] "Greece approves austerity bill on first reading," *Financial Times*, October 19, 2011.

[24] The EFSF's mandate is to safeguard financial stability in Europe by providing financial assistance to euro area Member States.
Source: European Stabilization Facility website: http://www.efsf.europa.eu/about/index.htm.

[25] Greece swears in unity cabinet and PM Lucas Papademos," BBC News Europe, November 11, 2011.

204   *The Politics of Market Discipline in Latin America*

declared that his "overriding concern was to restore confidence in the Portuguese economy and stimulate growth to lift the country out of recession."[26]

Still, the head of global economics with Fitch Ratings denied any intention to remove the negative outlook it placed on Portugal in September as a result of the budget proposals, and reiterated that the measure implied a probable credit downgrade within 12 to 18 months.

Even though other agencies had also warned Portugal of a possible downgrade of its long-term debt rating, the government emphasized that budget measures to cut the deficit were for the good of the economy and not designed to comply with the recommendations of international economists or ratings agencies.[27]

A troubled Greek economy and rumors of a Spanish downgrade triggered a sell-off of Portuguese debt in February 2009, with share prices in Lisbon falling by more than 4 percent and yields on ten-year government bonds reaching 4.8 percent, the highest level for almost a year. The cost of insuring Portuguese debt reached a record high in the same period, forcing the Portuguese finance minister, Fernando Teixeira dos Santos, to reaffirm the country's commitment to take the necessary measures to cut the deficit to less than 3 percent by 2013.

Further downgrades of Greek and also Portuguese sovereign debt triggered additional sell-offs in stock and debt markets in April, when the country's ten-year bond yield rose to its highest value in a decade. The government's limited access to international capital markets increased its dependence on funding from the European Central Bank. According to Standard & Poor's, the government would need to "implement fiscal consolidation over and above its current plans" if it were to meet its deficit targets by 2013.[28]

Despite complaining that a speculative attack was taking place against the euro and Portugal's sovereign debt, the government responded once again with promises to implement the austerity measures planned for 2011, now explicitly targeted at regaining the confidence of international financial markets after the downgrade. The third austerity package announced in less than two weeks since the onset of the crisis included an increase of the capital gains tax and of the income tax of high earners, a crisis tax on wages and big companies, the introduction of new road tolls, and cuts in unemployment and other welfare payments. The

---

[26] "Portugal vows to cut deficit by two thirds," *Financial Times*, January 27, 2010.
[27] "Portugal vows to cut deficit by two thirds," *Financial Times*, January 27, 2010.
[28] "Portugal to rush through austerity measures," *Financial Times*, April 28, 2010.

Who Governs? 205

government also revealed the decision to postpone indefinitely the building of a new international airport, among other infrastructure plans that included high-speed train links and hospital and school renovations, previously defended as vital to lifting Portugal out of recession and creating jobs.

Even though analysts recognized that the Portuguese fiscal situation was not as worrisome as in Greece, and that the government was putting forward all measures demanded by risk agencies and investors, it was also clear to them that none of these would matter in the event of a turn in market sentiment. In such a scenario, speculations about whether Portugal would be the next economy to collapse could easily turn into a self-fulfilling prophecy.

Additional downgrades seemed to confirm these expectations and to aggravate the crisis; each downgrade was followed by higher costs of capital that increased indebtedness, and by the announcement of new austerity measures that reduced growth prospects, justifying the next downgrade.

In September 2010, the Portuguese government announced one more package explicitly designed to reassure markets that deficit-reduction targets would be met and emergency funding would be avoided. It included new increases in the VAT and further wage cuts in public-sector jobs, as well as a freeze in state pensions in 2011 and a 25 percent reduction in social payments.[29]

Different from Greece, where the opposition sided with protesters against austerity measures, in Portugal the support of the center-right Partido Social Democrata (PSD) was considered by investors as important as the measures themselves. An economist affirmed in the *Financial Times* that "one of the biggest concerns in international markets has been whether the minority government has the capacity to implement the deficit-cutting measures it has announced."[30]

Yet the fiscal package of September 2010 received the full support of the opposition PSD, whose leader Pedro Passos Coelho had backed the government in the approval of an accelerated, tougher fiscal austerity package, arguing that "political stability was needed to face the pressure of international financial markets."[31]

The priority of regaining market confidence became more explicit as the crisis deepened in Portugal. Prime Minister Sócrates announced measures under extreme pressure from the European Union "to send a clear

---

[29] "Portugal announces austerity package," *Financial Times*, January 29, 2010.
[30] "Portugal pledges tough measures to cut deficit," *Financial Times*, May 03, 2010.
[31] "Portugal Country Report," Economist Intelligence Unit, September 2010, p. 10.

206   *The Politics of Market Discipline in Latin America*

message to international bond markets that it had the will and the capacity to control its public finances." José Manuel Barroso, president of the European Commission and himself a former prime minister of Portugal, declared to the *Financial Times* that "It is important that Portugal doesn't let us down.(...) [the country] cannot deviate a millimeter from its budget commitments."[32] Yet the bailout of Ireland later that year struck a major blow against these efforts.

Amid tense negotiations to approve another austerity package and a twenty-four-hour general strike called by its two trade union confederations, the Portuguese prime minister managed to approve the 2011 budget, which unions considered brutal. The bill once again increased the VAT, cut public wages by 5 percent, froze state pensions, and chopped welfare payments, in the hope that the difficult measures would strengthen market confidence.[33]

Analysts considered the cut in civil-service wages, in particular, as "one of the most consequential and politically costly measures contained in the budget, intended as a signal to international investors that Portugal was willing to make difficult decisions to control its public finances."[34]

Days later, the opposition leader Pedro Passos Coelho for the first time admitted the possibility that the country might need IMF help, while Moody's announced its intention to downgrade the Portuguese debt once again. A senior analyst attested to the sell-fulfilling nature of Portugal's crisis, affirming that Portugal's solvency was not in question, but the elevated price the country was forced to pay to finance its debt imposed severe risks: "If bond yields remained high, the government could face difficulties in meeting its funding needs."[35]

Despite a strong consensus among Portuguese economists, bankers, and business owners that all efforts should be directed to avoiding a bailout, in January it was already considered just a matter of time.

Increased tensions weakened the political support for the socialist government. As the bailout was accepted as inevitable, the formerly supportive center-right opposition demanded the resignation of Prime Minister Sócrates. The PSD leader Pedro Passos Coelho denounced the need to resort to outside funds as an unacceptable political failure that revealed that Sócrates was no longer in a position to lead the country.

---

[32] "Portugal announces austerity package," *Financial Times*, September 29, 2010.
[33] "Portugal seeks to boost market confidence," *Financial Times*, November 28, 2010.
[34] "Portugal Country Report," Economist Intelligence Unit, December 2010, p. 13.
[35] "Moody's warns Portugal on bond rating," *Financial Times*, December 21, 2010.

Who Governs?

In March 2011, the Portuguese government announced further austerity measures, once again aimed at calming nervous financial markets and reducing prospects of a bailout. The new package, drafted with input from the European Central Bank and the European Commission as an additional guarantee that Lisbon would meet its fiscal targets, included up to 10 percent cuts in state pensions above €1,500 a month, as well as reductions in health spending, unemployment benefits, and other welfare payments. State infrastructure projects would be further delayed, and new government concessions launched to increase revenue. Labor market reforms would encompass cuts in lay-off compensation payments. Once again, the measures announced did not convince investors about Portugal's prospects, and a downgrade by Moody's raised costs of capital to unprecedented levels.

The defeat in a parliamentary vote on the new austerity policies – the fourth package in twelve months – put additional pressures on the socialist minority government. Claiming that the new measures were limited and ineffectual, and demanded unjust sacrifices from the most vulnerable members of society, the PSD called for snap elections. Concerns over a potential political crisis served only to heighten the yields on Portuguese sovereign bonds.

The crisis culminated with the resignation of Prime Minister Sócrates and an election in June 2011. The irony of the situation was that the PSD's refusal to approve new austerity measures and the political turmoil that followed made the same measures even more urgent to calm panicked investors. After an S&P downgrade to one level above junk, Portugal finally submitted its formal request for a €78 billion bailout package from the European Union and the IMF.

As expected, the two-party coalition led by the PSD won the majority of seats in the general election. In a melancholic repetition of history, the new prime minister Pedro Passos Coelho pledged to do "whatever it takes" to avoid the Greek path, exactly the same words his predecessor used at the onset of the crisis. Not surprisingly at this point, the pledge did not prevent Moody's from once again downgrading Portuguese bonds, this time to junk, in the first blow taken by the new government.

Notably, markets barely moved in response to the election; as stated in the *Financial Times*, "what markets know is that whichever party is in power, it will have to implement structural reforms."[36]

The new government's program brought no surprise; fresh austerity measures, on top of previous initiatives aimed at cutting the country's

---

[36] "Portugal: Different leader, same problems," *Financial Times*, June 6, 2011.

budget deficit to zero in less than five years, were expected to reduce public-sector wages and pensions by about 20 percent compared with 2010.

The PSD administration also promised to accelerate the privatization program, create a "solidarity tax" on highest incomes, extend the public-sector wage freeze to 2012 and 2013, further downsize public jobs, increase hours of work with no additional pay in the private sector, abolish summer and Christmas bonuses for employees earning more than €1,000 a month, and further cut welfare payments for most other workers, along with expenditures on health and education.

In a last resort to recover confidence, Passos Coelho announced intentions to introduce constitutional limits for the budget deficit and public debt.

Spain

José Luis Zapatero was reelected as prime minister, in March 2008, promising to launch a fiscal stimulus that included funds for a two-year partial moratorium on mortgage payments by the unemployed, tax benefits, and financial incentives designed to help home buyers and promote job creation.

The plan allowed about 500,000 jobless people with mortgages of less than €170,000 to postpone half their monthly payments for the following two years and repay the money only after January 2011. In addition, the government provided banks with liquidity aid in the form of asset purchases and loan guarantees, reaching up to €250 billion.

Zapatero also announced a €1,500 per job subsidy for companies that hired unemployed workers with families to support, and increased expenditures on infrastructure and the auto industry.

In March 2009, however, the Spanish government announced the first bailout of a caja. Even though there were clear distinctions between cajas and banks, this decision sparked a confidence crisis in the Spanish financial system as a whole. A run on the banks caused new bailouts, furthering investors' panic and threatening the long-term sustainability of the country's debt. The government responded by raising capital requirements for all banks and, three months later, finally announced details of a rescue fund of up to €99 billion to help the Spanish banking system.

Besides advancing stimulus policies, the socialist government initially resisted economists' suggestions for changing labor regulation and increasing labor market flexibility in Spain. Among the measures markets demanded were to reduce the costs of firing two-thirds of the workforce that were on permanent contracts.

Who Governs? 209

As economic conditions further deteriorated, with deficits soaring and no signs of economic recovery, Zapatero revealed his intention to raise taxes by 1.5 percent of the GDP – about €15 billion – to balance the books. The announcement marked a U-turn in the government's tax strategy – in previous years, Zapatero had cut income and company taxes and offered a €400 annual rebate for all Spanish taxpayers. That plan was opposed by the People's Party (PP), which defended tax and expenditure cuts.

The changed strategy was consolidated after the budget deficit exceeded 8 percent of the GDP in 2009. The Spanish finance minister produced an outline of austerity measures designed to reduce the deficit in 2010 and 2011 and calm market fears.

In January 2010, Zapatero unexpectedly announced proposals to raise the retirement age from 65 to 67 years, provoking the fury of trade unions at home. The level of popular anger against the measure forced the government to backdown.

Days after the pension reform proposal, Zapatero announced a revised Stability Program for 2009–13 to the European Commission, which recognized the deterioration in the government's fiscal position in the past two years, and presented the outlines of a recovery strategy, under which deficit should be reduced by 2.1 percentage points of GDP a year between 2010 and 2013, to be achieved mainly through reductions in personnel costs and public investment. Toward this end, public-sector wages should be reduced as share of GDP by 1.9 percentage points, equivalent to a 4 percent nominal spending reduction between 2009 and 2013.

The government also promised public-sector wage moderation, but did not quantify this proposal. Public investment spending was budgeted to fall by 14 percent between 2009 and 2013, from 4.8 percent to 2.9 percent of GDP. As reported by the Economist Intelligence Unit, "the main objective of the austerity plan was to convince investors of the government's determination to keep the public finances under control."[37]

The measures were opposed by unions, and prompted a sudden drop in the government's popularity. Before the announcement of the austerity program, the Spanish Socialist Workers' Party (PSOE) was only 1.5 points behind the PP in election polls. Afterwards, this gap widened to 9 points.

In May 2010, after investors ditched Spanish assets during the Greek panic, the socialists finally abandoned the strategy of spending their way out of recession and, "under pressure from the financial markets, the

---

[37] "Spain Country Report," Economist Intelligence Unit, March 2010, p. 14.

210 *The Politics of Market Discipline in Latin America*

EU, IMF and the United States, announced a new round of austerity measures" which included budget cuts of €15 billion over two years.[38]

Measures included an average cut of 5 percent in 2.8 million public-sector salaries from June 2010, followed by a freeze in 2011; a €6 billion cut in public-sector investment, €1.2 billion in savings by regional and local governments and a €600 million reduction between 2010 and 2011 in official development aid; the abolition of a €2,500 child-birth allowance from 2011 (which was a flagship PSOE policy during the election campaign of 2008); the suspension of annual cost-of-living adjustments for most pensioners in 2011, ending twenty-five years of increases. The austerity measures determined that a total of €6 billion of investment spending would disappear over the following two years.

Economists kept insisting that budget cuts alone would not solve Spain's problems, and that it was even more urgent to reform the labor market and pensions, yet investors reacted with skepticism when Zapatero finally announced intentions to launch both reforms. According to *The Economist*, the prime minister adopted austerity measures and labor reforms *unwillingly*, his hand being forced by the markets[39]:

> Only a shove by the markets, the European Union or, on this occasion, America's Barack Obama, can get him [Zapatero] to act against his left-wing instincts.[...] he shows no willingness to force reforms past the unions. He will do what he has to do, but always the minimum and without enthusiasm, says José Luis Álvarez, of the ESADE business school.

The prime minister declared so himself. In an interview to the Spanish newspaper *El País*, Zapatero confessed to having lost sleep waiting to see financial markets' reactions to his austerity measures: "Let's say I spent the night waiting for the Nikkei."[40]

In June 2010, Spain's 2.6 million civil servants were called out on strike to protest pay cuts and in anticipation of labor reforms, in the first show of union muscle after the prime minister announced the austerity package. Whereas labor leaders estimated that three-quarters of public servants followed the strike order, central and regional governments claimed that no more than 12 percent did. Trains, planes, ports, schools, and hospitals functioned, and only a few public services were suspended.

Measures were harsh; in some cases, severance packages were slashed from forty-five days' worth of salary per year worked to twenty-five.

---

[38] "Spain Country Report," Economist Intelligence Unit, June 2010, p. 13.
[39] "Zapatero's cuts," *The Economist*, May 20, 2010.
[40] "He pasado noches sin dormir," *El País*, July 25, 2010.

Who Governs? 211

Deregulation made it easier for employers to temporarily dismiss workers during crises.

At the same time that unions called a general strike to protest the reforms, Spain's borrowing costs reached record levels, reflecting investors' persisting pessimism. Neither austerity measures, nor reforms, or the relatively good standing of the banking system were enough to calm markets, and sovereign bonds were downgraded once again in March 2011, causing heavy financial market losses.

In a scenario of relatively low public debt, investors still feared that the need for additional bank rescues could elicit a debt crisis. In January 2011, Spanish banks still had the equivalent of 42 percent of the GDP in loans to property developers and construction companies. The cajas were another source of worry, although their number had been successfully reduced from forty-five to seventeen. In January 2011, the government established September as the deadline for cajas to either boost capital ratios or face partial nationalization.

In April 2011, Zapatero finally announced that he would not run for a third term. A resounding victory for the opposition conservative PP in regional and municipal elections across Spain signaled that the party should easily win the general election scheduled for March 2012. The socialists saw their support nationwide fall by 19 percent compared to the poll held four years before. Overall, however, the PP's victory was interpreted to be more directly associated with the disillusion with the Left than with great advances on the Right. The number of invalid ballots rose to 4 percent, or the fourth most popular option, reflecting voters' disenchantment.

The dilemma of the socialist government between votes and capital, is evidenced in a quote from *The Economist*, which noted that Zapatero's popularity had proved inversely proportional to the "wisdom of his decision-making:"

> For two years he denied that Spain was in serious financial trouble. His support fell only slightly, despite recession and galloping unemployment. But last May, as contagion spread across the euro zone periphery, he executed a U-turn, embracing austerity and, to a lesser degree, reform. His ratings plunged ("The unhappy campers," *The Economist*, May 26, 2011).

Still, investors did not celebrate the PP's victory – bond yields rose and stock prices fell. Markets were believed to resent the president of the PP and most likely the future prime minister Mariano Rajoy's criticism of Zapatero's pension reform without having offered any alternative.

Markets expected Rajoy to "quickly pass an austerity package, cut corporate tax, and push through more labor reform with or without consent,"[41] but they feared the effect public demonstrations and the astounding electoral defeat of the socialists could have on the new government's resolve to advance unpopular measures deemed necessary to guarantee long-term solvency. Spain became a frequent stage for street protests by the so-called *indignados* (indignants). The demonstrators were by no means restricted to left-wingers, even though leftist groups seemed to retain control.

With unemployment at 21 percent and bond yields reaching new historic highs after a warning from Moody's of a possible downgrade, Prime Minister Zapatero called early elections in November 2011, in an attempt to "reduce pressure on Spanish debt."[42] His last proposal in office was to put a "German-style" constitutional cap on budget deficits, amidst socialists' complaints that this would be a severe tie on government's hands.

Mariano Rajoy was elected the new prime minister, after the PP won an absolute majority in the November general elections. The PP's manifesto promised a slimmer state, with lower business taxes, looser employment laws, and less red tape, to spur growth and employment.[43]

CONCLUSION

This chapter examined the economic crisis that hit the eurozone periphery after 2008 to argue that, in bad times, market discipline works in developed countries not very differently from what previous chapters have shown to be the case in the emerging markets.

As the crisis advanced and the risks of sovereign default increased, creditors' range of concerns went far beyond macroeconomic adjustment, encompassing microeconomic policies related to wages, regulation, and the structure of the state, on the basis of their impact on long-term debt sustainability.

The austerity measures and structural reforms deemed necessary to rebuild market confidence were signaled to governments, both implicitly – through risk rating reports, downgrades, sell-off, or through the specialized media – or explicitly – tied to rescue packages. The urgent need for additional funds to meet financial obligations and avoid a default that could ultimately lead to the dismantling of the eurozone, posed too strong a pressure for any of the three socialist governments – in Spain, Portugal, and Greece – to resist, with or without a rescue package.

---

[41] "The people of the People's Party," *The Economist*, June 16, 2011.
[42] "You've only got to put up with me for four more months," *The Economist*, June 29, 2011.
[43] "Rajoy the reformer," *The Economist*, November 5, 2011.

Who Governs? 213

As a result these countries watched, from 2008 on, socialists governments' embrace of an orthodox economic agenda oriented toward confidence building in the international financial community. In many ways, a phenomenon comparable to the policy switches that occurred in Latin American democracies in periods of dollar scarcity, studied in Chapter 4, aggravated by Europe's common currency.

Socialists in Portugal, Spain, and Greece were elected on the promise of boosting economic recovery through a more active presence of the state and, after more or less resistance, switched to an investor-oriented agenda similar to that promoted by their conservative counterparts. Party cohesiveness, support from the opposition, unions, and public protests all affected the costs involved in this decision, but in none of these countries did they prevent switches from occurring.

These cases, compared to those in emerging markets explored in previous chapters, suggest that there is no fundamental or qualitative difference between the ways international bondholders behave in developed and emerging economies. During currency booms, leftist governments in emerging markets acquire substantial room to maneuver to advance policies that confront market preferences, and to which investors frequently respond with complacency.

During currency crises, conversely, governments in developed economies are also subject to investors' demands on supply-side policies, in addition to macroeconomic equilibrium. As in emerging economies, the scarcity of funding in periods when financial requirements are high leaves countries vulnerable to investor sentiment and heavily constrain the adoption of programs that deviate from markets' agenda.

Ultimately, when the conflict between voters' and markets' demands seemed to have reached levels that could not be solved by democratic means, countries like Greece and Italy appointed technocratic leaders expected to "do the right thing," freed from electoral pressures that traditionally affect politicians. At its core, a path that challenges the fundamental assumptions that justify the democratic practice.

10

Conclusion: Markets' Vote and Democratic Politics

In the years of exuberance that preceded the global financial crisis of 2008, the very notion of an existing trade-off between votes and capital seemed outdated in Latin American emerging economies. On the contrary, the decade was marked by exceptional optimism, both in financial markets and among voters.

Evidence of this win–win scenario, dramatic decreases in sovereign bond yields occurred in parallel to very high levels of presidential popularity and a wave of reelections in the region, irrespective of the quality or ideology of the administration.

Moreover, different from the 1980s and 1990s when most leftist governments in Latin America abandoned their original program in favor of a neoliberal agenda, the 2000s witnessed a widespread "move to the Left," which became subject to much debate among political economists focused on the region.

Following the "great recession," an opposite trend observed in Europe – an alleged "move to the right" – has also attracted increasing attention of the specialized media[1] and academics (Lindvall 2011; Magalhães 2012).

Left-wing parties lost vote share in the majority of elections held since 2009 (Bartels 2011)[2]; most importantly, however, left-leaning governments have to a large degree abandoned their agenda in favor of orthodox economic policies, as seen in the previous chapter. Bartels finds

---

[1] "Center-Right Parties Gain in Europe," *The New York Times*, November 9, 2009; "The voters take their revenge," *The Economist*, June 17, 2004; "Swing low, swing right," *The Economist*, June 11, 2009.
[2] Even though Bartels (2011) documented the Left's loss, he argues that this was, more than an ideological shift, an evidence of retrospective vote in Europe.

214

Conclusion 215

that, all else equal they may have spent slightly less on stimulus programs than their right-wing counterparts.

The theory presented in this book suggests that these trends are different manifestations of the same mechanism; they reflect substantial changes in creditors' capacity to influence policymaking, which in both cases were prompted by exogenous economic conditions.

Whereas an unprecedented boom in commodity prices, coupled with high international liquidity, provided leftist governments in the emerging world with increased room to maneuver in the 2000s, capital scarcity following the American subprime mortgage crisis contributes to explain the peak of market discipline in Europe after 2008. With the crisis, resources to fund current account deficits were suddenly no longer available to countries that had become used to growing with foreign savings, the same way Latin American emerging markets did in the early 1990s. In an attempt to reattract these funds, left-wing governments have acquiesced to markets' demands, which extended to include not only macroeconomic orthodoxy, but also policies and institutional changes that should be implemented toward this end.

REINSTATING THE ARGUMENT

The conventional wisdom among students of the political consequences of financial globalization is that capital mobility affects policymaking in distinct ways in developed and emerging economies. It has been argued that bondholders' influence is stronger in the latter, where low domestic savings make governments more dependent on foreign finance and low levels of societal organization limit citizens' capacity to influence the political agenda.

Moreover, scholars have contended that the range of policies subject to market pressures is also different in emerging and developed economies. In the former, a negligible risk of sovereign default allows investors to make allocative decisions based on a relatively narrow range of indicators related to governments' macroeconomic agenda. In the emerging world, however, where default risk is frequently considerable, bondholders have incentives to closely follow a broader range of policies, as well as politics itself, to calculate governments' capacity and willingness to pay sovereign debt. Thus, in the emerging markets bondholder influence is not only strong but also broad.

This book challenged both claims, by showing that market discipline varies substantially in the emerging world, over time and among countries, and so does the range of policies over which it is exerted. I argued that to understand this variation in the particular case of Latin

American low-savings-commodity-exporting economies, it is necessary to consider cycles of currency booms and crises that are exogenous to governments and investors' decisions, and that are driven by fluctuations on commodity prices and international interest rates.

During currency booms, which occur when commodity prices are high and international interest rates are low, low demand and high supply of hard currency reduce governments' need to attract additional flows of financial capital, providing those on the Left with room to deviate from investors' preferred policies.

Under currency crises, conversely, when commodity prices are low and international interest rates are high, high demand and low supply of hard currency boost governments' need to attract capital inflows, forcing the Left toward adopting investor-oriented agenda.

Because currency booms and crises affect governments' capacity – and arguably willingness – to pay sovereign debt, they also influence the range of policies bondholders are likely to consider when making investment decisions. In good times, a negligible risk of default increases markets' complacency with more redistributive or interventionist microeconomic policies, provided that leftist government advance them within the limits of macroeconomic orthodoxy.

The long-term implication of this theory is that, in countries more vulnerable to cycles of currency booms and crises, the effectiveness of market discipline changes markedly over time, with the international scenario sometimes creating room for a leftist agenda that deviates from markets' preferences.

This creates incentives for the Left to commit with radical redistribution in such countries, independently of whether it will be or not capable of advancing it. Ultimately, this prevents a long-term convergence of the Left toward the Right; voters recognize ideological differences, as do investors, who perceive these countries as riskier and policymaking as more volatile.

In economies less vulnerable to these currency cycles, the effectiveness of market discipline does not vary significantly over time. Thus, once the Left learns the constraints imposed by investors' capacity to flee the economy, it moderates its agenda accordingly. Attempts to return to a radical discourse should not be credible, either to voters or to markets. These cases should confirm the predictions of efficiency theories of globalization, as increased capital mobility should promote a convergence of the Left toward an investor-oriented economic agenda.

Conclusion

CONTRIBUTION OF THE BOOK

Most studies devoted to the politics of financial globalization in the emerging markets in the past decade attempted to apply theories developed in the context of the Organisation for Economic Co-operation and Development (OECD) to the reality of these economies. In doing so, scholars resorted to large-N statistical analyses to identify broad associations between increased capital mobility and the size of the state, often captured by levels of social expenditures, as well as to investigate the intervenient role of partisanship in this relation.

While offering a fruitful starting point for the study of globalization in emerging economies, this literature lacked a clear specification of the mechanisms through which the internationalization of finance affects policymaking. It also suffered serious limitations from an empirical perspective, the most important being its inadequacy to deal with the simultaneous effects of trade and financial liberalization, and democratization, processes that occurred concurrently in most emerging markets and that should affect partisanship, policymaking, and the State.

Departing from this previous strategy, this book aimed to shed light on the *micro-foundations* of the confidence game between investors and governments in Latin American emerging economies. With a particular focus on the period that surrounds national elections, the analysis used a variety of theoretical approaches and empirical evidence to establish an important mechanism through which market discipline works.

I started by proposing a simple model that demonstrated why, other conditions fixed, capital should flee economies when elections bring about a left turn in government, and do the opposite when the Right wins. The model also showed why investors' increased mobility should curb leftist governments' capacity to deviate from markets, economic policy preferences, and force the Left to converge toward a conservative agenda. Finally, it explored the role of uncertainty in the relations between investors and governments, examining the conditions under which this uncertainty should forestall ideological convergence in the long run.

To probe the predictions of the model, this book started by establishing how financial markets, and in particular bondholders, effectively respond to government ideology in emerging economies, as well as how this response changes during currency booms and crises. The analysis revealed that investors perceive the Left as riskier, and reduce their position in countries where a left-wing candidate is anticipated to win the presidency. Yet investors' risk perception also depends on the international scenario, with market sentiment worsening in bad times of low commodity prices and high international interest rates, and improving when the opposite occurs.

Interestingly, in "good times" bondholders also seem to be indifferent between a "moderate left," which advances redistributive and interventionist microeconomic agenda within the limits of macroeconomic orthodoxy, and conservative governments. Negative reactions are restricted to the so-called radical left, which deviates from market preferences both in the micro- and macroeconomic realm.

Next I examined the conditions under which markets' response to ideology influenced policymaking. A study of presidential elections held in Latin America since re-democratization revealed an important source of variation in investors' capacity to influence government's economic agenda. It showed that among leftist candidates, the ones elected during currency crises were the most likely to renounce campaign promises and switch to a neoliberal program. Political factors matter; party institutionalization offers some barrier to switches, whereas the constitutional powers in the hands of the president facilitate them. Somewhat surprisingly, switches are more likely to occur in institutionalized party systems, and I hypothesized that this happens because in such systems presidents can rely on voters' long-term electoral commitment.

The case studies presented in Chapters 5 to 8 detailed the confidence game between investors and governments that occurs during elections, and revealed how exogenous conditions determine the effectiveness of market discipline. They explored the process through which markets' reactions to the Left during elections were translated into political pressures for the adoption of conservative economic programs, and how this dynamic varied among periods of currency booms and crises.

Chapter 9 complemented this analysis by demonstrating that, as much as in good times investors's influence over emerging market governments is narrower than claimed in the globalization literature, in bad times it becomes broader even in the developed world.

Even though this book investigates the workings of market discipline in Latin America, the claims made here can be extended to emerging market democracies in other regions, where financial integration has increased dramatically in the past decade or so. Besides the shorter term hypothesis that market discipline is more effective during currency crises, and less so during booms, it should be possible to observe whether left-wing governments persist in the long run in economies more vulnerable to these cycles, compared to those more stable in which the Left should move rightward.

Conclusion 219

IMPLICATIONS FOR DEMOCRACY

This book examined the trade-offs democratic governments face as they become increasingly exposed not only to citizens' but also to financial investors' demands. These trade-offs can be particularly pressing when voters and investors disagree about the direction policymaking should take.

In response to the criticisms directed to the primacy of markets over politics after the global crisis of 2008, a column in *The Economist* argued that "if you don't want to be bothered about the bond markets, don't borrow from them."[3] It added "the finance ministers of Norway and Saudi Arabia have no cause to worry about their borrowing costs because they are net creditors."

In fact, if policies demanded by financial markets always imposed losses on citizens that exceeded the benefits associated with capital inflows, investors' influence would not pose a problem for democratic governments. Ultimately, electoral pressures would limit other incentives governments might have to respond to mobile capital holders. Not borrowing, as suggested by *The Economist*, could be a reasonable option. In some way, irrespective of the legal barriers imposed by "holdouts," this seems to have been the conclusion reached by presidents Néstor Kirchner and Cristina Fernández in Argentina.

If, conversely, most policies demanded by creditors were also broadly favorable to citizens, investors' influence would not be problematic for democratic governments. In this win–win game, not rarely pictured by the specialized media and assumed in academic work, in responding to markets governments would end up advancing voters' interests as well. Their real motivation, for any practical purpose, would be irrelevant.

The trade-off between votes and capital is complex exactly because financial investment carries numerous advantages while also frequently imposing harsh costs. This complexity arises as governments risk losing benefits associated with receiving these funds by responding to voters' demands, or to anger voters by paying the sometimes exceedingly high costs of satisfying creditors' preferences.

Apart from the important debate about the economic consequences of the volatility of international capital flows, from a political standpoint the experience of emerging economies after financial integration has been one in which voters were, on many occasions, left with comparably little say on policymaking.

---

[3] "Voters versus creditors," *The Economist*, November 19, 2011.

Once the constraints imposed by capital mobility are acknowledged, and the left adopts conservative economic policies, very often leftist voters have nowhere to go in their search for alternative agendas. In more volatile economies, where this convergence does not occur, leftist governments' capacity to advance a redistributive program is still quite contingent on external conditions, at least when it comes to Latin American emerging markets. Moreover, the uncertainty about how long these conditions will persist also creates deleterious short-term incentives likely to compromise much needed investment in the long term.

Democratic theory emphasizes the centrality of electoral mechanisms of accountability, and the quality of democracies is frequently believed to depend on some measure of governments' responsiveness to citizens' preferences. At the same time, students of the politics of financial globalization, regardless of their identification with convergence or divergence theories, acknowledge that the influence of mobile capital holders on policymaking is strengthened as global investment options expand. Moreover, many among them acknowledge that measures oriented toward confidence building are not always the most sensible in the longer term.

The question, then, becomes how much room to maneuver governments should have to respond to citizens' demands for a system to be conceived of as a healthy democracy. Can a political system be recognized as democratic if politicians compete for office under stable and fair rules, yet the policies they implement are fundamentally the same?

Even the weakest form of accountability established by theories of retrospective voting is not necessarily valid in a world of mobile capital, as it subsumes that policy competition necessarily follows electoral competition. Accepting that voters in emerging democracies evaluate their incumbents ex post, how far can they punish a government for implementing policies that constitute "the only game in town?"

Consider the Brazilians who elected Lula da Silva in the expectation that he would reverse the policies adopted by the former center-right government, as promised during the presidential campaign. Their only realistic alternative available for punishing the PT in the following election would be to vote for the center-right candidate of the same party of Lula's predecessor, who promised by and large the same policies that the PT historically rejected but ended up adopting in office. In that sense, a choice not very different from that available to the post-crisis Portugal or Spain, and that points to the existing limits on the prospects of democratic responsiveness in a scenario of increased financial integration.

References

Abbas, S. M. Ali, Alexander Klemm, Sukhmani Bedi, and Junhyung Park. 2012. "A Partial Race to the Bottom: Corporate Tax Developments in Emerging and Developing Economies." *IMF Working Paper.*

Acosta, Alberto, Denise Gorfinkiel, Eduardo Gudynas, and Rocio Lapitz. 2005. *El otro Riesgo Pais: Indicadores y Desarollo en la Economia.* Quito: Ediciones Abya-Ayala.

Agnoli, Myriam Quispe and Diego Vilán. 2007. "Financing Trends in Latin America." BIS Papers No. 36: Document prepared for the BIS-FRB Atlanta meeting "Recent Financing Trends in Latin America: A Bumpy Ride Towards Stability," held in Mexico City, May 24–25, 2007.

Agullo, Juan. 2006. "La Politica Social desde los Sectores Populares de los Barrios Urbanos." In *Balance y Perspectivas de la Politica Social en Venezuela,* ed. Thais Maingon. Caracas: Instituto Latinoamericano de Investigaciones Sociales (ILDIS)/ CENDES, pp. 309–29.

Alesina, Alberto. 1987. "Macroeconomic Policy in a Two-Party System as a Repeated Game." *The Quarterly Journal of Economics* 102(3):651–78.

Alesina, Alberto and Howard Rosenthal. 1995. *Partisan Politics, Divided Government and the Economy.* New York: Cambridge University Press.

Alesina, Alberto and Lawrence Summers. 1993. "Central Bank Independence and Macro-economic Performance: Some Comparative Evidence." *Journal of Money, Credit, and Banking* 25(2):151–62.

Amaral, Oswaldo E. 2012. "O que aconteceu com os radicais? Uma análise das mudanças nas clivagens no interior do PT." Paper prepared for the workshop "The PT from Lula to Dilma: Explaining Change in the Brazilian Workers' Party," Brazilian Studies Programme, University of Oxford, January 27, 2012.

Ameringer, Charles D. 1992. *Political Parties of the Americas, 1980s to 1990s.* Westport, CT: Greenwood Press.

Ananchotikul, Sudarat and Barry Eichengreen. 2007. "Managing Commodity Booms: Lessons of International Experience." Paper prepared for the African Economic Research Consortium – Centre for the Study of African Economies, Department of Economics, Oxford University.

References

Avelino, George, David S. Brown, and Wendy Hunter. 2005. "The Effects of Capital Mobility, Trade Openness, and Democracy on Social Spending in Latin America, 1980–1999." *American Journal of Political Science* 49(3):625–41.

Avendaño, Rolando, Helmut Reisen, and Javier Santiso. 2008. "The Macro Management of Commodity Booms: Africa and Latin America's Response to Asian Demand." OECD Development Centre: Working Paper No. 270.

Baiocchi, Gianpaolo. 2006. "Lula at the Crossroads? Workers' Party and Political Crisis in Brazil." *Economic and Political Weekly* 41(2):657–79.

Baiocchi, Gianpaolo and Sofia Checa. 2008. "The New and the Old in Brazil's PT." In *Leftovers: Tales of the Latin American Left*, pp. 105–29. New York: Taylor and Francis.

Barbosa, Nelson and José Antônio Pereira de Souza. 2010. In Chapter 6 *Brasil, entre o passado e o futuro*, ed. Emir Sader and Marco Aurélio Garcia. São Paulo: Editora Fundação Perseu Abramo.

Bartels, Larry M. 2008. *Unequal Democracy: The Political Economy of the New Gilded Age*. Princeton: Princeton University Press.

Bartels, Larry M. 2011. "Ideology and Retrospection in Electoral Responses to the Great Recession." Prepared for presentation at a conference on "Popular Reactions to the Great Recession," Nuffield College, Oxford, June, 24–26 2011.

Beckerman, Paul. 2001. "Dollarization and Semi-Dollarization in Ecuador." Policy Research Working Paper 2643. Washington, DC: The World Bank.

Beckerman, Paul. 2005. "The IMF and Argentina, 1991–2001." Santiago: Economic Commission on Latin America and the Caribbean. Macroeconomia del Desarollo.

Bellas, Dimitri, Michael G. Papaioannou, and Iva Petrova. 2010. "Determinants of Emerging Market Sovereign Bond Spreads: Fundamentals vs. Financial Stress." *IMF Working Paper 10/281.*

Biglaiser, Glen. 2004. "The Expansion of Neoliberal Economic Reforms in Latin America." *International Studies Quarterly* 48:561–78.

Biglaiser, Glen and DeRouen Jr., Karl. 2007. "Sovereign Bond Ratings and Neoliberalism in Latin America." *International Studies Quarterly* 51:121–138.

Blake, Charles. 1998. "Economic Reform and Democratization in Argentina and Uruguay: The Tortoise and the Hare Revisited?" *Journal of Interamerican Studies and World Affairs* 40(3):1–26.

Block, Steven and Paul M. Vaaler. 2004. "The Price of Democracy: Sovereign Risk Ratings, Bond Spreads and Political Business Cycles in Developing Countries." *Journal of International Money and Finance* 23:917–46.

Block, Steven, Paul M. Vaaler, and Burkhard N. Schrage. 2005. "Counting the Investor Vote: Political Business Cycles Effects on Sovereign Bonds Spreads in Developing Countries." *Journal of International Business Studies* 36:62–88.

Block, Steven A., Paul M. Vaaler, and Burkhard N. Schrage. 2006. "Elections, Opportunism, Partisanship and Sovereign Ratings in Developing Countries." *Review of Development Economics* 10(1):154–70.

Bobbio, Norberto. 1994. *Left and Right: The Significance of a Political Distinction*. Cambridge: Polity Press.

References 223

Boito Jr., Armando and Laura Randall. 1998. "Neoliberal Hegemony and Unionism in Brazil." *Latin American Perspectives* 112(4):71–93.

Boix, Carles. 2000. "Partisan Governments, the International Economy, and Macroeconomic Policies in Advanced Nations, 1960–93." *World Politics* 53(1):38–73.

Boix, Carles. 2003. *Democracy and Redistribution*. Cambridge: Cambridge University Press.

Botero, Juan, Simeon Djankov, Rafael Porta, and Florencio C. Lopez-De-Silanes. 2004. "The Regulation of Labor." *The Quarterly Journal of Economics* 11(1):51–81.

Bresser-Pereira, Luiz Carlos. 2001. "Incompetência e Confidence Building por trás de 20 Anos de Quase-Estagnação da América Latina." *Revista de Economia Política* 21(1):141–66.

Broder, Pablo. 2005. *Dos Anos en la Era Kirchner*. Buenos Aires: Planeta.

Buckley, Ross P. 2008. *The International Financial System: Policy and Regulation*. New York: Wolters Kluwer.

Burgo, Ezequiel. 2011. *7 Ministros – La Economía Argentina: Historias Debajo de la Alfombra*. Buenos Aires: Planeta.

Buxton, Julia. 2003. "Economic Policy and the Rise of Hugo Chávez." In *Venezuelan Politics in the Chavez Era: Class, Polarization and Conflict*, ed. Steve Ellner and Daniel Hellinger, pp. 27–54. Boulder, CO: Lynne Rienner.

Calvo, G., L. Leiderman and C. Reinhart. 1993. "Capital Inflows and Real Exchange Rate Appreciation in Latin America: The Role of External Factors." *International Monetary Fund*, IMF Staff Papers, Vol. 40 No. 1, March 1993, 108–51.

Calvo, Guillermo, Leonardo Leiderman, and Carmen M. Reinhart. 1996. "Inflows of Capital to Developing Countries in the 1990s." *Journal of Economic Perspectives* 10(2):123–39.

Cameron, Maxwell A. and Lisa L. North. 1998. "Development Paths at a Crossroads: Peru in Light of the East Asian Experience." *Latin American Perspectives* 25(1).50 66.

Campello, Daniela. 2013. *Globalization and Democracy: The Politics of Market Discipline in Latin America*. Cambridge: Cambridge University Press.

Campello, Daniela. 2014. "The Politics of Financial Booms and Crises: Evidence from Latin America." *Comparative Political Studies* 47(2):260–286.

Campello, Daniela and Cesar Zucco Jr. 2012. "Merit or Luck? International Determinants of Presidential Popularity in Latin America." Paper presented in the 2012 meeting of the International Political Economy Society, Charlottesville.

Carcanholo, Marcelo Dias. 2006. "Orthodox Economic Policies of the Lula Administration." *Economic and Political Weekly* 41(2):679–700.

Carreirão, Yan de Souza. 2007. "Raízes Sociais e Ideológicas do Lulismo." *Opinião Pública* 13(2):307–39.

Castañeda, Jorge G. 2006. "Latin America's Left Turn." *Foreign Affairs* 24(3):363–95.

Castañeda, Jorge G. 2008. *Left Overs: Tales of the Latin American Left*. New York: Routledge.

224 References

Castro, Marcus Faro de and Maria Izabel Valladão de Carvalho. 2003. "Globalization and Recent Political Transitions in Brazil." *International Political Science Review* 24(4):465–90.

Cerny, Philip. 1995. "The Dynamics of Financial Globalization: Technology, Market Structure, and Policy Response." *Policy Sciences* 27:319–42.

Cohen, Benjamin. 1996. "Phoenix Risen: The Resurrection of Global Finance." *World Politics* 48(2):268–96.

Collier, Paul. 2007. "Plumbing for Latin American Capital Markets." BIS Papers No.36: Document prepared for the BIS-FRB Atlanta meeting "Recent financing Trends in Latin America: A Bumpy Ride Towards Stability," held in Mexico City, May 24–25, 2007.

Comesaña, Antón Costas. 2004. "Un Año de Lula: Esperando el Crecimiento." *Revista CIDOB d'Afers Internacionals* 65:29–38.

Conaghan, Catherine. 2011. "Rafael Correa and the Citizen's Revolution." In *The Resurgence of the Latin American Left*, pp. 260–82. Baltimore: Johns Hopkins University Press.

Conaghan, Catherine M., James M. Malloy and Luis A. Abugattas. 1990. "Business and the 'Boys': The Politics of Neoliberalism in the Central Andes." *Latin American Research Review* 25(2):3–30.

Corrales, Javier. 1998. "Do Economic Crises Contribute to Economic Reform? Argentina and Venezuela in the 1990s." *Political Science Quarterly* 112(4):617–44.

Corrales, Javier and Michael Penfold. 2011. *Dragon in the Tropics*. Washington, DC: Brookings Institution Press.

Correa, Rafael. 2003. "La Política Econômica del Gobierno de Lucio Gutiérrez." *Iconos. Revista de Ciencias Sociales* 16:6–10.

Correa, Rafael. 2013. "Ecuador's Path." *New Left Review* 77:89–104.

CRS Report, US. 2010. "Argentina's Defaulted Sovereign Debt: Dealing with the "Holdouts." Washington, DC: US Congress. Congressional Research Service Report for Congress.

Cuddington, John T. and Assilis Carlos. 1990. "Fiscal Policy, the Current Account and the External Debt Problem in the Dominican Republic." *Journal of Latin American Studies* 22(2):331–52.

Diniz, Eli. 2004. "Democracia y Desarrollo en Brasil: La Relevancia de la Dimensión Político-institucional." *Revista CIDOB d'Afers Internacionals* 65:61–77.

Dornbusch, Rudiger. 1989. "The Latin American Debt Problem: Anatomy and Solutions." In *Debt and Democracy in Latin America*, ed. Barbara Stallings and Robert Kaufman, pp. 7–22. Boulder, CO: Westview Press.

Drake, Paul. 1989. "Debt and Democracy in Latin America, 1920s–1980s." In *Debt and Democracy in Latin America*, ed. Barbara Stallings and Robert Kaufman, pp. 39–58. Boulder, CO: Westview Press

Drake, Paul. 1991. "Comment: The Political Economy of Latin American Populism." In *The Macroeconomics of Populism in Latin America*, ed. Rudiger Dornbusch and Sebastian Edwards, pp. 35–40. Chicago: University of Chicago Press.

Dreher, Axel, Jan-Egbert Sturm, and Heinrich W. Ursprung. 2008. "The Impact of Globalization on the Composition of Government Expenditures: Evidence from Panel Data." *Public Choice* 134(3–4):263–92.

References

Drezner, Daniel W. 2001. "Globalization and Policy Convergence." *International Studies Review* 3(1):53–78.

Dryzek, John S. 1996. *Democracy in Capitalist Times*. Oxford: Oxford University Press.

Duhalde, Eduardo. 2007. *Memorias del Incendio*. Buenos Aires: Editorial Sudamericana.

Edwards, Sebastian. 1998. "Capital Inflows to Latin America: A Stop-Go Story?" *NBER Working Paper Series* 6441(1):1–23.

Edwards, Sebastian. 2010. *Left Behind*. Chicago: University of Chicago Press.

Eichengreen, Barry, Andrew K. Rose, Charles Wyplosz, Bernard Dumas, and Axel Weber. 1995. "Exchange Market Mayhem: The Antecedents and Aftermath of Speculative Attacks." *Economic Policy* 10(21):249–312.

Fernández-Villaverde, Jesús and Lee Ohanian. 2010. "The Spanish Crisis from a Global Perspective." *FEDEA-Fundación de Estudios de Economía Aplicada* Documento de Trabajo 2010-03 February 2010, 1–58.

Fleury, Sonia. 2004. "Primer Año del Gobierno Lula: la Difícil Transición." *Revista CIDOB d'Afers Internacionals* 65:39–59.

Flores-Macías, Gustavo A. 2010. "Statist vs. Pro-Market: Explaining Leftist Governments' Economic Policies in Latin America." *Comparative Politics* 42(4):413–33.

Flores-Macías, Gustavo A. 2012. *After Neoliberalism? The Left and Economic Reforms in Latin America*. Oxford: Oxford University Press.

Garrett, Geoffrey. 1998. "Global Markets and National Politics: Collision Course or Virtuous Circle?" *International Organization* 52(4):787–824.

Gavin, Michael, Ricardo Hausmann, and Leonardo Leiderman. 1995. "Macroeconomics of Capital Flows to Latin America: Experience and Policy Issues." *RES Working Papers, Inter-American Development Bank* 4012(3):389–431.

Gerchunoff, Pablo and Lucas Llach. 2003. *El Ciclo de la Ilusion y el Desencanto – Un siglo de Politicas Economicas Argentinas*. Buenos Aires: Ariel.

Goldfrank, Benjamin and Brian Wampler. 2008. "From Petista Way to Brazilian Way: How the PT Changes in the Road." *Revista Debates* 2(2):245–71.

Griffith-Jones, Stephany. 2000. "International Capital Flows to Latin America." Serie Reformas Economicas 55. Prepared for the project Growth, Employment and Equity: Latin America in the 1990s.

Gunson, Phil, Greg Chamberlain, and Andrew Thompson. 1989. *The Dictionary of Contemporary Politics of South America*. Cornwall: TJ Press.

Gunson, Phil, Greg Chamberlain, and Andrew Thompson. 1991. *The Dictionary of Contemporary Politics of Central America and the Caribbean*. Cornwall: TJ Press.

Haggard, Stephan and Robert Kaufman. 1995. *The Political Economy of Democratic Transitions*. Princeton: Princeton University Press.

Harrington, Carrie. 2011. "The Spanish Financial Crisis." Iowa City: The University of Iowa Center for International Finance and Development.

Hays, Jude, Helmut Stix, and John R. Freeman. 2000. "The Electoral Information Hypothesis Revisited." Earlier versions of this paper were presented at the 1999 Meeting of the Midwest Political Science Association and at the Conference on "Globalization and Democracy," University of Minnesota.

References

Helleiner, Eric. 1994. *States and the Reemergence of Global Finance*. Ithaca, NY: Cornell University Press.

Hellinger, Daniel. 2003. "Political Overview: The Breakdown of Puntofijismo and the Rise of Chavismo." In *Venezuelan Politics in the Chavez Era: Class, Polarization and Conflict*, ed. Steve Ellner and Daniel Hellinger, pp. 27–54. Boulder, CO: Lynne Rienner.

Hellwig, Timothy, Eve Ringsmuth, and John Freeman. 2008. "The American Public and the Room to Maneuver: Responsibility Attributions and Policy Efficacy in an Era of Globalization." *International Studies Quarterly* 52(4):855–80.

Hernandez, Ramon and Roberto Giusti. 2006. *Carlos Andres Perez – Memorias Proscritas*. Caracas: Los Libros de El Nacional.

Hibbs, Douglas. 1977. "Political Parties and Macroeconomic Policies." *American Political Science Review* 71(4):1467–87.

Hirschman, Albert O. 1977. "Exit, Voice and the State." *World Politics* 31(1):90–107.

Hojman, David E. 1996. "Poverty and Inequality in Chile: Are Democratic Politics and Neoliberal Economics Good for You?" *Journal of Interamerican Studies and World Affairs* 78(2–3):73–96.

Hornbeck, J. F. 2010. "Argentina's Defaulted Sovereign Debt: Dealing with the "Holdouts"." Congressional Research Service. July 2, 2010.

Hunter, Wendy. 2008. "The Workers' Party: Still a Party of the Left?" In *Democratic Brazil Revisited*, pp. 15–32. Pittsburgh: Pittsburgh University Press.

Hunter, Wendy. 2011. "The PT in Power." In *The Resurgence of the Latin American Left*, pp. 306–25. Baltimore: Johns Hopkins University Press.

Hunter, Wendy and Natasha Borges Sugiyama. 2009. "Democracy and Social Policy in Brazil: Advancing Basic Needs, Preserving Privileged Interests." *Latin American Politics and Society* 51(2):29–58.

Hurtado-Larrea, Osvaldo. 2006. *Los Costos del Populismo*. Quito: CORDES.

IMF, Independendent Evaluation Office. 2004. "The IMF and Argentina, 1991–2001." Washington, DC: International Monetary Fund. Evaluation Report.

Izquierdo, Alejandro, Randall Romero, and Ernesto Talvo. 2008. "Booms and Busts in Latin America: The Role of External Factors." *IADB Working Paper* 89(631):2–31.

Jones, Mark. 2005. "The Role of Parties and Party Systems in the Policy Making Process. State Reform, Public Policies, and Policymaking Processes." Paper prepared for the Workshop on State Reform, Public Policies, and Policymaking Processes. Inter-American Development Bank, Washington, DC.

Kaufman, Robert. 2011. The Political Left, the Export Boom, and the Populist Temptation. In *The Ressurgence of the Latin American Left*, pp. 93–116. Baltimore: Johns Hopkins University Press.

Kaufman, Robert R. and Alex Segura-Ubiergo. 2001. "Globalization, Domestic Politics, and Social Spending in Latin America: A Time-Series Cross-Section Analysis, 1973-97." *The Quarterly Journal of Economics* 53(4):553–87.

Keohane, Robert and Helen Milner. 1996. "Internationalization and Domestic Politics: An Introduction." In *Internationalization and Domestic Politics*,

References 227

ed. Robert Keohane and Helen Milner, pp. 25–47. Cambridge: Cambridge University Press.

Kitschelt, Herbert, Peter Lange, Gary Marks, and John D. Stephens. 1999. *Continuity and Change in Contemporary Capitalism*. Cambridge: Cambridge University Press.

Kurtz, Marcus. 2004. "The Dilemmas of democracy in the Open Economy: Lessons from Latin America." *World Politics* 56(4):262–302.

Kurtz, Marcus J. and Sarah M. Brooks. 2008. "Embedding Neoliberal Reform in Latin America." *World Politics* 60(4):231–80.

Kurzer, Paulette. 1993. *Business and Banking: Poliitcal Change and Economic Integration in Western Europe*. Ithaca, NY: Cornell University Press.

Lander, Edgardo. 2007. "Venezuelan Social Conflict in a Global Context." In *Venezuela: Hugo Chávez and the Decline of an "Exceptional Democracy,"* ed. Steve Ellner and Miguel Tinker Salas, pp. 27–54. Lanham, MD: Rowman & Littlefield.

Lander, Edgardo and Luis A. Fierro. 1996. "The Impact of Neoliberal Adjustment in Venezuela, 1989–1993." *Latin American Perspectives* 23(3): 50–73.

Lavagna, Roberto. 2011. *El Desafio de La Voluntad – Trece Meses Cruciales en La Historia Argentina*. Buenos Aires: Sudamericana.

Leblang, David A. 2002. "The Political Economy of Speculative Attacks in the Developing World." *International Studies Quarterly* 46:69–91.

Leblang, David A. and William Bernhard. 2000. "The Political Economy of Speculative Attacks in the Developing World." *International Organization* 54(2):291–324.

Leblang, David and William Bernhard. 2006. *Democratic Processes and Financial Markets*. Cambridge: Cambridge University Press.

Levine, Daniel H. 2001. Diez Tesis Sobre la Decadencia y Crisis de la Democracia en Venezuela. In *Venezuela en TransiciÛn: Elecciones y Democracia 1998–2000*, ed. Jose Vicente Carrasquero, Thais Maignon, and Friedrich Welsch, pp. 27–54. Caracas. RedPol CDB Publicaciones.

Levitsky, Steven and Maria Victoria Murillo. 2003. "Argentina Weathers the Storm." *Journal of Democracy* 14(4):152–66.

Licio, Elaine Cristina, Rennó Lucio R. e Castro Henrique Carlos de O. de. 2009. "Bolsa Família e Voto na Eleição Presidencial de 2006: em Busca do Elo Perdido." *Opinião Pública* 15(1):43.

Lindblom, Charles. 1977. *Politics and Markets: The World's Political Economic Systems*. New York: Basic Books.

Lindert, Peter H. and Peter J. Morton. 1989. "How Sovereign Debt Has Worked." In *Developing Country Debt and the World Economy*, ed. Jeffrey D. Sachs, pp. 225–36. Chicago: University of Chicago Press.

Lindvall, Johannes. 2011. "The Political Effects of Two Great Crises." Unpublished Manuscript, Lund University.

Lopez Maya, Margarita. 2005. *Del Viernes Negro al Referendo Revocatorio*. Caracas: Editorial Melvin.

Lora, Eduardo. 2001. "Structural reforms in Latin America: What has been reformed and how to measure it." Washington, DC: IADB Research

228 *References*

Department Working Paper Series 466. Updated version of Working Paper 348.

Lora, Eduardo, Ugo Panizza, and Myriam Quispe-Agnoli. 2004. "Reform Fatigue: Symptoms, Reasons, and Implications." *Economic Review – Federal Reserve Bank of Atlanta* (2nd quarter): 1–28.

Luna, Juan Pablo. 2008. "Estructura Programatica e Institucionalización del Sistema de Partidos." Presented at the Institucionalizacion de los Sistemas de Partidos en America Latina – CIDOB, Barcelona.

Luongo, José Luis Silva. 2007. *De Herrera Campins a Chávez*. Caracas: Editorial Alfa.

Lustig, Nora and Darryl McLeod. 2011. "Inequality and Poverty Under Latin America's New Left Regimes." Tulane University Economics Working Paper Series Working Paper 1117.

Magalhães, Pedro C. 2012. "Economy, Ideology, and the Elephant in the Room: A Research Note on the Elections of the Great Recession in Europe." unpublished manuscript, Institute of Social Sciences of the University of Lisbon.

Mainwaring, Scott and Timothy Scully. 1995. *Building Democratic Institutions: Party Systems in Latin America*. Stanford: Stanford University Press.

Mainwaring, Scott and Matthew Shugart. 1997. *Presidentialism and Democracy in Latin America*. Cambridge: Cambridge University Press.

Mainwaring, Scott and Mariano Torcal. 2006. "Party System Institutionalization and Party System Theory after the Third Wave of Democratization." In *Handbook of Party Politics*, ed. Richard Katz and William Crotty, pp. 140–81. Thousand Oaks, CA: Sage.

Malkiel, Burton G. 2003. "The Efficient Market Hypothesis and Its Critics." *The Journal of Economic Perspectives* 17(1):59–82.

Marcano, Cristina and Alberto Barrera Tyska. 2005. *Hugo Chávez Sin Uniforme: Una Historia Personal*. Buenos Aires: Debate.

Mauceri, Philip. 1995. "State Reform, Coalitions and the Neoliberal Autogolpe in Peru." *Latin American Research Review* 30(1):7–37.

Maxfield, Sylvia. 1998. "Effects of International Portfolio Flows on Government Policy Choice." In *Capital Flows and Financial Crises*, ed. Miles Kahler, pp. 69–92. Cornell: Cornell University Press, 1998 (first printed).

Meltzer, Allan H. and Scott F. Richard. 1981. "A Rational Theory of the Size of Government." *The Journal of Political Economy* 89(5):914–27.

Meneguello, Rachel and Oswaldo E. Amaral. 2006. "Ainda novidade: Uma revisão das transformações do Partido dos Trabalhadores no Brasil." *Brazilian Studies Program*, St Antony's College, Oxford University.

Mitchell, Neil J. 1997. *The Conspicuous Corporation: Business, Public Policy, and Representative Democracy*. Ann Arbor: University of Michigan Press.

Mollo, Maria de Lourdes Rollemberg and Alfredo Saad-Filho. 2006. "Neoliberal Economic Policies in Brazil (1994–2005): Cardoso, Lula and the Need for a Democratic Alternative." *New Political Economy* 11(1):99–123.

Moser, Christopher. 2007. "The Impact of Political Risk on Sovereign Bond Spreads – Evidence from Latin America." Proceedings of the German Development Economics Conference, Göttingen 2007 / Verein für Socialpolitik, Research Committee Development Economics, No. 24

References   229

Mosley, Layna. 2003. *Global Capital and National Governments*. Cambridge: Cambridge University Press.

Mosley, Layna and David Andrew Singer. 2008. "Taking Stock Seriously: Equity-Market Performance, Government Policy, and Financial Globalization." *International Studies Quarterly* 52:405–25.

Murillo, María Victoria, Virginia Oliveros and Milan Vaishnav. 2011. "Economic Constraints and Presidential Agency." In *The Ressurgence of the Latin American Left*, pp. 93–116. Baltimore: Johns Hopkins University Press.

Nicolau, Jairo and Vitor Peixoto. 2007. "As Bases Municipais da Votação de Lula em 2006." *Cadernos Fórum Nacional* 6:20.

Nooruddin, Irfan and Joel W. Simmons. 2009. "Openness, Uncertainty, and Social Spending: Implications for the Globalization – Welfare State Debate." *International Studies Quarterly* 53(3):841–66.

Oatley, Thomas. 1999. "How Constraining Is Capital Mobility? The Partisan Hypothesis in an Open Economy." *American Journal of Political Science* 43(4):1003–27.

O'Donnell, Guillermo. 1985. "External Debt: Why Don't Our Countries Do the Obvious?" *CEPAL Review* 27(3):389–431.

Orestein, Mitchell A. and Martine R. Haas. 2005. "Globalization and the Future of Welfare States in the Post-Communist East-Central European Countries." In *Globalization and the Future of the Welfare State*, ed. Miguel Glatzer and Dietrich Rueschmeyer, pp. 130–52. Pittsburgh: University of Pittsburgh Press.

Pachano, Simon. 2005. "Ecuador: Cuando la Inestabilidad se Vuelve Estable." *Iconos. Revista de Ciencias Sociales* 23:37–44.

Palermo, Vicente. 2005. "El gobierno de Lula y el PT." *Nueva Sociedad* 192: 4–11.

Pastor, Manuel and Carol Wise. 1997. "State Policy, Distribution and Neoliberal Reform in Mexico." *Journal of Latin American Studies* 29(2):419–56.

Payne, J.Mark, Daniel Zovatto G., Fernando C. Florez, and Andres A. Zavala. 2002. *Democracies in Development: Politics and Reform in Latin America*. Washington DC: Inter-American Development Bank and the International Institute for Democracy and Electoral Assistance [Producer]. Johns Hopkins University Press [distributor].

Payne, J.Mark, Daniel Zovatto G., Fernando C. Florez, and Andres A. Zavala. 2003. *La Politica Importa: Democracia y Desarrollo en America Latina*. Washington, DC: Inter-American Development Bank and the International Institute for Democracy and Electoral Assistance [Producer]. Johns Hopkins University Press [distributor].

Penfold-Becerra, Michael. 2001. "El Colapso del Sistema de Partidos en Venezuela: Explicacion de una Muerte Anunciada." In *Venezuela en Transiciûn: Elecciones y Democracia 1998–2000*, ed. Jose Vicente Carrasquero, Thais Maignon, and Friedrich Welsch, pp. 27–54. Caracas: RedPol CDB Publicaciones.

Persson, Torsen and Guido Tabellini. 2002. *Political Economics – Explaining Economic Policy*. Cambridge, MA: MIT Press.

Petkoff, Teodoro. 1997. *Por Que Hago lo que Hago*. Caracas: Alfadil Ediciones.

230 *References*

Potrafke, Niklas. 2009. "Did Globalization Restrict Partisan Politics? An Empirical Evaluation of Social Expenditures in a Panel of OECD Countries." *Public Choice* 140:105–24.

Przeworski, Adam. 2007. "Political Rights, Property Rights, and Economic Development." Working Paper. Department of Politics, New York University.

Przeworski, Adam and Covadonga Meseguer. 2005. "Globalization and Democracy." In *Globalization and Egalitarian Distribution*, Chapter 7, ed. Pranab Bardhan, Samuel Bowles, and Michael Wallerstein. Princeton: Princeton University Press.

Przeworski, Adam and Michael Wallerstein. 1982. "The Structure of Class Conflict in Democratic Societies." *American Political Science Review* 76(2): 215–38.

Quinn, Dennis. 1997. "The Correlates of Change in International Financial Regulation." *American Political Science Review* 91:561–78.

Quispe-Agnoli, Myriam and Elena Whisller. 2006. "Official Dollarization and the Banking System in Ecuador and El Salvador." Atlanta: Federal Reserve Bank of Atlanta. Economic Review.

Reinhart, Carmen. 2005. "Some Perspectives on Capital Flows to Emerging Market Economies." National Bureau of Economic Research.

Reinhart, Carmen and Kenneth Rogoff. 2009. *This Time Is Different: Eight Centuries of Financial Folly*. Princeton: Princeton University Press.

Renno, Lucio and Anthony Spanakos. 2009. "Speak Clearly and Carry a Big Stock of Dollar Reserves: Sovereign Risk, Ideology, and Presidential Elections in Argentina, Brazil, Mexico, and Venezuela." *Comparative Political Studies* 42(1):1292–316.

Roberts, Kenneth. 1996. "Economic Crisis and the Demise of the Legal Left in Peru." *Comparative Politics* 29(1):69–92.

Roberts, Kenneth. 2003. "Social Polarization and the Populist Resurgence in Venezuela." In *Venezuelan Politics in the Chavez Era: Class, Polarization and Conflict*, ed. Steve Ellner and Daniel Hellinger, pp. 55–72. Boulder, CO: Lynne Rienner.

Roberts, Kenneth M. 2011. "The Left after Neoliberalism." In *The Resurgence of the Latin American Left*, pp. 260–82. Baltimore: Johns Hopkins University Press.

Roberts, Kenneth and Steven Levitsky. 2011. *The Ressurgence of the Latin American Left*. Baltimore: Johns Hopkins University Press.

Robinson, William I. 2000. "Neoliberalism, the Global Elite, and the Guatemalan Transition: A Critical Macrosocial Analysis." *Journal of Interamerican Studies and World Affairs* 42(4):89–107.

Rodriguez, Enrique. 2006. "Politica Social Actual: Una Vision desde el Gobierno." In *Balance y Perspectivas de la Politica Social en Venezuela*, ed. Thais Maingon, pp. 269–90. Caracas: Instituto Latinoamericano de Investigaciones Sociales (ILDIS)/ CENDES.

Rodrik, Dani. 1998. "Why Do More Open Economies Have Bigger Governments?" *The Journal of Political Economy* 106(5):997–1032.

Rodrik, Dani. 2000. "How Far Will International Economic Integration Go?" *The Journal of Economic Perspectives* 14(1):177–86.

References

Rogoff, Kenneth. 1985. "The Optimal Degree of Commitment to an Intermediate Monetary Target." *Quarterly Journal of Economics* 100(4):1169–90.

Rosario, Espinal. 1995. "Economic Restructuring, Social Protest and Democratization in Dominican Republic." *Latin American Perspectives* 22(3):63–79.

Rudra, Nita. 2002. "Globalization and the Decline of the Welfare State in Less-Developed Countries." *International Organization* 56(2):7411–45.

Rudra, Nita. 2008. *Globalization and the Race to the Bottom in Developing Countries: Who Really Gets Hurt?* Cambridge: Cambridge University Press.

Sachs, Jeffrey D. 1989. "Introduction." In *Developing Country Debt and the World Economy*, ed. Jeffrey D. Sachs, pp. 1–36. Chicago: University of Chicago Press.

Samuels, David. 2004. "Presidentialism and Accountability for the Economy in Comparative Perspective." *American Political Science Review* 98(3): 425–36.

Samuels, David. 2008. "Brazilian Democracy under Lula and the PT." In *Constructing Democratic Governance in Latin America*, 3rd ed., pp. 15–32. Baltimore: Johns Hopkins University Press.

Santiso, Javier. 2003. *The Political Economy of Emerging Markets – Actors, Institutions and Financial Crises in Latin America*. New York: Palgrave MacMillan.

Santiso, Javier. 2006. "Markets and Institutions in Middle Income Countries: Foreign Investors in Emerging Democracies." Presentation made in the Casa de América, Madrid, 8–9 June 2006. Source: Merrill Lynch, December 2003.

Santiso, Javier and Emmanuel Frot. 2010. "Portfolio Managers and Elections in Emerging Economies: How Investors Dislike Political Uncertainty." SITE Working Paper Series 9, Stockholm Institute of Transition Economics, Stockholm School of Economics.

Santiso, Javier and Juan Martínez. 2003. "Financial Markets and Politics: The Confidence Game in Latin American Emerging Markets." *International Political Science Review* 24(3):363–95.

Singer, André. 2009. "Raízes Sociais e Ideológicas do Lulismo." *Novos Estudos* 85:83–102.

Singer, Matthew M. and Guillermo Rosas. 2007. "Perceptions of Economic Inequality and Presidential Approval: Evidence from Argentina." *Observatory on Structures and Institutions of Inequality in Latin America: Working Paper Series* (WPS5):1–40.

Song, Ho Keun and Kyung Zoon Hong. 2005. "Globalization and Social Policy in South Korea." In *Globalization and the Future of the Welfare State*, ed. Miguel Glatzer and Dietrich Rueschmeyer, pp. 179–202. Pittsburgh: University of Pittsburgh Press.

Stallings, Barbara. 1987. *Banker to the Third World*. Berkeley and Los Angeles: University of California Press.

Stallings, Barbara. 1992. "International Influence on Economic Policy: Debt, Stabilization, and Structural Reform." In *The Politics of Economic Adjustment*, ed. Stephan Haggard and Robert R. Kaufman, pp. 41–88. Princeton: Princeton University Press.

Stokes, Susan. 2001. *Mandates and Democracy: Neoliberalism by Surprise in Latin America*. Cambridge: Cambridge University Press.

Strange, Susan. 1986. *Casino Capitalism*. New York: Basil Blackwell.

Swank, Duane. 1992. "Politics and the Structural Dependence of the State in Democratic Capitalist Nations." *American Political Science Review* 86(1):38–54.

Thorp, Rosemary. 1998. *Progresso, Pobreza e Exclusão: Uma História Económica da América Latina no Século XX*. Washington: BID.

Thorp, Rosemary and Whitehead, Laurence, ed. 1987. *Latin American Debt and the Adjustment Crisis*. Pittsburgh: University of Pittsburgh Press.

Tomz, Michael. 2007. *Reputation and International Cooperation: Sovereign Debt Across Three Centuries*. Princeton: Princeton University Press.

Wantchekon, Leonard. 2003. "Clientelism and Voting Behavior Evidence from a Field Experiment in Benin." *World Politics* 55(3):399–422.

Weisbrot, Mark, Jake Johnston, and Stephan Lefebvre. 2013. "Ecuador's New Deal: Reforming and Regulating the Financial Sector." Washington, DC: Center for Economic and Policy Research.

Weiss, Wendy. 1997. "Debt and Devaluation: The Burden on Ecuador's Popular Class." *Latin American Perspectives* 24(4):9–33.

Weyland, Kurt. 1996. "Risk Taking in Latin American Economic Restructuring: Lessons from Prospect Theory." *International Studies Quarterly* 40(2):185–208.

Weyland, Kurt. 2002. *The Politics of Market Reform in Fragile Democracies: Argentina, Brazil, Peru, Venezuela*. Princeton: Princeton University Press.

Weyland, Kurt. 2004. "Critical Debates on Neoliberalism and Democracy in Latin America: A Mixed Record." *Latin American Politics and Society* 46(1):135–57.

Weyland, Kurt. 2009. "The Rise of Latin America's Two Lefts: Insights from Rentier State Theory." *Comparative Politics* 41(2):145–64.

Weyland, Kurt, Raúl L. Madrid and Wendy Hunter. 2010. *Leftist Governments in Latin America: Successes and Shortcomings*. New York: Cambridge University Press.

Whitehead, Laurence. 2006. "The Political Dynamics of Financial Crises in Emerging Democracies." In *Statecrafting Monetary Authority: Democracy and Financial Order in Brazil*, pp. 13–36. Center for Brazilian Studies, University of Oxford.

Wibbels, Erik. 2006. "Dependency Revisited: International Markets, Business Cycles, and Social Spending in the Developing World." *International Organization* 60:433–68.

Wibbels, Erik and Moises Arce. 2003. "Globalization, Taxation, and Burden-Shifting in Latin America." *International Organization* 57:111–36.

Wilson, Bruce M. 1994. "When Social Democrats Choose Neoliberal Economic Policies: The Case of Costa Rica." *Comparative Politics* 26:149–68.

Yi, Dae Jin. 2011. "Globalization, Democracy, and the Public Sector in Asia." *Asian Survey* 51(3):472–96.

Zucco Jr., Cesar. 2008. "Stability Without Roots: Party System Institutionalization in Brazil." Presented at the Institucionalizacion de los Sistemas de Partidos en America Latina – CIDOB, Barcelona.

Index

Acción Democratica (AD, Venezuela), 136, 138, 151n19
Agenda Venezuela, 141–42
agrarian reform, 90, 93, 95, 97, 107–8, 149
Alarcón, Fabián, 122
Alckmin, Geraldo, 108, 116
Alfonsín, Raúl, 6, 67, 160–61
Alvarado, Juan Velasco, 142
Another Brazil Is Possible (Um Outro Brasil é Possível), 93
Argentina, 6, 21, 67
  balance of payments in, 164–65, 179
  collapse and default in, 7, 81, 159–60, 166–73
  commodity exports of, 14, 180, 182, 185
  debt renegotiation under Kirchner and, 173–78
  dollarization of economy, 166, 172, 190
  income inequality in, 172
  macreconomic policies under N. Kirchner, 178–79
  Menem and, 160–66
  microeconomic policies under N. Kirchner, 178–83
  sovereign risk and, 52–53, 173–74
  trade balance in, 163
  vivir con lo nuestro under N. Kirchner and, 176–78
  See also Fernández, Cristina de Kirchner; Kirchner, Néstor

Bachelet, Michelle, 50
  See also Chile
balance of payments in Argentina, 164–65, 179
Banco Latino, 141

BNDES. *See* Brazilian National Development Bank (Banco Nacional de Desenvolvimento Econômico e Social)
boliburguesía, 151
Bolsa Família program, 105–8, 111–12, 116
boom (commodity boom), 20, 81, 89, 120, 160, 187–88
Boom (variable), 73, 75–77, 82
Brady Plan, 6, 48
  Ecuador and, 122–23
Brazil, 6, 24
  Cardoso and, 90–92
  commodity exports of, 14, 113
  confidence crisis of 2002, 1–2
  currency booms and crisis and, 81, 89, 105, 108
  income inequality in, 107
  presidential campaign of 1989 and, 89–90
  sovereign risk and, 52–53
  See also da Silva, Lula; Rousseff, Dilma; Workers' Party (PT)
Brazilian Central Bank (BACEN), 1–2, 94, 99, 101
Brazilian National Development Bank (Banco Nacional de Desenvolvimento Econômico e Social), 50, 106, 110
Brazilian Social Democratic Party (Partido Social Democrata Brasileiro, PSDB), 90–91
Bremmer, Ian, 51
Broad Front, 50
  See also Uruguay
Bucaram, Abdalá, 122

Caldera, Rafael, 136–37, 140–42
Campins, Luis Herrera, 138

234   *Index*

capital account liberalization, 7
capital mobility, 4, 12–13, 21, 220
  income of the poor as function of
    taxation and, 31–34, 38–40, 43–44
  redistribution politics and model, 23,
    27–31
Cardoso, Fernando Henrique, 90–96,
  99–100, 103–4, 106
Carta ao Povo Brasileiro (Letter to the
  Brazilian People), 94n9
Cavallo, Domingo, 169–70, 171
central bank independence, 54, 71, 132
Central Única dos Trabalhadores (CUT),
  104
Chávez, Hugo, 27, 48–50, 88, 136–38,
  157–59
  boom and consolidation, 150–53
  confrontation and instability and,
    149–50
  economic growth and, 151–53
  exogenous shocks, 25
  first year of presidency of, 145–49
  policy switches of, 20–21, 50, 76–77,
    137, 145–49, 156–59
  popularity of, 151, 153
  presidential election of 1998 and,
    142–45
  reelection of under socialist agenda,
    153–57
  See also Venezuela
Chile
  commodity exports of, 14
  sovereign risk and, 52–53
  See also Bachelet, Michelle; Lagos,
    Eduardo
Christian Social Party (Partido Social
  Cristiano, COPEI), 138
Coelho, Pedro Passos, 206–8
Collor de Mello, Fernando, 89–90
Colombia, 71
  commodity exports of, 14
  economic policies of, 51
commodity exports, 14, 17–19, 36, 40, 42,
  47, 61, 216
  in Argentina, 180, 182, 185
  in Brazil, 113
  in Mexico, 114
commodity price boom (2004), 21–22, 25,
  39, 105, 113–16, 119, 159–60,
  215–16
  Argentina and, 187–88
commodity prices, 3, 14–16, 18–19, 22,
  36, 40, 47, 52, 55–56, 188, 216
  high, 3, 16, 19, 36, 47, 61, 188, 216,
    218
  low, 15–16, 19, 37, 80, 123, 166, 189,
    216–18
  move to leftist governments in 2000s
    and, 39
compensation theories, 9–11

complete information, 35
Confederación de Nacionalidades
  Indígenas del Ecuador (CONAIE),
  123, 125, 130
Confederación Ecuatoriana de
  Organizaciones Sindicales Libres
  (CEOSL), 130
confidence crisis, 1, 19, 22, 51, 64, 88, 94,
  97, 99, 116
  in Argentina, 161, 165, 186
  in Ecuador, 118
  in Greece, 195, 199
  in Spain, 208
confidence game, investor influence as,
  7–8, 12, 24, 64, 80, 88, 198, 217–18
constitutional powers, 73–75, 129, 218
  policy switches and, 68–69
Convertibility Law (Argentina), 162–66,
  173
  Cavallo plan, 162, 169–72
  convertibility plan, 160–62, 186–87
COPOM (Comitê de Política Monetária),
  104
Correa, Rafael, 2, 20, 24, 27, 49, 129–35,
  159, 188
  currency pressures and, 118–21
  government revenues and spending
    under, 132–33
  See also Ecuador
currency booms and crisis, 216–18
  Brazil and, 89, 105, 108, 159
  in developed world, 212–13
  Ecuador and, 81, 119, 131, 134, 159
  government revenues and, 17
  leftist presidents and governments and,
    3–4, 14, 19, 25, 37–42, 45, 64–67,
    80–81, 134–35, 213
  policy switches and, 37–42, 45, 67,
    74–86, 213
  policy switches model of, 70–74, 82–86
  sovereign risk and, 47
  Venezuela and, 81, 137, 141, 158–59

Dahik, Alberto, 122
Da Lula Monster, 93
da Silva, Lula, 1–2, 19–20, 26, 40, 42, 50,
  87–88, 118
  in 2004-2005, 105–7
  Bolsa Família program of, 105–8,
    111–12, 116
  first year of presidency of (2003),
    98–105
  political discourse of 2006 and 2010,
    108–17
  presidential campaign of 1989 and,
    89–90
  presidential campaign of 2002 and,
    92–98
  presidential campaign of 1994 and 1998
    and, 90–92

Index

presidential election of 2010 and, 115–17
See also Brazil; Workers' Party (PT)
Debt Club, 71, 125
debt crisis of 1980s, 48, 66, 89, 122
Venezuela and, 138
debt renegotiation, 96, 108, 173–78
decreasing capital specificity, 28
default, 4, 6, 13, 16, 21, 46, 53, 166, 189–91, 197, 212, 215–16
in Argentina, 7, 25–26, 48, 81, 119, 159–60, 166–73, 175–76, 178, 182–86
Brazil and, 90, 93, 97, 112, 115
in Ecuador, 48–49, 123, 127, 132, 188
Greece and, 200, 202
in Mexico, 5, 56, 89, 164
De La Rúa, Fernando, 21, 22n15, 62, 83, 166–71, 178, 186–87
democracy, implications of, 219–20
democratization, 35, 37
dollarization
of Argentinian economy, 166, 172, 190
of Ecuadorian economy, 70, 119, 121–23, 125, 127–28, 130, 190
dollar scarcity, 64, 66, 72, 80, 134, 159, 200, 213
Duhalde, Eduardo, 172–73, 187

economic growth, 36
in Venezuela under Chávez, 151–53
economic policymaking, government ideology and, 48–51, 218
Ecuador, 24
Brady Plan and, 6, 123
commodity exports of, 14
currency booms and crisis and, 81, 119, 131, 134, 159
currency pressures in, 118–20
dollarization of economy, 70, 119–25, 127–28, 130, 190
government revenues under Correa, 132–33
market discipline in, 118–20, 134–35
neoliberal agenda in, 20
oil and oil prices and, 17–18
sovereign risk and, 52–53, 126, 131–32
See also Correa, Rafael; Gutiérrez, Lucio
efficiency theories, 9, 118
Eichengreen, Barry, 72
EMBIg. *See* Emerging Market Bond Index Global (EMBIg)
Emerging Market Bond Index Global (EMBIg), 54–55, 57, 59–61
in Ecuador during 2002 election, 126
in Ecuador during 2006 election, 131
in Venezuela during 1998 election, 144
European Central Bank, 190, 195n9, 196, 198, 204, 207

European Commission, 190, 198, 206–7, 209
eurozone, 25, 190–91, 191n3, 192–94, 196, 200, 212
See also Greece; Portugal; Spain
exchange market pressure (EMP), 72
Exército Revolucionário Bolivariano (Revolutionary Bolivarian Army), 142
exogenous shocks, 3, 14, 21, 23–24, 35–38, 40–42, 81, 159, 187–88, 191, 215–16, 218
Argentina and, 166–67
Chávez and, 25, 158

Cristina Fernández de Kirchner, 21, 48, 183–87
See also Argentina
financial crisis, 141
of 2008, 1, 10, 53, 185, 190, 212, 214, 219
Asian, 56, 91, 122, 143
in Brazil, 1, 92, 94
in Ecuador, 120
Mexican, 89, 91, 122
Russian, 56, 91, 122, 166
financial globalization
investor's behavior and, 35
in Latin American emerging markets, 4–12
market discipline and, 27–28
optimal taxation and, 33–34
Flores-Macías, Gustavo, 22n15
Fome Zero (No Hunger, Brazil), 105–6
Franco, Itamar, 90–91
Frechette, Myles, 2
Free Trade Area of the Americas (FTAA), 71, 125
Frente Unitario de los Trabajadores (FUT), 130
Fujimori, Alberto, 77

García, Alan, 6, 67, 77
Garcia, Marco Aurélio, 100, 106
Germany
sovereign risk in *vs.* Greece, Portugal and Spain, 191–92
Gini coefficient, 157
Good Economic Times (GET) index, 55–58, 60
government ideology
economic policymaking and, 48–51, 218
investors response to sovereign risk and, 45–54, 57–62
investors response to sovereign risk model, 53–57, 62
sovereign bondholders and, 46–47, 217
government revenues, 16–17
Gran Viraje (Great Turnaround) plan in Venezuela, 139–40

Index

Great Recession (2008), 190–95
  developed countries response to, 195–212
Greece, 190–95
  government response to financial crisis and, 198–204
  sovereign risk in *vs.* Germany, 191–92
Gutiérrez, Lucio, 20, 22, 24, 27, 121, 124–32, 159, 188
  currency pressures and, 118–21
  income inequality and, 70, 125
  leftist, state-oriented agenda of during 2002 election, 70–71
  See also Ecuador

holdout creditors, Argentina, 175–76, 184, 187, 219
Humala, Ollanta, 21, 52, 88
  See also Peru
hyperinflation, 6, 73, 90, 160–61, 161–62, 167, 173, 177, 186–87

ideological convergence, 20, 27
ideology. *See* government ideology
income inequality, 4, 50–51, 52 n.12, 80
  in Argentina, 172
  in Brazil, 107
  capital mobility and, 31–34
  Gutiérrez and, 70, 125
  left–right "policy distance" and, 34–35
  in Uruguay, 50
  in Venezuela, 140
income of the poor, 23
  capital mobility and, 31–34, 38–40, 42–44
  left–right "policy distance" and, 34–35
  model of optimal taxation and, 30–31, 37–41, 43–44
inflation, 73, 89
Instituto Nacional de Estadística y Censos de la Republica Argentina (INDEC), 163, 184
Inter-American Development Bank, 73, 92, 128, 147, 171
International Center for the Settlement of Investment Disputes (ICSID), 176
international interest rates, 3, 5, 15–16, 18, 36, 40, 47, 52, 80, 188, 216, 218
  Good Economic Times (GET) index and, 55
internationalization of finance in Latin America
  historical perspective, 4–7
International Monetary Fund (IMF), 5, 71, 188, 193, 198–200, 206–7, 210
  Argentina and, 159, 165–70, 178, 182–85
  Brazil and, 91–94, 97–98, 100, 104

Ecuador and, 119, 124, 127–28, 130, 134, 188
Venezuela and, 137–39, 141–42, 146–48
investor behavior, 13, 16, 23–25, 39–40
  model of, 28
  uncertainty and economic volatility and, 35–37
investor income, maximization of, 42–44
investor influence
  as confidence game, 7–8, 12, 24, 64, 80, 88, 198, 217–18
  leftist governments during currency cycles and, 14
investor-oriented agenda, 2, 27–28, 35, 213, 216
  in Ecuador, 132
investor response to government ideology, 45–46, 51–53, 57–62
  sovereign risk model of, 53–57, 62
Izaguirre, Maritza, 145

January 21 Patriotic Movement (Partido Sociedad Patriótica 21 de Enero), 124
justicialismo (Partido Justicialista or Partido Peronista), 49, 62, 83, 161, 169, 188–89

Kirchner, Néstor, 21, 48, 159–60, 173
  balance of payments and, 179
  debt renegotiation and, 173–78
  macreconomic policies of, 48, 178–79, 187–88
  microeconomic policies of, 48, 178–83, 187–88
  vivir con lo nuestro under, 160, 176–78
  See also Argentina

Lagos, Eduardo
  economic policies of, 50
  See also Chile
Latin American elections, 2, 5, 12–13, 35
  state-oriented and market-oriented campaigns and, 65–66
  See also leftist presidential candidates
Latin American emerging economies, 4–12, 35
  capital account liberalization, 7
  investor behavior in uncertain, 36
  sovereign risk and, 47
  total public foreign debt outstanding and stock market capitalization of, 8
  See also by country
Lavagna, Roberto, 177
leftist governments, 27, 45–46, 48
  capital mobility and income of the poor and, 31–34
  currency booms and crisis and, 3–4, 14, 19, 25, 37–42, 64–67, 80–81, 134–35, 213, 218

Index

237

in developed world, 190
move to in 2000s, 39, 48, 124, 214
radical Left, 88
responsible Left, 88
sovereign bondholders and, 46–47
sovereign risk and, 64
leftist presidential candidates and elections
currency booms and crisis model, 70–74, 82–86
policy switches during currency booms and crisis and, 3–4, 20–22, 37–42, 45, 64–67, 74–86, 88–89, 213, 218
See also Chávez, Hugo; Correa, Rafael; da Silva, Lula; Gutiérrez, Lucio; Kirchner, Néstor
Letter to the Brazilian People (Carta ao Povo Brasileiro), 94n9
Lopez Murphy, Ricardo, 168–69
Luis Inácio Lula da Silva. *See* da Silva, Lula
Lulameter, 93
Lusinchi, Jaime, 67, 138

Machinea, José Luis, 166–68
Mahuad, Jamil, 123–24
market discipline
in bad financial times, 37–42, 45, 190
in Brazil, 118, 188
Brazilian Workers' Party and, 88
currency booms and crisis' effect on leftists governments and, 3–4, 19–23, 25, 37–42, 45, 64–67, 80–81, 134–35, 159, 189–90
defined, 28
in developed world, 188–90, 212
in Ecuador, 118–20, 134–35, 159, 188
during elections, 2–3, 12–13
exogenous shocks and, 14, 159, 188, 218
financial globalization and, 27–28
in Venezuela, 157, 159
vulnerable and nonvulnerable economies and, 19–22
Meirelles, Henrique, 99
Menem, Carlos, 21, 22n15, 160–66, 186
See also Argentina
Mercosur, 164
Mexico, 122
commodity exports of, 14, 114
economic policies of, 51
misiones (missions, Venezuela), 151, 153
Mitterand, François, 88
Movimento Sem Terra (MST, landless peasant movement in Brazil), 104, 107
Movimiento Nacionalista Revolucionario, 83
Movimiento Popular Democrático (MPD), 125
Movimiento Quinta República (MVR), 151

Mujica, José
economic policies of, 50
See also Uruguay

nationalization, 46, 48–49, 54, 137, 140, 157, 211
in Argentina, 178–80, 183, 187–88
in Venezuela, 49, 156–57
neoliberal agenda, 4, 9, 19, 21 n.14, 48, 50–51, 218
in Brazil, 1, 26
currency crises and, 24, 26, 42, 45
in Ecuador, 20, 27, 70, 124–25, 131
market confidence and, 89
neoliberalism, 27, 67, 70, 80, 89, 103, 124–25, 131, 138–42, 186
policy switches to, 67
state-oriented and market-oriented campaigns and, 65–66, 71
in Venezuela prior to 1998, 138–42
Noboa, Álvaro, 124, 130
Noboa, Gustavo, 123

OECD, 5, 9–11, 16, 36, 189–90, 192, 194, 196, 200, 217
oil and oil prices, 4, 17–18, 49–50, 123
in Brazil, 105, 111, 113–14
in Ecuador, 118–20, 124–25, 128–29, 131–34
in Venezuela (before Chávez), 136–42, 145
in Venezuela (under Chávez), 20, 143, 145, 147–52, 154, 156–59
Organisation for Economic Cooperation and Development. *See* OECD
orthodox policy switches, 1, 19–20, 22, 22n15, 24–25, 27, 39, 48, 50–51, 71, 80, 188–89, 191, 213–16, 218
in Argentina, 159–61, 168–69, 186
in Brazil, 87–88
in Ecuador, 134–35
in eurozone, 191–92
in Venezuela, 136–37, 140, 143, 145–48, 158
See also policy switches

Palocci, Antonio, 99, 104
Papaconstatinou, George, 202
Papandreou, Georges, 194–95, 200, 203
Paris Club, 146, 171, 175 n.27, 185
Partido dos Trabalhadores. *See* Workers' Party (PT)
Partido Renovador Institucional Acción Nacional (PRIAN, Ecuador), 129
Partido Roldosista Ecuatoriano, 62, 124
Partido Social Cristiano (PSC), 124, 130
Partido Social Democrata (PSD, Portugal), 205–8
partisan theories, 28, 34, 46, 48

238

Index

party and party system institutionalization, 22n15, 35, 73–75, 128
  policy switches and, 69–70, 218
Pérez, Carlos Andrés, 136, 138–41
Peronismo, 161, 172–73, 186
Peru, 6, 14, 17, 21, 48, 67, 77, 88
  commodity exports of, 14
  economic policies of, 51
  sovereign risk and, 51–53
  See also Humala, Ollanta
petrodollars, 4, 121
Petróleos de Venezuela (PDVSA), 143, 150, 154, 156
Plano Real (Real Plan, Brazil), 90
policy convergence, 4, 9, 12, 19–20, 23, 26–27, 80–81
  in Brazil, 20, 118
  in Ecuador, 27, 118
  in Venezuela, 141, 150
policy distance, income inequality and, 34–35
policy switches
  Chávez in Venezuela and, 20–21, 50, 76–77, 137, 145–49, 156–59
  constitutional strength, 68–70, 218–19
  Correa in Ecuador and, 20, 128–29, 134, 188
  currency booms and crisis and leftist governments agendas, 3–4, 20, 37–42, 45, 64–67, 74–86, 88–89, 213
  currency booms and crisis model, 70–74, 82–86
  Gutiérrez in Ecuador and, 20, 128–29, 134, 188
  Kirchner in Argentina and, 187
  Lula in Brazil and, 19–20, 87–89
  oil boom and, 156–59, 188
  party and party system institutionalization, 69–70, 128, 218
  See also orthodox policy switches
political risk. *See* sovereign risk
Portugal, 190–96
  government response to financial crisis, 198–99, 204–8
  sovereign risk in *vs.* Germany, 191–92
presidential elections, 2–4, 12, 24, 26–28, 35–37, 39, 45, 47, 55, 59, 61, 64–66, 70–71, 75, 78–80, 83–86, 218
  in Argentina, 160–61, 166, 173–74
  in Brazil, 1, 26, 40–41, 88–93, 95–96, 98, 100–101, 104–10, 115–16
  in Ecuador, 119–21, 123–27, 129–31
  in Peru, 51, 76–77
  sovereign risk and, 60
  summary of data on, 62–63
  in Venezuela, 76–77, 138, 142–44, 149, 151, 153–57
Primavera Plan (Argentina), 160–61

privatization, 46, 54, 71, 90–91, 93–95, 123, 141, 148, 156–57, 162–64, 169, 179, 186, 198, 201, 203, 208
Programa de Aceleração Crescimento (PAC), 109–10

radical Left, 88
real minimum wage, 111
Real Plan (Plano Real, Brazil), 90
redistribution, 25, 36, 42, 45, 51, 128, 135, 139–42, 216, 220
  capital mobility and financial integration and, 23, 29–34
  defined, 28
  in good financial times, 4, 20, 22, 39, 45, 112, 120, 134–35, 157–59, 187, 189, 216, 218
  Left and, 9, 19–20, 28
  optimal taxation and, 23, 33–34
responsible Left, 88
right-leaning governments
  sovereign bondholders and risk perception and, 46–47, 64
  See also neoliberal agenda
risk. *See* sovereign risk
Rodríguez Saá, Adolfo, 171–72, 187
Römer, Henrique Salas, 143
Rousseff, Dilma, 2, 26, 50, 62–63, 116
  See also Brazil

Serra, José, 93, 98, 116
Social Christian Party of Venezuela (COPEI), 136, 138
Social Christian Party of Venezuela (Partido Social Cristiano, COPEI), 136, 138, 151n19
sovereign bondholders, 46–47, 64, 217
sovereign risk
  in Argentina, 173–74
  in Ecuador, 126, 131–32
  in good *vs.* bad financial times, 47, 53
  investor response to government ideology and, 45–53, 57–62
  investor response to government ideology model, 53–57, 62
  in Portugal, Greece and Spain *vs.* Germany, 191–92
  in Venezuela, 52–53, 144, 153–55
Spain, 190–97
  government response to financial crisis, 198–99, 208–12
  sovereign risk in *vs.* Germany, 191–92
Switch (dependent variable), 70–72
  See also orthodox policy switches; policy switches
Syriza (Greek left-wing party), 194, 201

trade balance in Argentina, 163
Tsipras, Alex, 201

Index 239

twenty-first century socialism (Venezuela), 131, 153, 158

Unión Cívica Radical (UCR), 83, 160, 166–68
Uribe, Álvaro, 71
Uruguay, 6
  commodity exports of, 14
  income inequality in, 50
  sovereign risk and, 52–53
  See also Broad Front; Mujica, José; Vázquez, Tabaré

Vázquez, Tabaré, 2, 50
  See also Uruguay
Venezuela, 3, 6, 25, 67, 136–37
  commodity exports of, 14
  currency booms and crisis and, 81, 137, 141, 158–59
  income inequality in, 140
  neoliberalism in prior to 1998, 138–42

oil and oil prices and, 17–18
sovereign risk and, 52–53, 144, 153–55
  See also Chávez, Hugo
Vivir con lo nuestro (Argentina), 160, 176–78

Weyland, Kurt, 22, 142
Workers' Party (PT, Brazil), 1–2, 26, 50, 81, 87, 91–100, 102, 104–8
  market discipline and, 88
  1989 presidential campaign and, 88–89
World Bank, 54
  Argentina and, 161, 171, 176
  Brazil and, 92, 121
  Ecuador and, 128, 130
  International Center for the Settlement of Investment Disputes (ICSID), 176
  Venezuela and, 147

Zapatero, José Luis, 197, 208–12

For EU product safety concerns, contact us at Calle de José Abascal, 56–1°,
28003 Madrid, Spain or eugpsr@cambridge.org.

www.ingramcontent.com/pod-product-compliance
Ingram Content Group UK Ltd.
Pitfield, Milton Keynes, MK11 3LW, UK
UKHW020358060825
461487UK00008B/708